IMAGES
of America

ALPINE

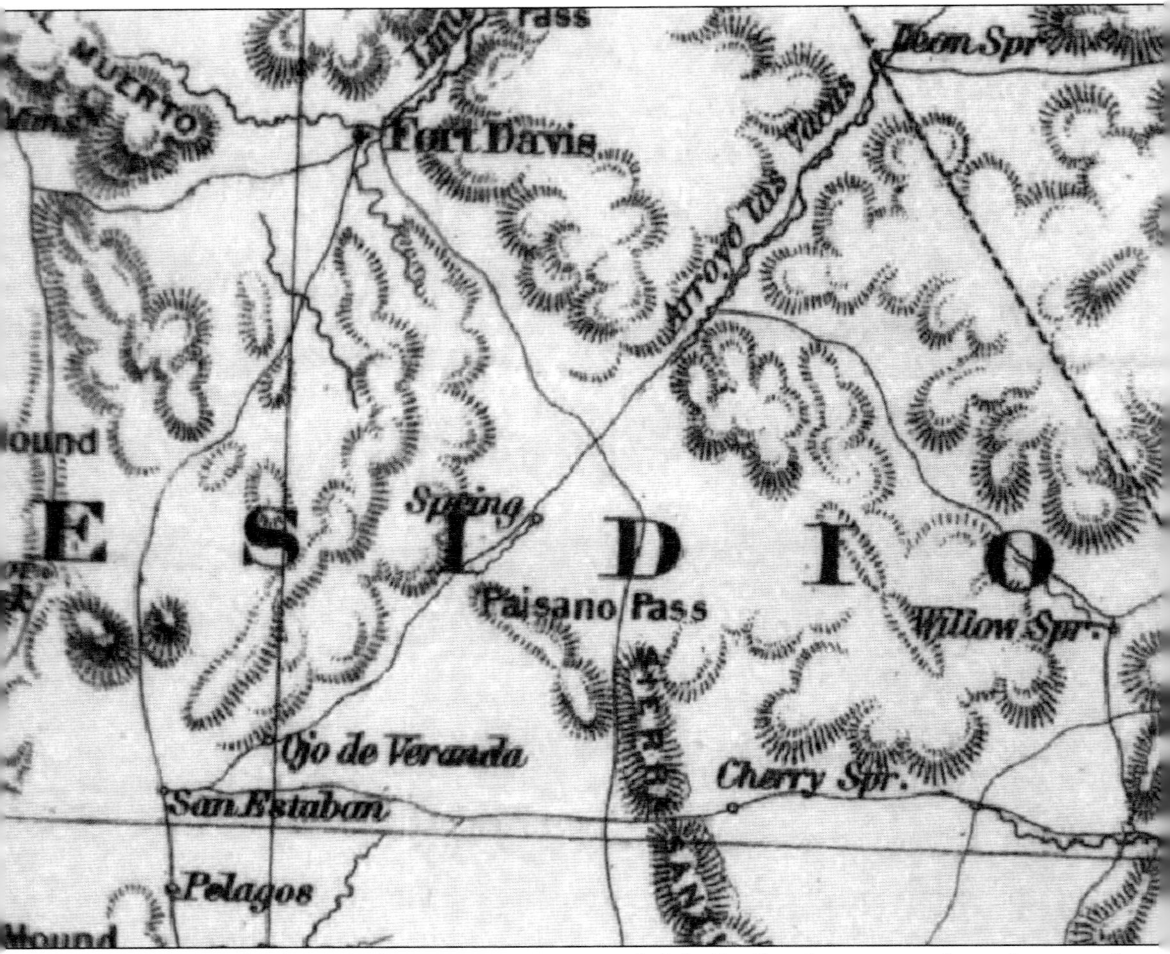

For thousands of years before Euro-Americans settled the Big Bend, native people used a network of trails that spanned the region. This 1873 railroad map, one of the earliest charts of the area, shows the location of these ancient paths. The spring that became Alpine is shown near the center of the map. (Detail of Texas and Pacific Railway Map, Library of Congress Geography and Map Division.)

On the Cover: The old adobe Catholic church Nuestra Senora de Guadalupe stands prominently in the foreground on the northern toeslope of A Mountain. This photograph is part of a larger panorama taken of Alpine in 1904 (see pages 22–23). In the distance, Henderson Mesa creates the northern edge of Alpine Valley. (Courtesy of the Archives of the Big Bend.)

IMAGES
of America

ALPINE

David W. Keller

ARCADIA
PUBLISHING

ISBN 978-0-7385-7894-1

Published by Arcadia Publishing
Charleston, South Carolina

Printed in the United States of America

Library of Congress Control Number: 2010920452

For all general information, please contact Arcadia Publishing:
Telephone 843-853-2070
Fax 843-853-0044
E-mail sales@arcadiapublishing.com
For customer service and orders:
Toll-Free 1-888-313-2665

Visit us on the Internet at www.arcadiapublishing.com

To the town's many photographers and chroniclers, especially John and Lizzie Thain, Frank Duncan, W. D. Smithers, Charles Hunter, Carl Williams, and Clifford Casey

CONTENTS

Acknowledgments 6

Introduction 7

1. Osborne to Alpine: Birth of a Railroad Town (1882–1909) 11
2. Coming of Age: Growth and Development (1910–1919) 29
3. The Prosperous Years: Alpine's Florescence (1920–1939) 43
4. Riding High: Ranching the Highlands 59
5. Coming Together: Social Events and Organizations 73
6. The Intellectual Frontier: Sul Ross State University 83
7. The Years Between: Decades after World War II 101
8. Modern Alpine: The Last Frontier 111

Acknowledgments

The images used in this book were selected from a body of more than 500 photographs derived from many sources. The majority came from the Clifford B. Casey Collection at the Archives of the Big Bend, Bryan Wildenthal Memorial Library, and the Museum of the Big Bend, both at Sul Ross State University in Alpine, Texas. Additional photographs came from *The Brand*, a publication of Sul Ross State University, News and Publications at Sul Ross State University, the *Alpine Avalanche*, the Marfa and Presidio County Museum, the Harry Ransom Humanities Research Center, the University of Texas at Austin, the U.S. Natural Resources Conservation Service in Alpine, the Charles Deering McCormick Library of Special Collections at Northwestern University Library in Chicago, Illinois, the Perry-Castaneda Library Map Collection at the University of Texas at Austin, the Dolph Briscoe Center for American History at the University of Texas at Austin, and the Prints and Photographs Division at the Library of Congress in Washington, D.C.

A large number of photographs also came from family collections, most notably the Smith and Roberts collections. A special thanks to Rusty Hill, Willeen Austin, Travis Roberts, Ofelia Valadez, Carl Williams, Ted Gray, Bill Ivey, King and Becky Terry, Mike Hunter, Martin Theophilus, Karen Williams, Robert Halpern, and Josh Ward for sharing their photograph collections. Many contributed time and effort to this project, some beyond the call of duty. Thanks to Mary Bones, Mary Williams, B. J. Gallego, Melleta Bell, Jeri Garza, Michael Howard, Steve Lang, Jason Hennington, Lana Covington, Ray Hendryx, Michael Stevens, Tom Curry, and Mike and Cindy Perry. I would also like to thank those who helped inform this history, especially Ted Gray, Julia Nail Moss, Homer Mills, Carla McFarland, Keri Artzt, Lonn Taylor, Gary Dunshee, and Jack McNamara. Thanks to Paul Wright and Bob Mallouf for commenting on parts of the manuscript. Finally, thanks to my patient editors at Arcadia Publishing, Kristie Kelly and Hannah Carney.

INTRODUCTION

Alpine was just another railroad town, one of a great many along the Southern Pacific–Galveston, Harrisburg, and San Antonio Railway. But for millennia the site had also been an ancient Indian camp—a spring along the trail between La Junta on the Rio Grande and the Pecos River crossing to the northeast.

In the winter of 1684, Spanish explorer Juan Dominguez de Mendoza and his party, on their way east from El Paso del Norte, descended Paisano Pass into the treeless expanse of Alpine Valley where deer, antelope, and bison grazed on "grass that looked like a field of waving grain." The party made camp at the foot of Hancock Hill, beside a fresh water spring he dubbed "San Lorenzo." After having to forego erecting the customary cross for want of wood and almost being consumed by a prairie fire, the expedition continued east.

One hundred years later, a band of Mescalero Apaches camped at the spring were descended upon by Spanish general Juan de Ugalde during one of his extermination campaigns against Texas Indians. By the late 1850s, the spring had become an overnight stop on the Chihuahua Trail between Indianola, Texas, and Chihuahua City, Mexico. Because of the number of Indian attacks that took place, the spring became known as Charco de Alsate after a local Apache war chief. But a steady military campaign eventually drove the natives out of the region. By the early 1880s, the Apache presence was a thing of the past.

Sometime in the spring of 1882, hundreds of Chinese railroad workers labored down Paisano Pass, across Alpine Valley and continued east, leaving the Southern Pacific railway in their wake. Where it passed close to what we now call Kokernot Springs, a side-track, a water tank, and a boxcar depot bearing the name "Osborne" were left behind. An agent and a section foreman were assigned to the station. And Alpine was born.

Ranchers from South and East Texas had been driving sheep and cattle into the region ever since the Indian threat had been removed. But with the arrival of the railroad, the land rush was on full tilt. Alpine became county seat in 1887 when Brewster County was carved out of Presidio County. In 1897, Brewster gained adjacent Buchel and Foley Counties, making it—at 6,200 square miles—the largest in Texas. A new land law passed in 1905 that allowed settlers to claim an unprecedented eight sections, set off a second land rush. Between 1900 and 1910, the population of Brewster County more than doubled, and by 1907 the county contained a record-breaking 90,000 cattle—more than there ever had been or would be again. But the drought of 1910–1911 caused most newcomers to fail and triggered a permanent reduction in stocking rates.

Quicksilver mining in south Brewster County had taken place intermittently since the 1880s but began on a large scale as early as 1899, when the Marfa and Mariposa Mining Company set up shop. The Brewster County mines were productive enough that they soon made Texas the second leading state in the nation for quicksilver production. By World War I, around 20 percent of the entire quicksilver supply mined in the United States came from the Terlingua District. Although the mining traffic went to neighboring Marathon, Alpine likewise benefitted as taxes on the quicksilver trade filled the county coffers.

Alpine had outgrown two schoolhouses by 1910 when the city passed a bond issue to build a new elaborate brick school featuring a three-story crenellated tower. Later known as "Central School," the Gothic Revival building was so impressive that it helped inspire the Alpine Summer Normal, the only teacher's school between San Antonio and El Paso. It was such a resounding success that students, teachers, and citizens began to petition the legislature for a permanent college in Alpine. The bill finally passed in 1917 establishing the college, but with a strict set of conditions. Alpine met and exceeded them: incorporating, donating land on Hancock Hill, extending utilities, drilling a well, and making room—often in the citizen's own homes—for students to live.

Sul Ross State Normal College opened its doors in 1920. What had been a sleepy cowtown began its transformation to a college town. Over the next 10 years, the population of Alpine almost doubled and many of the town's most significant downtown buildings were constructed, including the Granada Theatre, which showed motion pictures, and the Mojave Theatre, which hosted traveling shows and theatrical performances. The Holland Hotel, originally built in 1908 by rancher John Holland, added a third floor to the rear of the building in 1923. Only five years later, a new 40-room "annex" was completed featuring a banquet hall, dining room, and coffee shop. Between the campus and the downtown area, the Spanish-styled College Apartments and rows of hollow tile and cast concrete cottages were built for student housing.

In 1923, Harvard graduate Horace Morelock arrived in Alpine to become the third, longest running, and most influential president in Sul Ross's history. During his 22 years, enrollment climbed, the curriculum broadened, new buildings were constructed, and Sul Ross was admitted to the American Association of Colleges. Morelock was also a major force behind the establishment of Big Bend National Park and—from the very beginning—one of Alpine's greatest champions.

In 1926, Prof. Victor Smith along with other Sul Ross faculty and area citizens founded the West Texas Historical and Scientific Society to support research and publish on the region's rich natural and historical resources. The society started what would become the Museum of the Big Bend and published 11 bulletins between 1926 and 1946, including one cosponsored by the Peabody Museum at Harvard University that established the foundation for serious archaeological study in the region.

With its sweeping views of the Davis Mountains, the stately Greek neoclassical college building on the hill, a prospering downtown area, and the Gothic, turreted Central School, Alpine had gained a sophistication that set it apart from other towns in the region. Academic and cosmopolitan, by the end of the decade, the town had easily established itself as the cultural and intellectual center of the Big Bend.

Alpine's newfound pride was not enough, however, to offset the debilitating effects of the depression and drought of the 1930s. By 1933, the school treasury had amassed a deficit of more than $7,000 due to unpaid taxes. Citizens organized the Alpine Relief Association to urge employers to only hire locals. The two main banks in town—First National and State National—merged to stay solvent. Then, in 1934, with the economy already in shambles, the region experienced the driest year on record. During the summer, as temperatures soared over 100 degrees, desperate ranchers gathered to apply to the federal Emergency Relief Program. A Drought Relief Office was established in Alpine that would eventually purchase over 27,000 cattle from Brewster County alone.

In spite of the troubles of the ranching industry, Sul Ross prospered during the 1930s. Throughout the decade, the college sponsored annual four-day weekend educational trips to Chihuahua City. In 1933, Sul Ross conferred its first master's degree, and for most of the decade the college hosted the Sul Ross Summer Art Colony, led by esteemed painters Xavier Gonzales and Julius Woeltz. And putting itself on the academic radar, both the Texas Academy of Science and the American Association for the Advancement of Science held meetings on campus.

Also during the 1930s, thanks to various New Deal programs and the labor of local relief workers, Alpine and the college gained some of their most attractive and historically significant buildings. In 1934, Kokernot Lodge and an outdoor theatre were dedicated on 35 acres around the historic spring. In 1936, the Works Progress Administration built the Centennial School out of adobe bricks. Meanwhile, the campus gained Lawrence Hall in addition to a men's dormitory, a greenhouse, a stadium for the tennis courts, a clubhouse, and a bowling alley. The crowning achievements, however, were 14 cottages, a two-story band house, and one of the most impressive museums in the state, all built out of native stone.

In 1941, a record 35 inches of rain fell in Alpine, signaling the end of the drought of the previous decade. World War II drove up demand for beef and fibers, and for a time the region became a sheep and goat raising empire. By 1945, there were almost 170,000 sheep and 68,000 goats (in addition to more than 66,000 cattle) in Brewster County. The Big Bend Wool and Mohair was bursting at the seams.

But the war also had the effect of nearly driving Sul Ross out of business, as construction activities ground to a halt and enrollment plummeted. Only 13 students graduated in 1945. Had it not been for a U.S. Navy pilot training program and the Women's Army Corps Training School, Sul Ross's days would have been numbered. Although enrollment rebounded quickly after the war ended, the conflict had exacted a toll on the region: Brewster County lost 38 men, many times the number lost during World War I.

For the next decade, both the school and town enjoyed a period of prosperity. In 1944, Big Bend National Park became the nation's 27th national park, and tourism slowly began to play a larger role in the local economy. In the late 1940s, Alpine gained a semiprofessional baseball team and world-class playing field as well as local radio station KVLF. But the successes of the 1940s were soon overshadowed by another drought so severe and long lasting that it nearly paralyzed ranching across the region. Although many ranchers received help during the 1950s and 1960s from the recently organized Big Bend Soil Conservation District, the region's cattle industry would never fully recover.

The drought of the 1950s finally broke by the end of the decade, and from 1966 to 1992 the region enjoyed some of the most abundant rainfall on record. But during the same years, Alpine slid into a sort of cultural slumber. Chain stores and fast food restaurants began to arrive, and modern construction styles threatened the town's character. Times were especially hard on historic structures. In 1964, the old adobe Catholic Church was razed. In 1968, the Hancock Building was demolished to make room for a new 10,000 square foot building for C. G. Morrison and Company. Only three years later, the Central School—the crown jewel of Alpine, now more than half a century old—was demolished. As if to punctuate this lackluster era, in 1969, the Holland Hotel—a business that had long been a symbol of Alpine's growth and prosperity—shut its doors for good.

Times were no better on campus. In 1966, the museum was deeded to the college, which promptly claimed the building for a Student Center and moved the museum into the old bowling alley. Space was so cramped that some collections were given back to their donors. In the meantime, enrollment was skyrocketing. In just over a decade, the number of students almost tripled; by 1974 enrollment stood at an all time high of nearly 3,000. To accommodate the growth, during the late 1960s, Mountainside dormitory, the Industrial Arts building, and the Bryan Wildenthal Memorial Library were constructed—but all in styles that departed from both the neoclassical design of the main campus and the native rock buildings that surrounded and accented it. But the spike in the student population wasn't to last. The next decade would see enrollment decline more precipitously than it had risen.

Hints of a cultural reawakening were in the air as early as the mid 1980s, with the reopening of the Holland Hotel and the first-annual Texas Cowboy Poetry Gathering in the state. By the early 1990s, several new businesses opened their doors. Kiowa Gallery, Front Street Books, and Quetzal imports all renovated and reoccupied historic buildings on Holland Avenue, setting a precedent for downtown revitalization. Within four years of opening, the Railroad Blues was hailed by *Texas Monthly* as "one of the best small town live music clubs in Texas." And in 1994, the first Gallery Night—now a bustling annual art festival—signaled the beginning of the "Alpine Renaissance." In the last decade, the Museum of the Big Bend returned to its original 1930s rock building, the Centennial school was remodeled, the Granada Theatre reopened as a performance hall and yoga studio, and an entire section of Murphy Street that had been shuttered for over 35 years was restored. And, as a crowning achievement, symbolizing a return to Alpine's glory days, in 2009 the Holland Hotel was restored to its original Spanish Colonial decor.

Today Alpine enjoys once again the mix of cultural events and academics that distinguished it during the early years of Sul Ross. Poised at the edge of one of the last great outdoor laboratories for the natural and cultural sciences, the Chihuahuan Desert Research Institute and university organizations such as the Borderlands Research Institute and the Center for Big Bend Studies conduct research, host conferences, and organize education programs. Meanwhile, the town has held firmly on to its ranching roots, with annual events such as the Cowboy Poetry Gathering, Trappings exhibit, and some of the best intercollegiate and ranch rodeos anywhere. In 2009, the Alpine Cowboys were reborn as the Big Bend Cowboys marking the first professional baseball played at Kokernot Field in 48 years. Alpine now boasts over a dozen art galleries, a respectable literary magazine, national public radio, a vibrant summer outdoor theatre program, a jazz ensemble, a Tahitian Dance troupe, a number of talented local bands, and a growing array of annual events.

Alpine has arrived at a juncture where its history, culture, and panoramic setting are celebrated once again at a scale in keeping with the pride and poise held in its earlier days. Slowly growing more sophisticated, intellectual, and cosmopolitan, the town retains its quaint, regional, rough-around-the-edges feel that keeps it unique. Cradled in the embrace of the Davis Mountains, Alpine remains a friendly West Texas town, and a gateway to one of the most majestic landscapes in the country.

One

Osborne to Alpine
Birth of a Railroad Town
(1882–1909)

On January 12, 1883, just west of the Pecos River, a silver spike was ceremoniously driven into the last crosstie connecting the lines of the Galveston, Harrisburg, and San Antonio and the Southern Pacific Railways. The two companies had built 639 miles of track in 19 months, averaging just over 0.5 miles a day per crew. That same day, the first passenger train rolled into Alpine, on its maiden voyage from New Orleans to California.

Later that year, Thomas O. Murphy registered with the Presidio County clerk a plat out of section 42, block 9 for his new town centered around the Southern Pacific depot. In exchange for water from the spring, the railroad agreed to change the name of the section from Osborne to Murphyville. But within a matter of years, the city fathers grew weary of the cumbersome and uninspiring name and, in 1888, by popular vote of the citizens, changed it to the more evocative Alpine.

The town grew only gradually. Before the 20th century, the economy was centered around the beef industry and the region's sprawling cattle ranches. Though flush with livestock, there were relatively few people in the area and much of the land in south Brewster County remained unsettled. But in spite of setbacks, including several major fires, Alpine enjoyed good fortune. In 1897 Brewster County, for which Alpine had become the county seat, gained adjacent Buchel and Foley counties. For the next decade, ample precipitation and good prices allowed the cattle industry to boom. And with the second land rush following the Eight-Section Act and vigorous mining activity in south Brewster County, Alpine was, by 1910, fast becoming a prosperous little Western town.

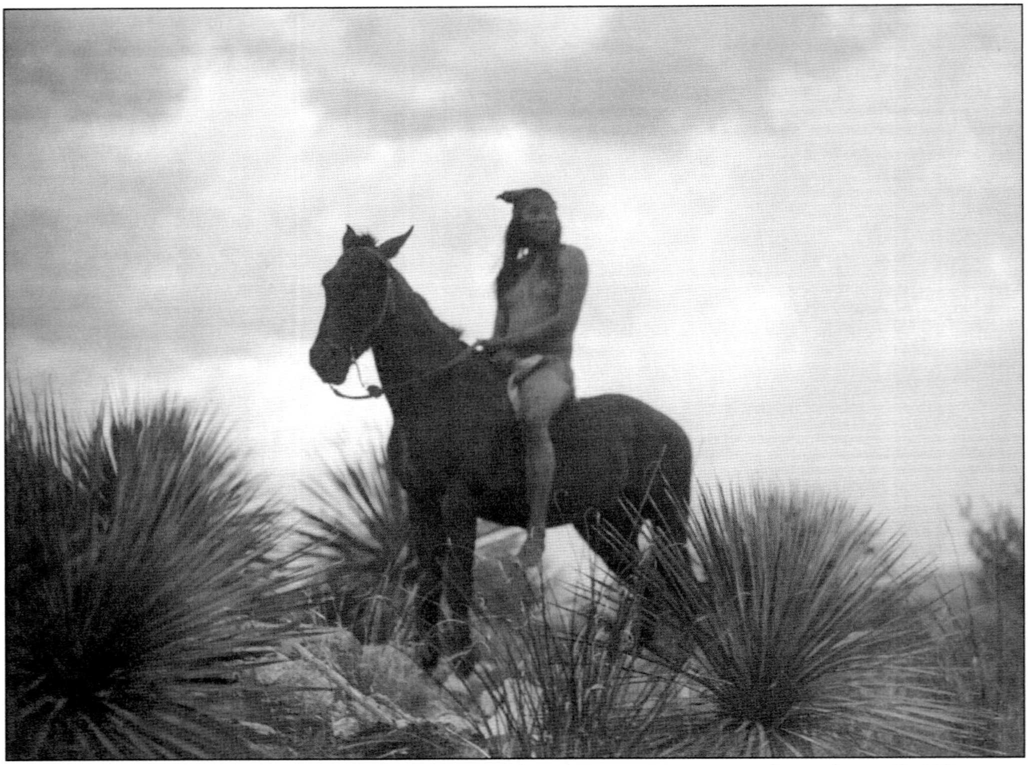

Native American groups resided in the Big Bend and Davis Mountains for at least 10,000 years. Apaches were relative newcomers to the region, arriving during the 1600s. Horses were not in common use until after the Pueblo Revolt of 1680. (Courtesy of the Charles Deering McCormick Library of Special Collections.)

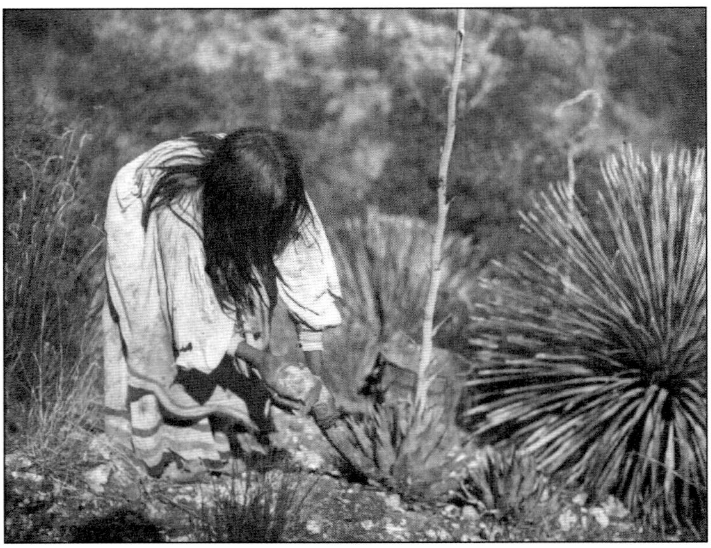

The resident Mescalero Apache, like native groups before them, utilized the starchy roots of the lechuguilla and sotol plants for food. These were cooked for up to 48 hours in earth ovens—pits dug into the ground and lined with rocks that had been heated in a fire. The food was placed inside, covered with more hot rocks, and sealed with dirt. (Courtesy of the Charles Deering McCormick Library of Special Collections.)

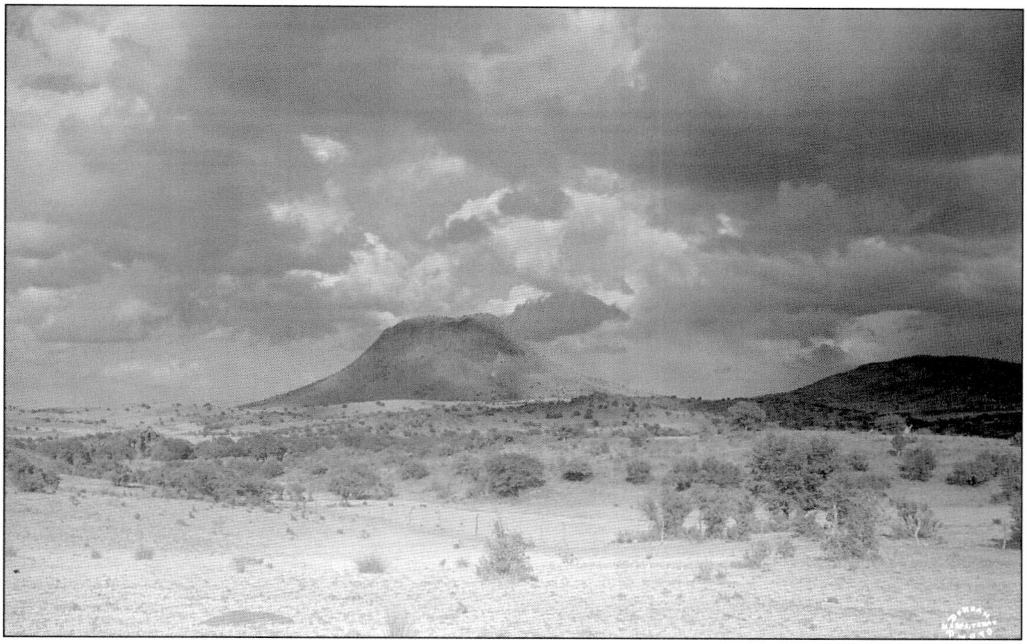

Paisano Peak looms like a sentinel on the horizon above Paisano Pass, an ancient passageway through a narrow section of the Davis Mountains. It was this pass through which Mendoza entered Alpine Valley in 1684, providing the first written description of the area. (Courtesy of the Marfa and Presidio County Museum.)

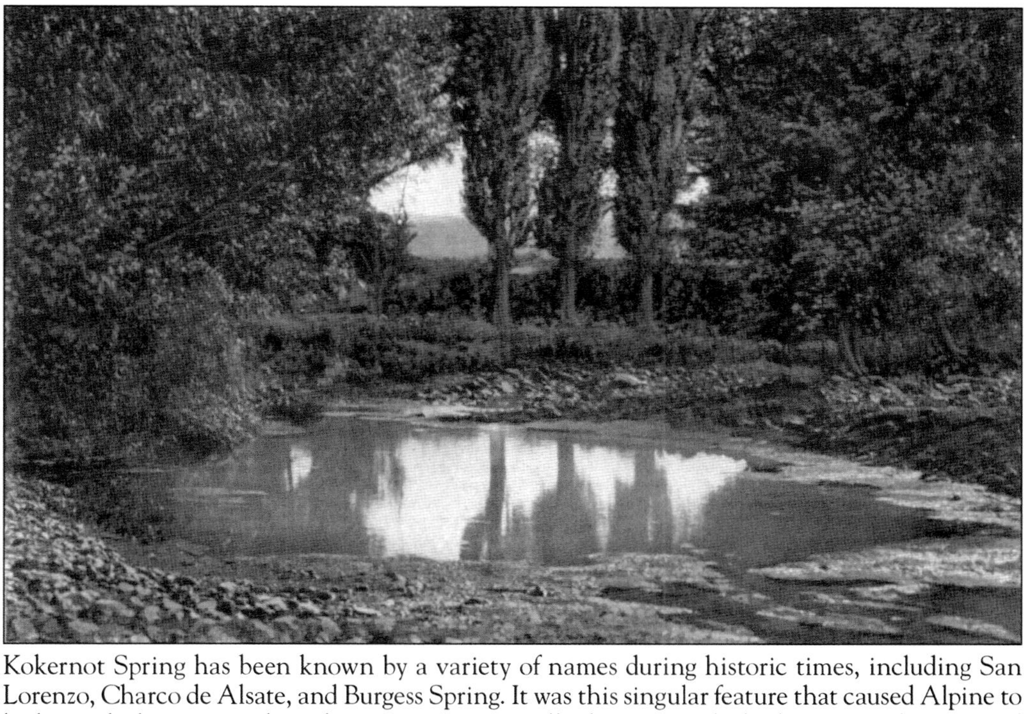

Kokernot Spring has been known by a variety of names during historic times, including San Lorenzo, Charco de Alsate, and Burgess Spring. It was this singular feature that caused Alpine to be located where it is today. This 1930 image actually shows a much shadier spring than existed in earlier times, when it was kept treeless by frequent prairie fires. (Courtesy of the Museum of the Big Bend.)

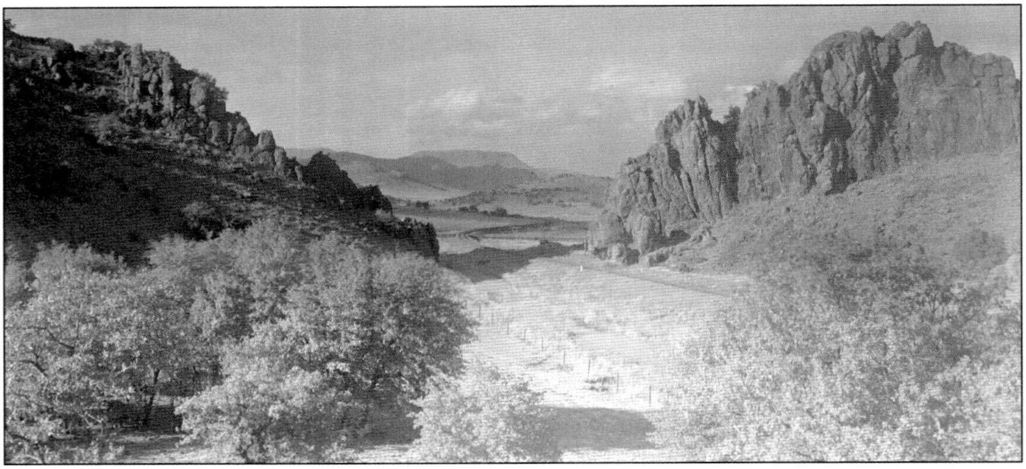

This rocky defile, the narrowest place through which the Southern Pacific line was built over Paisano Pass, was also, at 5,074 feet, the highest point on the entire railroad between New Orleans and Los Angeles. (Courtesy of the Marfa and Presidio County Museum.)

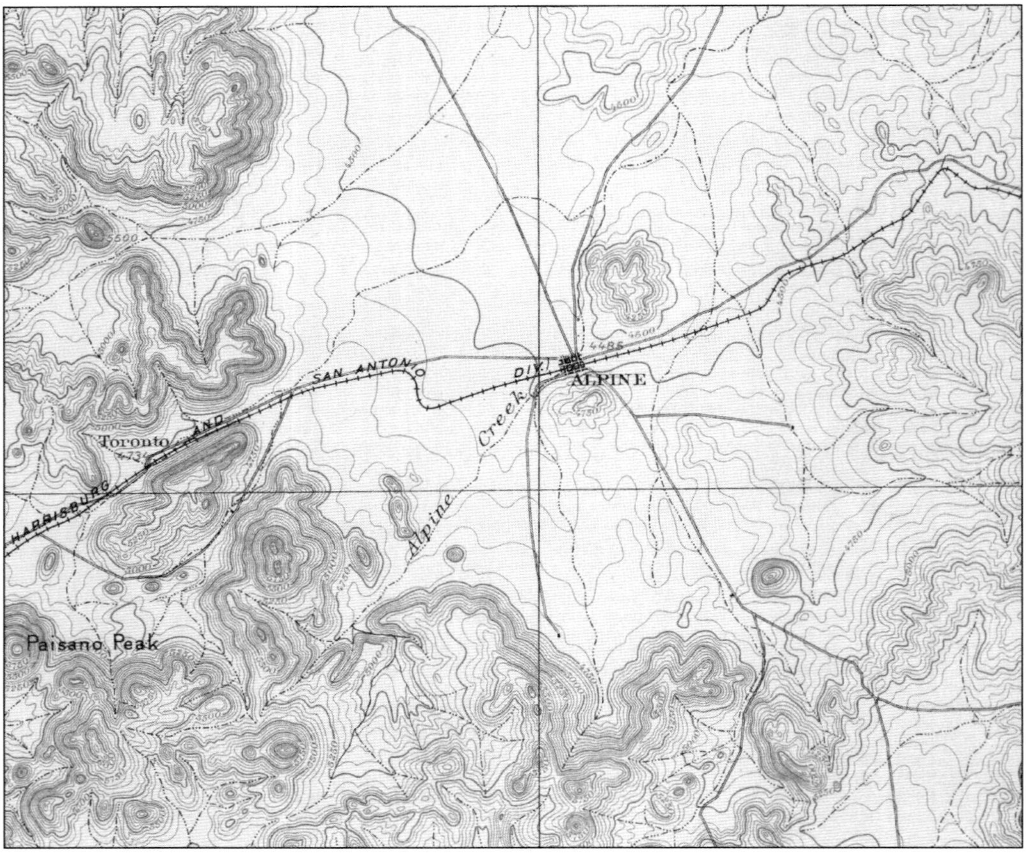

This 1895 map, the earliest accurate topographic chart made of the Alpine area, shows the route of the Southern Pacific–Galveston, Harrisburg, and San Antonio Railroad. The tracks descended through Paisano Pass and Toronto Canyon, across Alpine Valley, and onward to Strobel and Altuda—all section stops along the line. (Courtesy of the Perry-Castaneda Library Map Collection.)

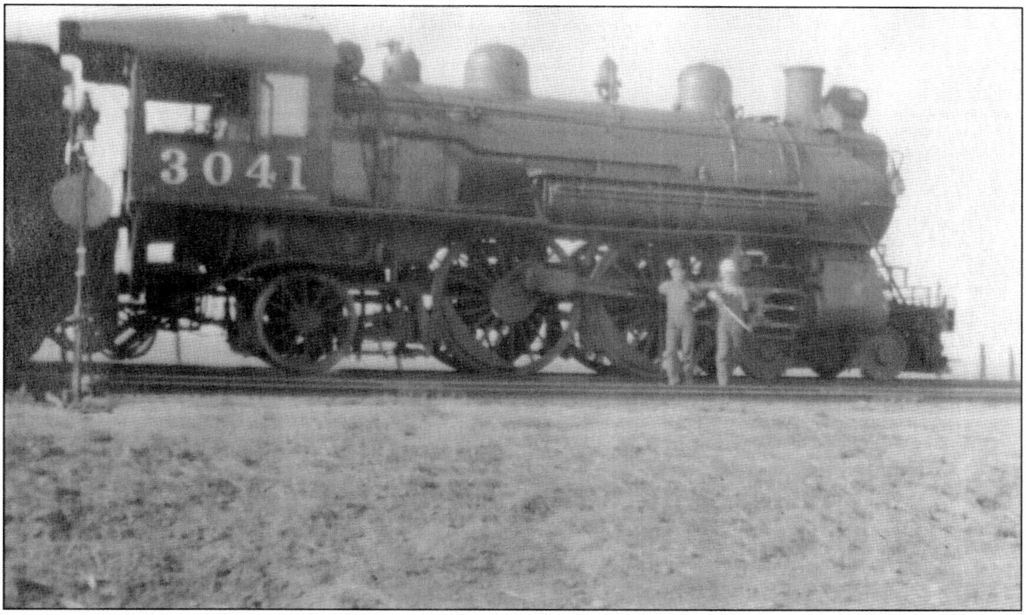

The railroad that gave birth to Alpine was a joint venture between the Galveston, Harrisburg, and San Antonio Railroad working westward and the Southern Pacific Railroad working eastward. These early steam locomotives were originally fueled with coal, although most were replaced with oil-burning locomotives after 1900. (Courtesy of the Smith collection.)

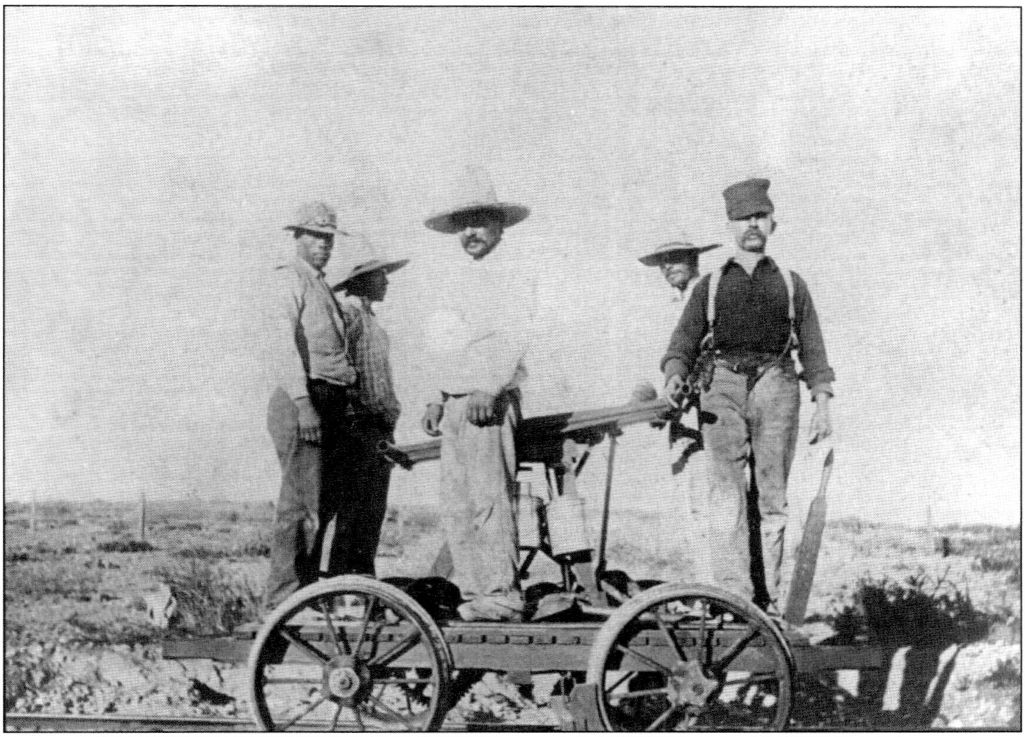

Crews were used to maintain sections of railroad, usually about 10 miles long. Alpine was set up as both a water stop and a section house. Crews typically consisted of an Anglo foreman and four to five usually Hispanic section workers. (Courtesy of the Archives of the Big Bend.)

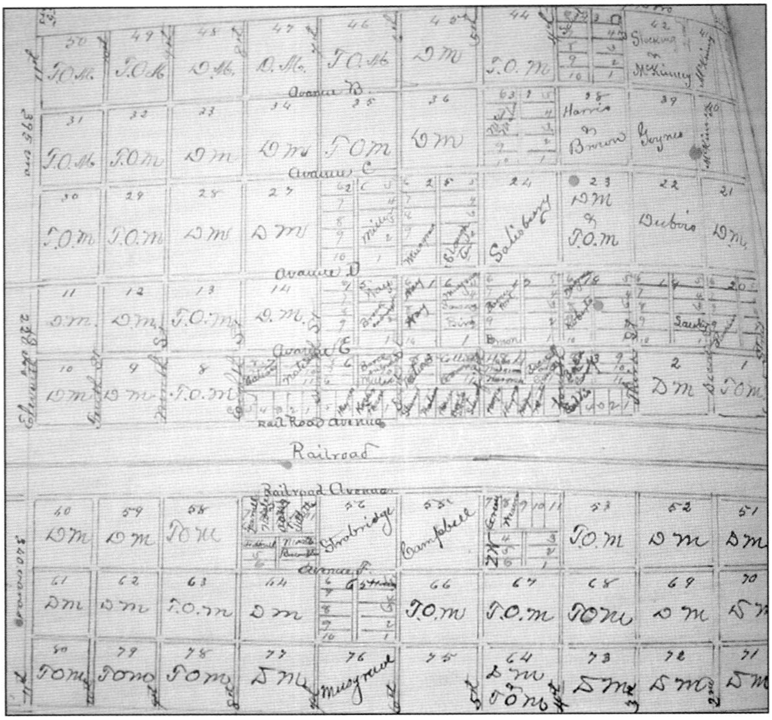

On November 10, 1883, Thomas O. Murphy registered with the Presidio County clerk a plat out of section 42 around the new Southern Pacific depot. The ink had scarcely dried when Murphy held a special sale of town lots, dubbing his new town Murphyville. (Courtesy of the Presidio County Courthouse.)

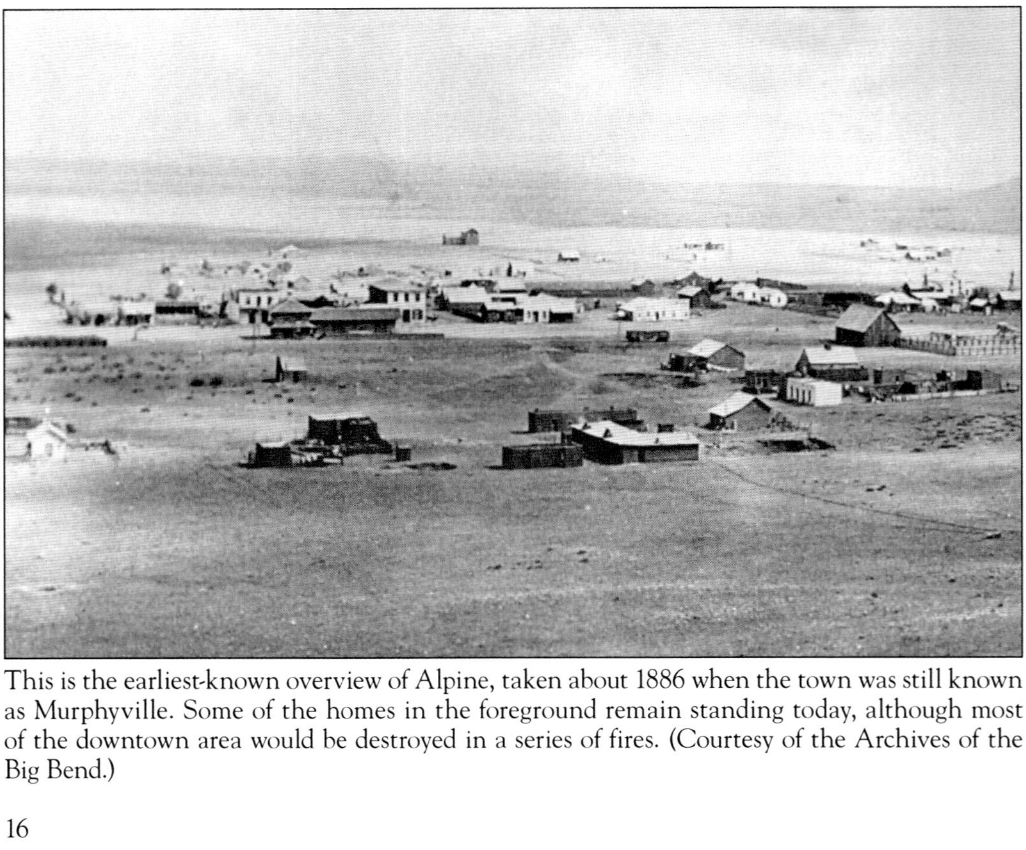

This is the earliest-known overview of Alpine, taken about 1886 when the town was still known as Murphyville. Some of the homes in the foreground remain standing today, although most of the downtown area would be destroyed in a series of fires. (Courtesy of the Archives of the Big Bend.)

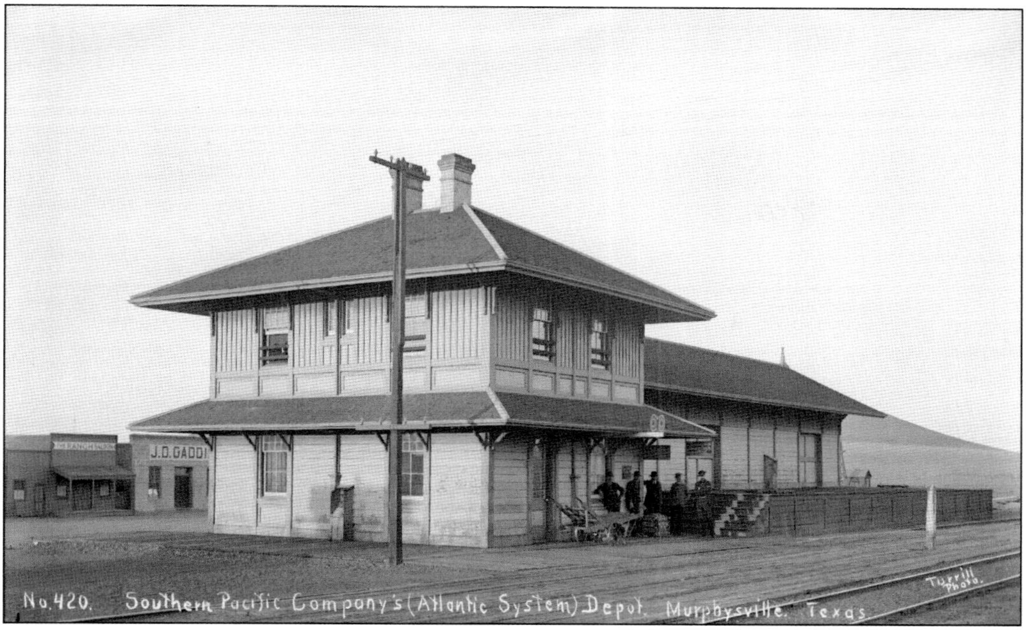

Alpine's first depot was the Southern Pacific's Standard Plan Number 22, built completely of redwood and sporting Victorian flourishes. This structure was Alpine's lifeline to the rest of the world—its nerve center. Trains hauling passengers, baggage, and mail arrived daily, and freight cars supplied the town and ranches with everything from stamps to building materials. (Courtesy of Center for American History, the University of Texas at Austin.)

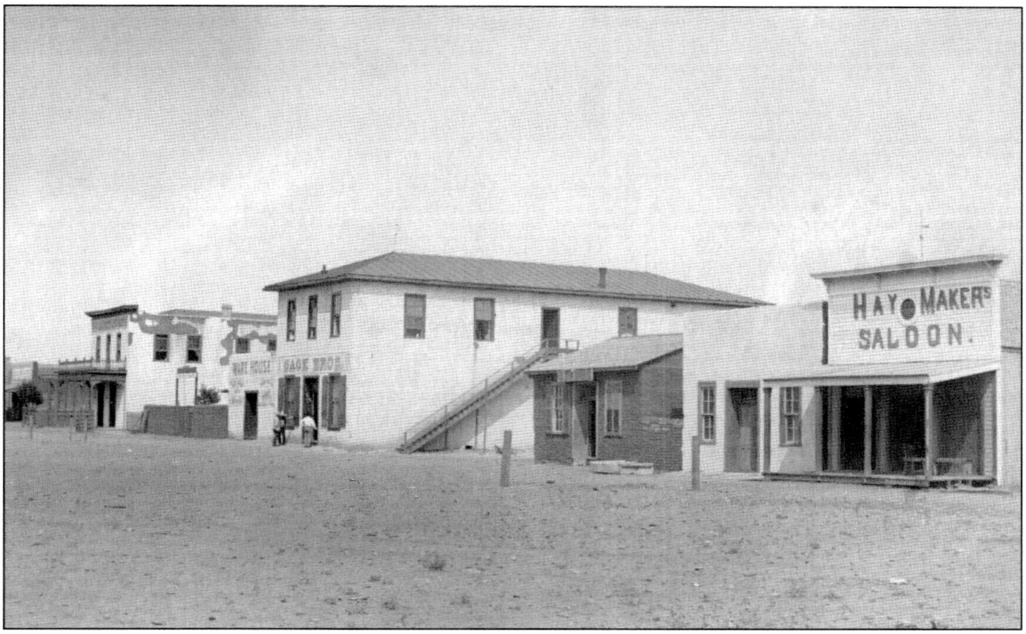

Front Street, now known as Holland Avenue, had two other saloons in addition to the Hay Maker Saloon shown in this c. 1886 photograph. Though generally a peaceful town, weekends could get rowdy as cowboys from surrounding ranches rode in to slake their thirst. The more distant two-story structure is the Garnett building; the nearer one is the Gage Brothers building. (Courtesy of the Archives of the Big Bend.)

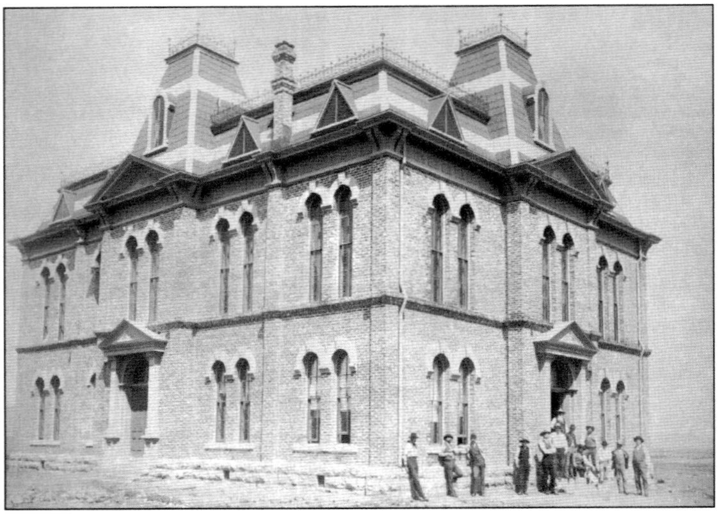

The Brewster County Courthouse, shown soon after its completion in 1888, was fairly typical of Second Empire style. The two-story brick structure features a mansard roof, arched windows, and a bracketed cornice. It was one of a handful in the state built by Tom Lovell and today is one of only 26 surviving courthouses in this style built before 1900. (Courtesy of the Archives of the Big Bend.)

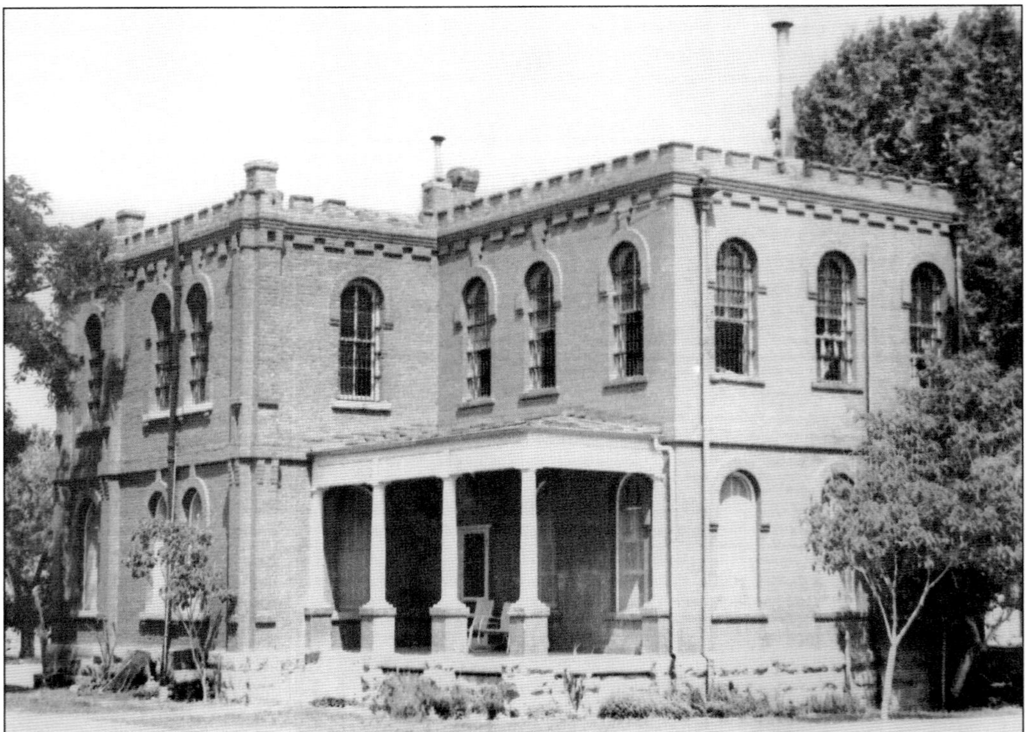

The Brewster County Jail is a two-story brick Gothic Revival structure. Resembling a small medieval castle, it featured a castellated parapet, brick corbelling around the cornice, and a belt course. Although the jail was built at the same time as the courthouse, the hoodmolds over the arched windows are the only stylistic element shared between the two structures. (Courtesy of the Archives of the Big Bend.)

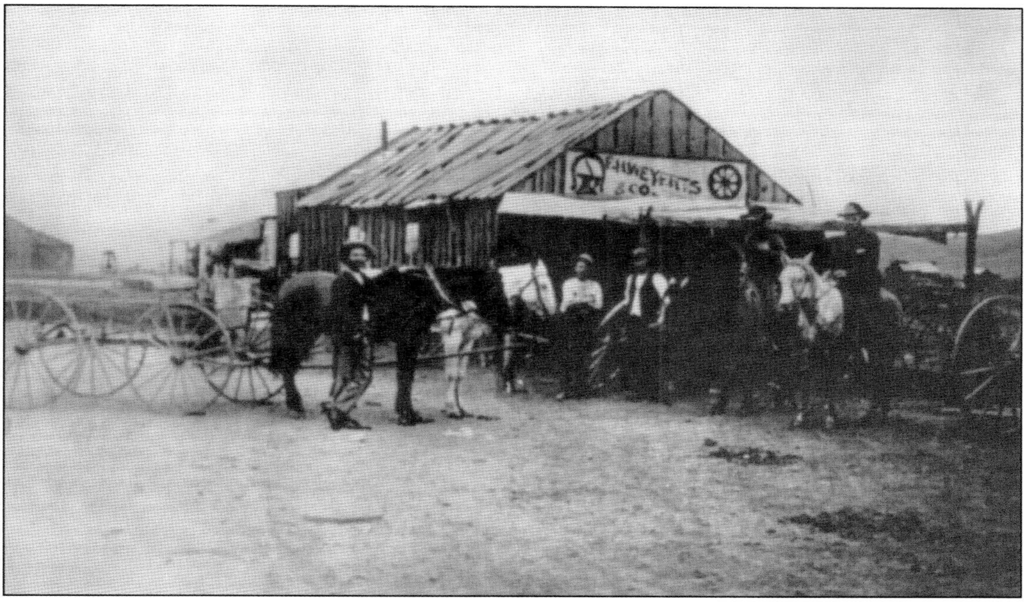

The F. H. Weyerts and Company blacksmith shop was originally of frame construction. But, perhaps inevitably, the structure burned down in the early 1890s. Weyerts soon rebuilt using adobe bricks made in a commercial adobe yard he established expressly for that purpose. (Courtesy of the Archives of the Big Bend.)

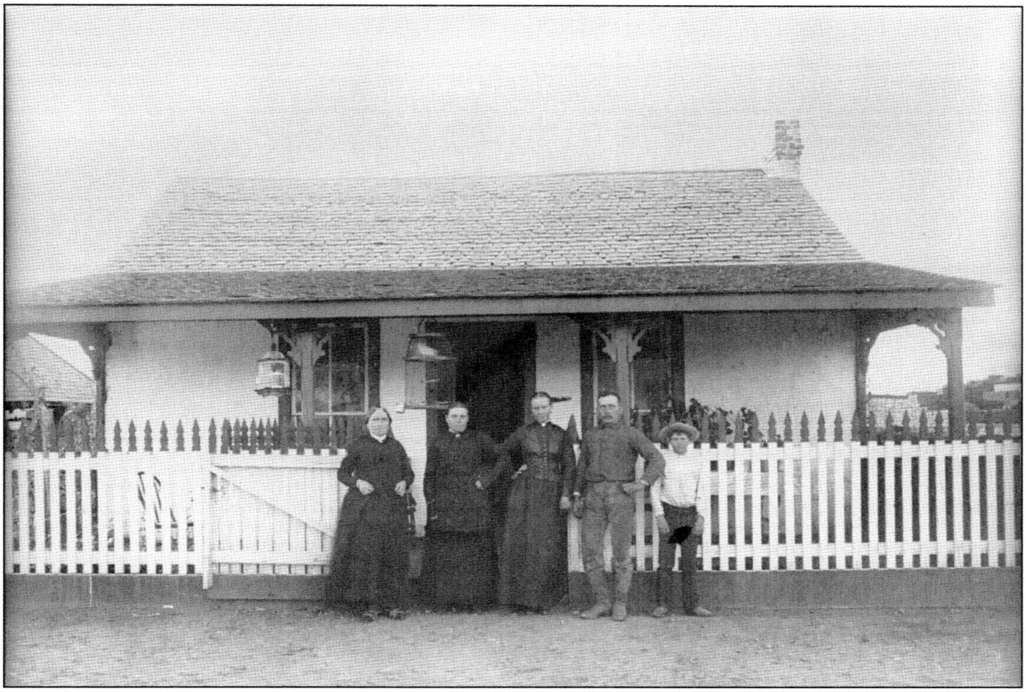

Members of the Frederick Weyerts family stand in front of their home on East Avenue E (where the First National Bank building is located today) in 1889. They are, from left to right, Anna, Metta, Ricka, Frederick, and A. W. Lentz. Anna was the mother of Metta and Frederick, and Ricka was Frederick's wife. The entire family had recently emigrated from Germany. (Courtesy of the Archives of the Big Bend.)

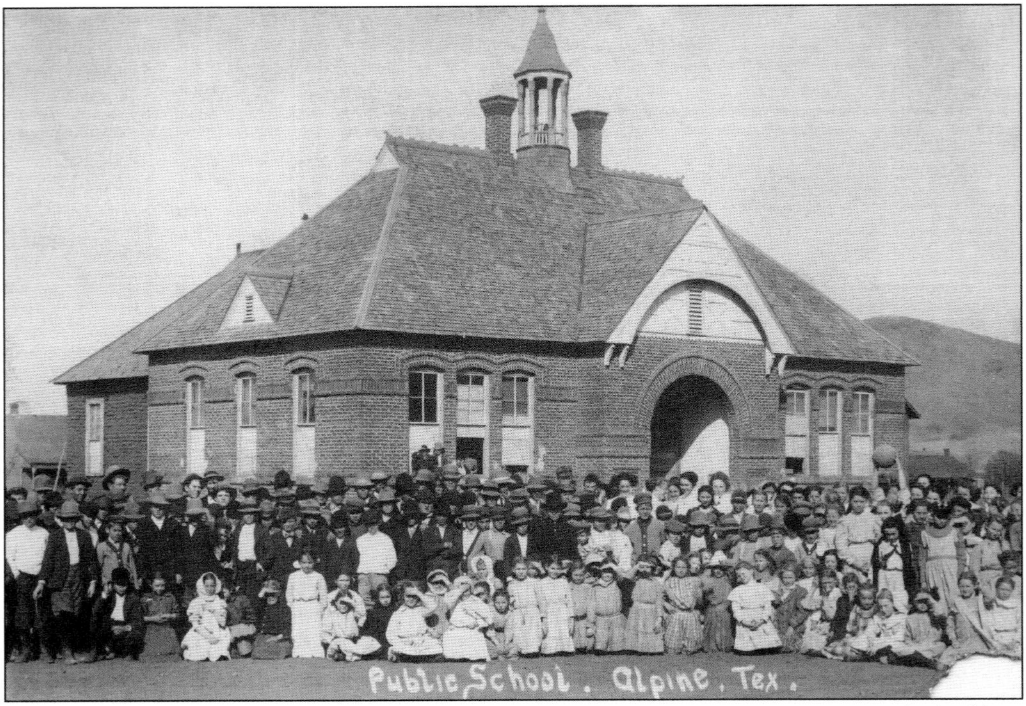

The second Alpine schoolhouse was built in 1891 on what is now Sul Ross Avenue. The building survives and has served in a variety of capacities including a Sul Ross dormitory, offices for the Soil Conservation Service, and, most recently, the Sunshine House senior center. (Courtesy of the Smith collection.)

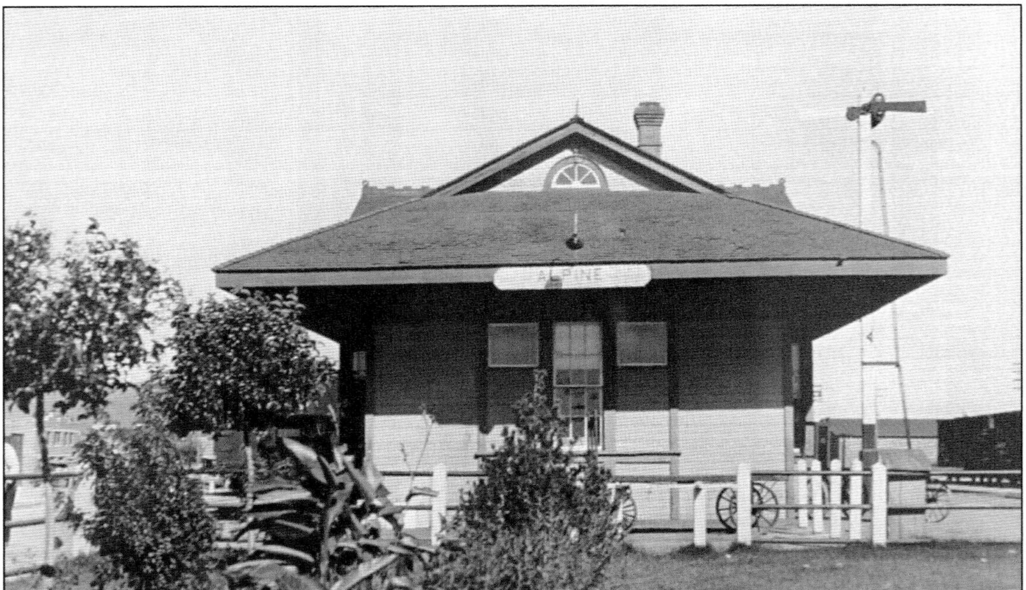

The second Alpine depot was built in 1902 after the original station burned down. Not as large or elaborate as the one it replaced, this depot was a single-story structure, with the freight dock and loading ramps on the east side, the passenger waiting room on the west end, and the agent and telegraph operator's office in the center. (Courtesy of the Archives of the Big Bend.)

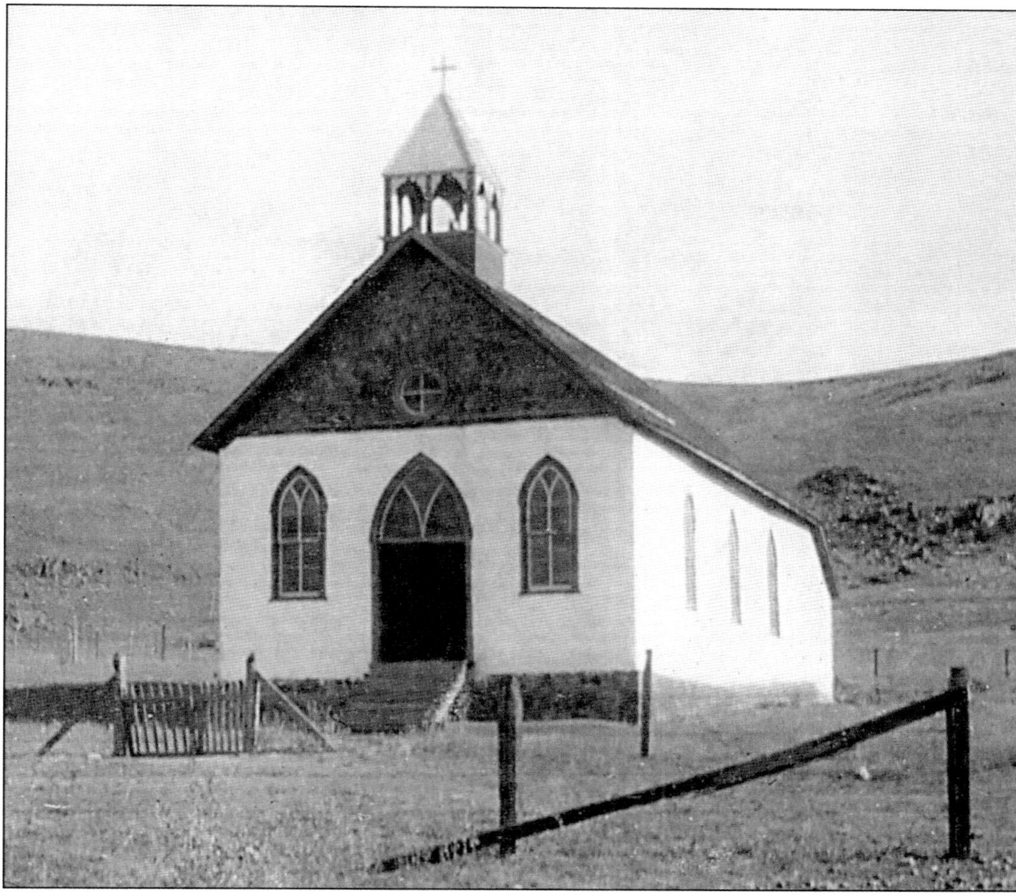

Nuestra Senora de Guadalupe Catholic Church was built of adobe along the flanks of A Mountain in 1900. In the 1920s, the church was renamed Our Lady of Peace. In the 1940s, a new sanctuary was built of native stone, after which the old church served as the Parish Hall. In 1964, the old adobe structure was demolished. (Courtesy of the Archives of the Big Bend.)

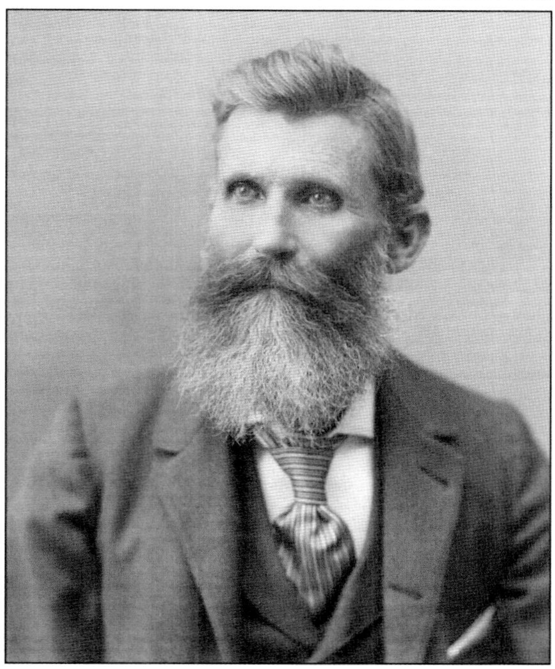

Capt. D. A. T. Walton, sheriff of Brewster County from 1902 to 1908, was a well-known lawman who had been a member of the Texas Rangers, fought in the Civil War, and served as sheriff of Bee County for 19 years before moving to Brewster County. He was succeeded by his son Allen J. Walton, who served until 1918. (Courtesy of the Archives of the Big Bend.)

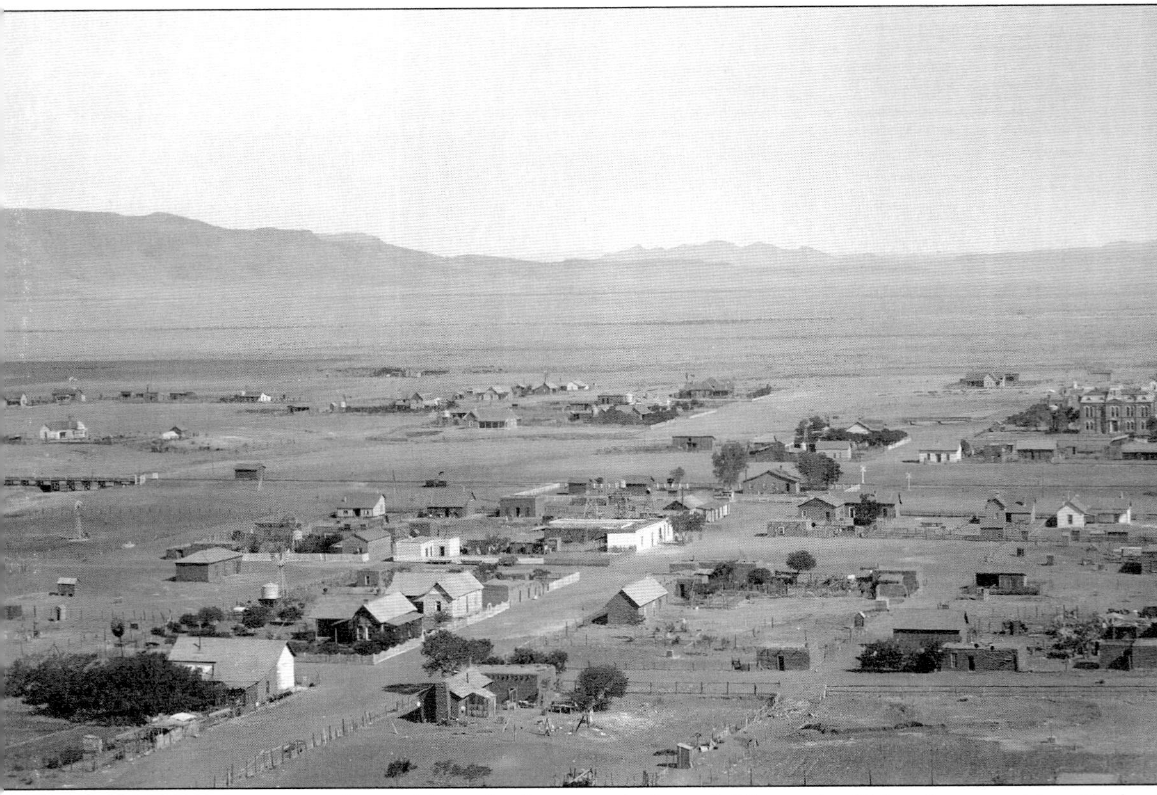

This 1904 panorama shows Alpine looking north from A Mountain. Taken by an unidentified photographer, it is the best of several early overviews taken of Alpine. The courthouse is near the center of the photograph, the railroad cattle yard on the far righthand side, and Nuestra Senora de Guadalupe Catholic Church in the lower-right foreground. Alpine grew slowly in the early years. When this photograph was taken, the town was just over two decades old, with a population

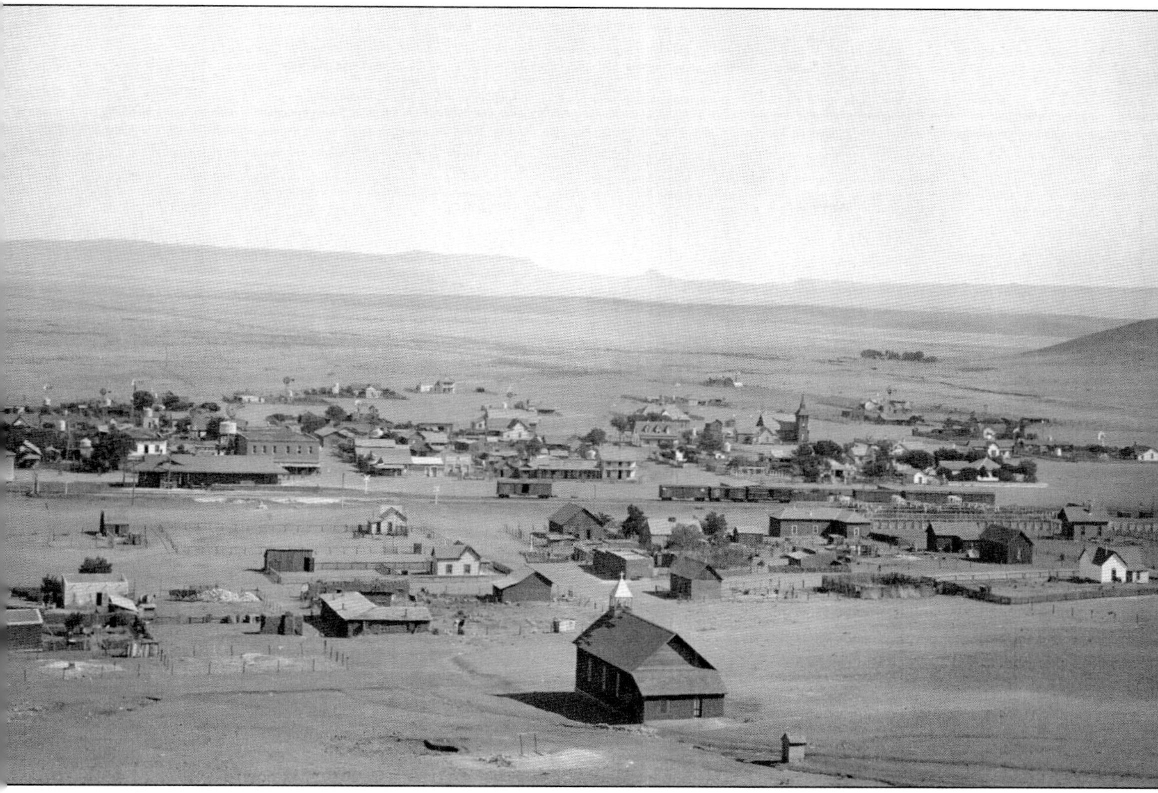

estimated at less than 400. It had not changed much since the early 1890s, when rancher and lawman E. E. Townsend first saw Alpine and described it as "a little cowtown spraddled across the railroad tracks as uncertain in conformity as a pair of ragged overalls." (Courtesy of the Archives of the Big Bend.)

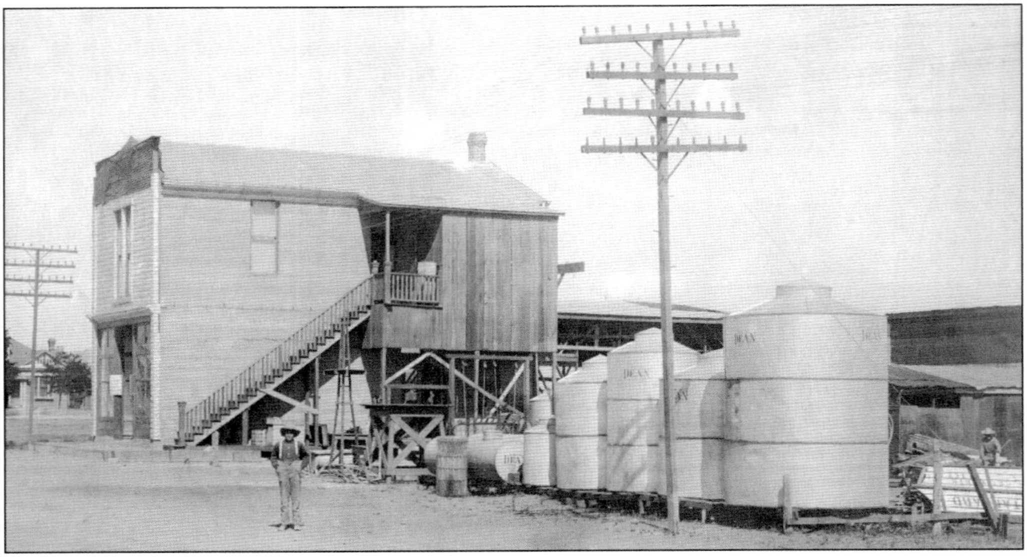

The Dean Manufacturing company, established in 1909, made many of the steel water tanks—like the ones seen here—as well as other sheet metal goods used by area ranchers. Still standing at the corner of Seventh and Sul Ross Avenue, the building was remodeled by Charles Livingston into a funeral parlor in 1928 and sold to Don Geeslin in 1961. (Courtesy of the Archives of the Big Bend.)

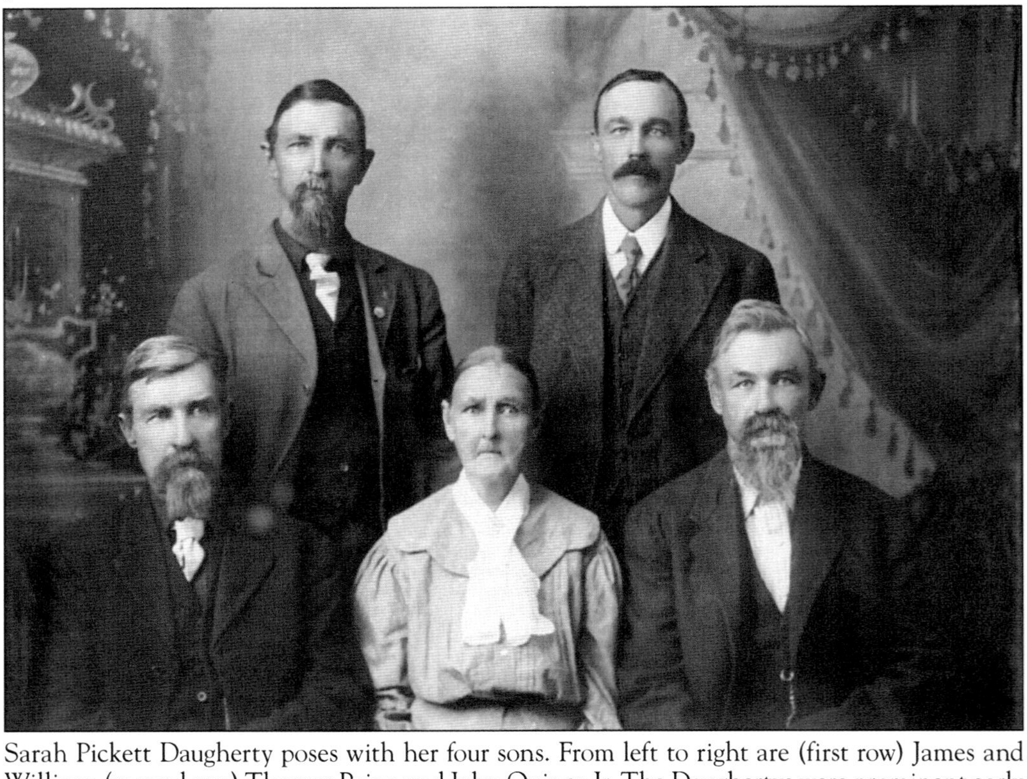

Sarah Pickett Daugherty poses with her four sons. From left to right are (first row) James and William; (second row) Thomas Paine and John Quincy Jr. The Daughertys were prominent early Alpine businessmen. James and John owned the first icehouse and received the first contract to supply electricity to the town. William constructed many of Alpine's finer homes and businesses. (Courtesy of the Archives of the Big Bend.)

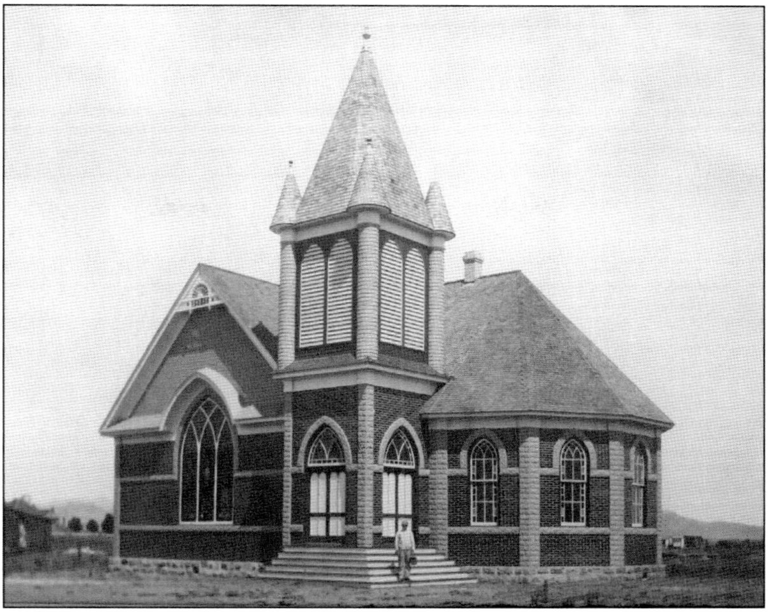

The First Christian Church of Alpine, was constructed in 1906 by William Daugherty, one of Alpine's earliest building contractors. Adapted from the High Victorian Gothic style, the church features a central bell tower, an asymmetrical floor plan, and limited use of vergeboards. (Courtesy of the Archives of the Big Bend.)

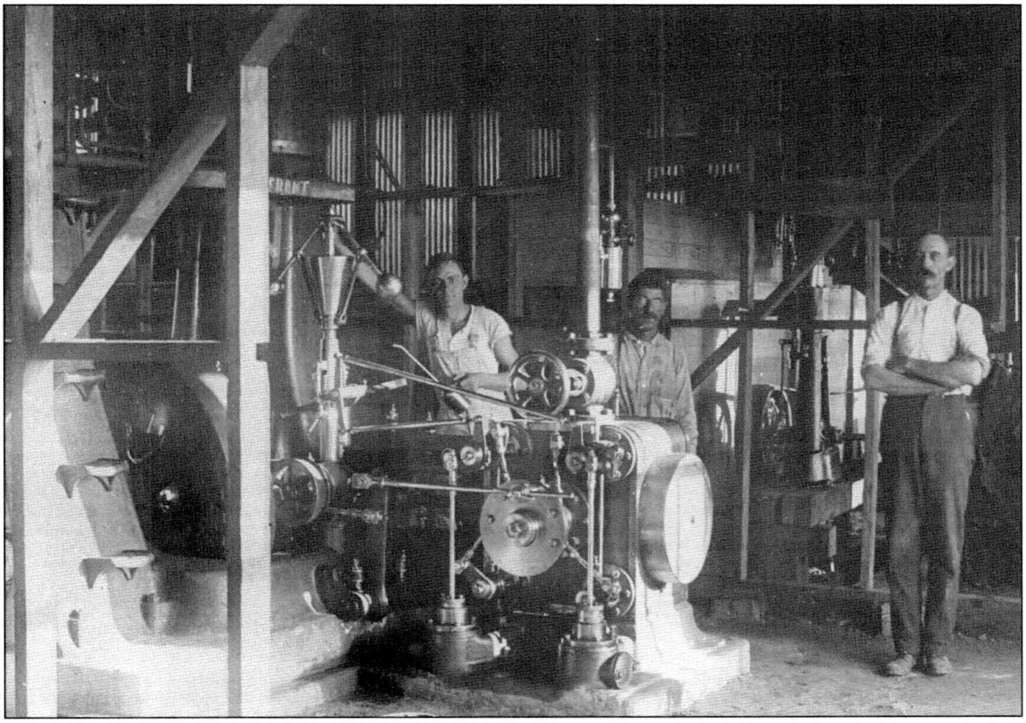

Alpine's first electric generator, owned by brothers James and John Daugherty (standing on right), was housed in a building adjacent to their Alpine Ice and Bottling works at South Seventh and Murphy Streets. A 10-year contract was entered to power lights in the courthouse for $36 per year. (Courtesy of the Archives of the Big Bend.)

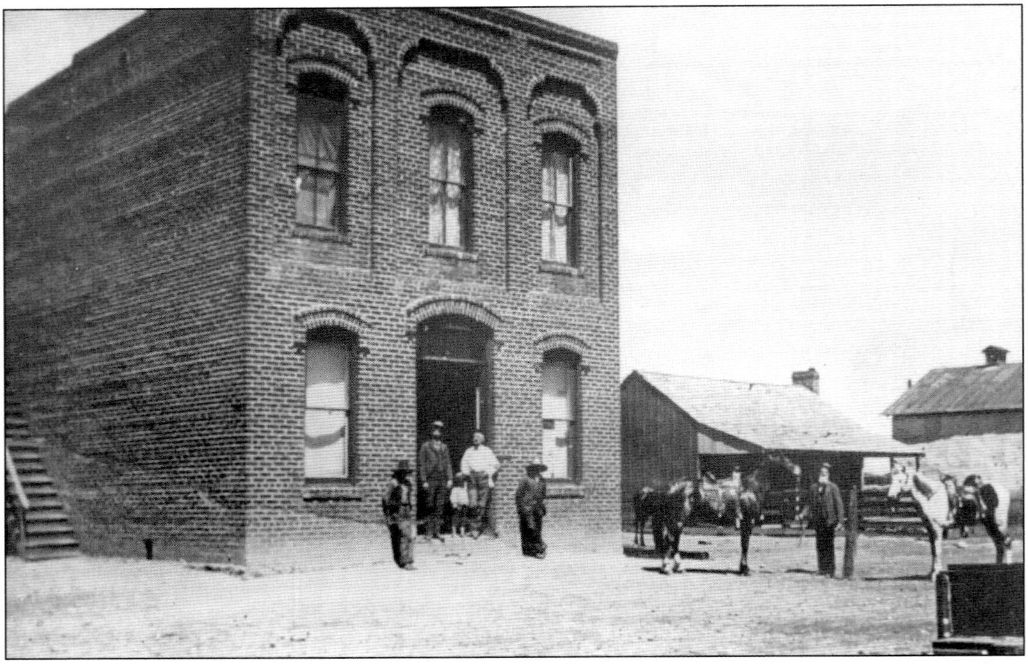

One of the earliest multistory buildings in Alpine, the Hancock Building was constructed in 1888 on North Fifth Street. It was used in a variety of capacities over the years, including as a post office, drugstore, saddle shop, and grocery store. During World War II, it was used by the United Service Organization. The building was demolished in the early 1960s. (Courtesy of the Archives of the Big Bend.)

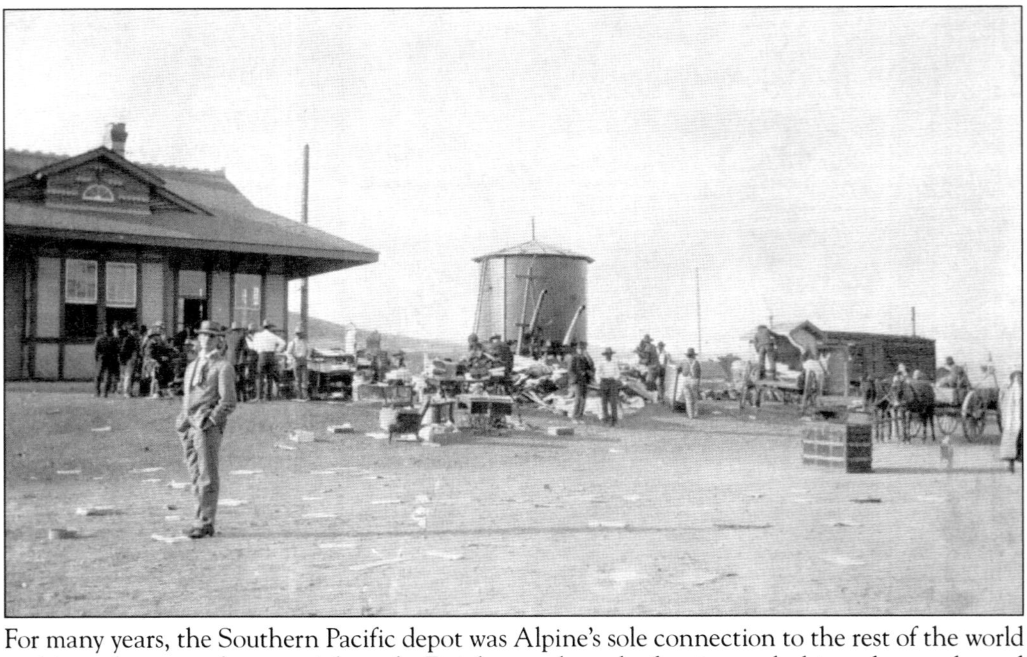

For many years, the Southern Pacific depot was Alpine's sole connection to the rest of the world and its only source for material goods. Freight cars brought furniture, clothing, dry goods, and other items to those who ordered them from suppliers or had them shipped from homes they had left behind. (Courtesy of the Archives of the Big Bend.)

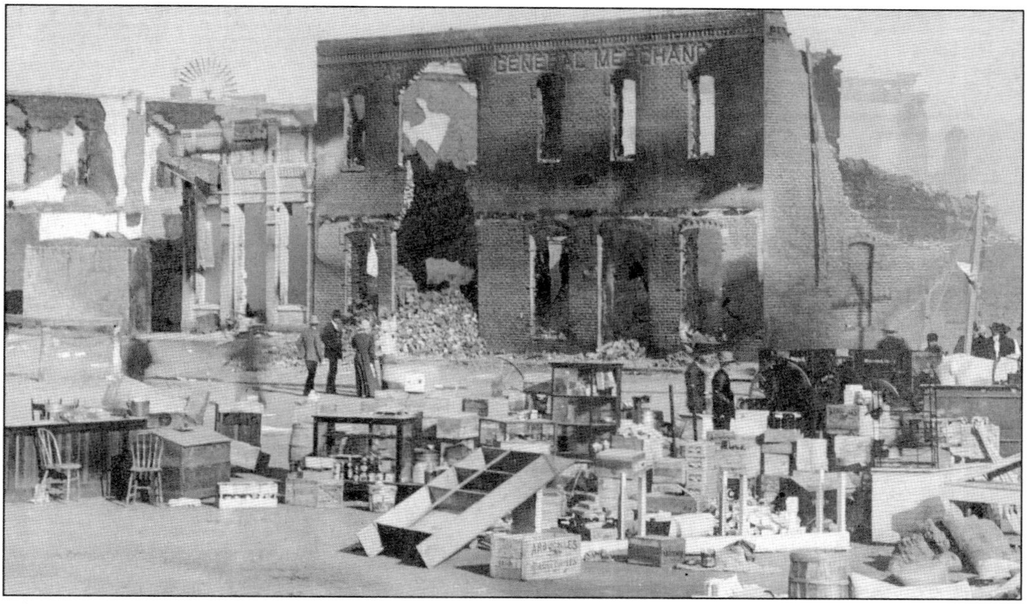

The fire of April 14, 1907, was the second of three major fires that would ravage downtown Alpine during the first two decades of the 20th century. Storekeepers and townspeople frantically moved what little could be saved out onto the street. Fires eventually spurred both better, more fire-resistant construction as well as public waterworks to help prevent future catastrophes. (Courtesy of the Archives of the Big Bend.)

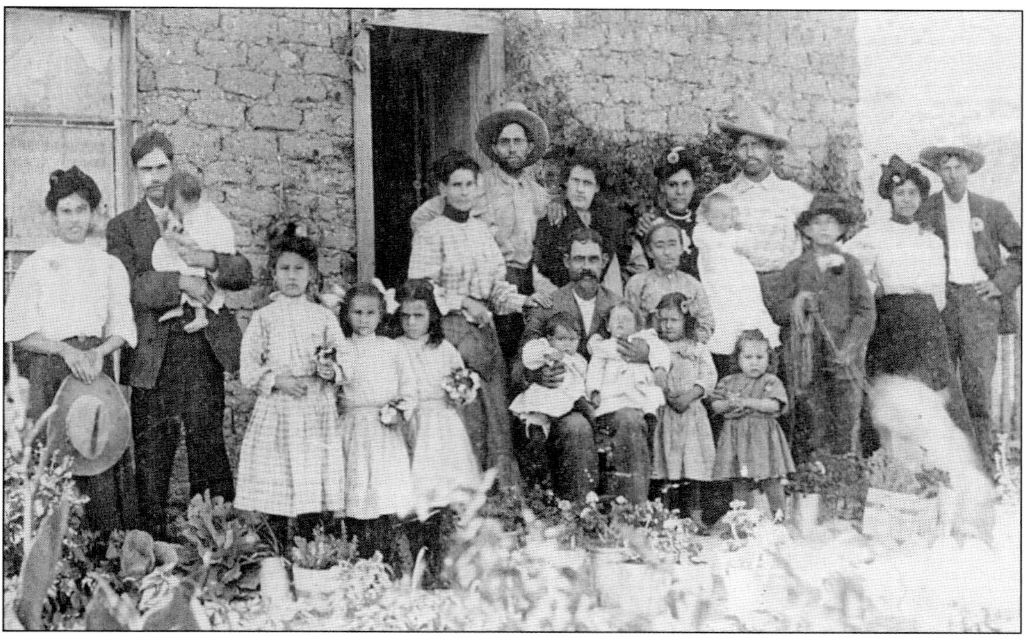

Wenserlado "Ben" Gallego and his family pose at their ranch 8 miles west of Alpine in 1907. Standing, from left to right, are Cesaria Mata, Joe "Jose" holding daughter Virginia, Juanita, Francisca, Leonor, Susie "Jesusita" Russell, John "Juan" Sr., Andrea Sotello, Ramona, Jim "Santiago," Celso, Victorina Almodova, and Pete Sr. Seated from left are Wenserlado and Juanita Mata (family friend) with children Dan, Ben, Lucinda, and Adela, daughter of John. (Courtesy of the Valadez collection.)

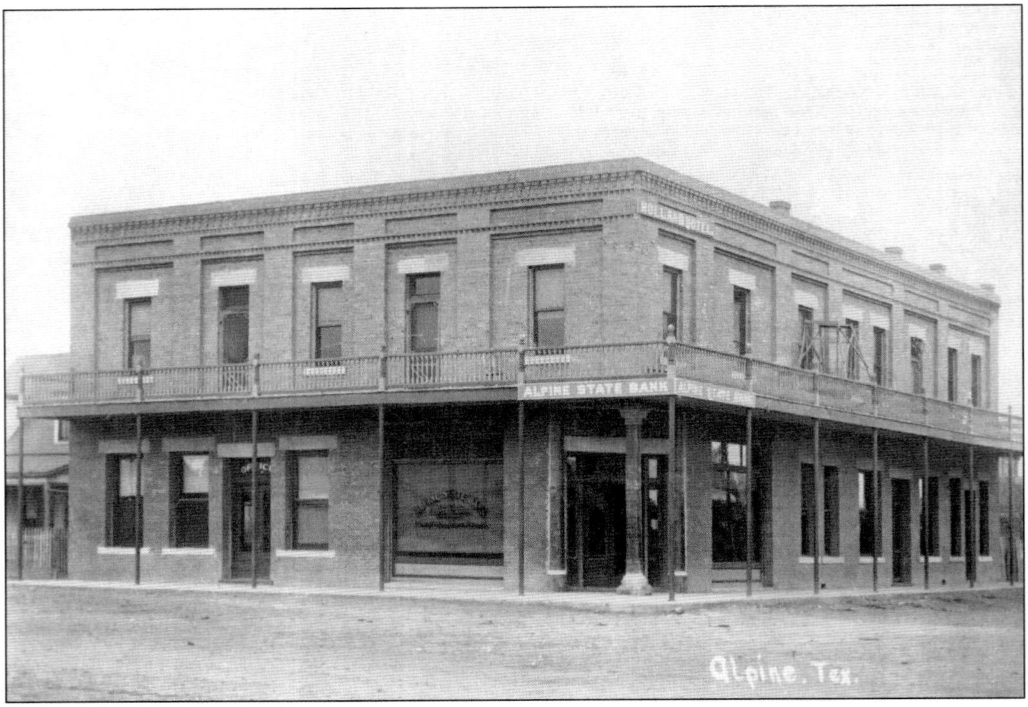

The original Holland Hotel was built in 1908 by rancher John Holland on the corner of North Sixth and Front Streets. The hotel served as Alpine's first upscale accommodations and became one of the town's most enduring institutions. (Courtesy of the Archives of the Big Bend.)

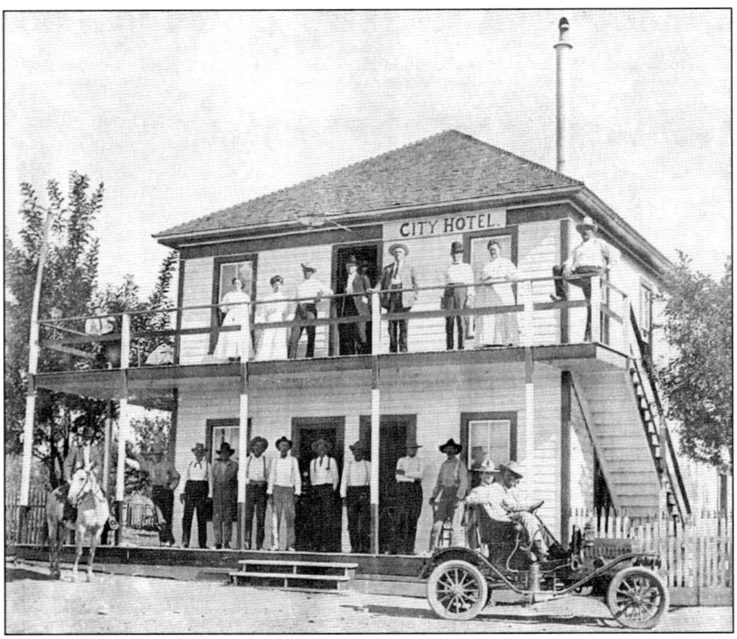

The City Hotel on Murphy Street, shown here in 1909, catered primarily to laborers and railway passengers. Later renamed the Ritchey Hotel, it was the more economical choice for cowboys who had come to town to oversee cattle shipments out of the Southern Pacific loading pens across the road. The Ritchey is one of few early frame constructed buildings that still stand today. (Courtesy of the Archives of the Big Bend.)

Two

COMING OF AGE
GROWTH AND DEVELOPMENT (1910–1919)

During the second decade of the 20th century, Alpine made great strides in spite of a series of setbacks. The droughts of 1910 and 1916 caused a slackening in the steady growth Alpine had enjoyed since its birth, as the natural increase was offset by an out-migration of defeated homesteaders. In 1911, Alpine suffered its third major fire that, once again, destroyed the downtown business district. And the Mexican Revolution, which shook the security of the border region and triggered a depopulation of the area along the Rio Grande, reached a climax in 1916 with the tragic raid on Glenn Springs causing the loss of three soldiers and one civilian.

But in spite of these difficulties, Alpine continued to grow. In 1910, the town gained an elaborate two-story brick schoolhouse with Gothic detailing that helped inspire the first session of the Alpine Summer Normal. Over the next several years, the Alpine State Bank was organized, and many of the more substantial downtown buildings were erected, including the Lackey-Hord building on Sixth and Holland Streets and the Masonic Lodge on the corner of Fifth Street and Avenue E. In 1913, the Kansas City, Mexico, and Orient Railway reached Alpine, generating great excitement and a celebration so large it temporarily doubled the population of the town.

And despite periods of drought, World War I guaranteed that beef prices would continue to climb; by the end of the decade, they stood at an all-time high. In 1918, the Highland Hereford Breeders Association formed to advertise the exceptional quality of the region's livestock. The end of World War I was cause for celebration in Alpine beyond the end of the conflict. Although legislation had passed in 1917 establishing Sul Ross Normal College, the war intervened to delay its construction. With the end of the war, construction proceeded. And with the promise of having its own college, the town's future looked more hopeful than ever.

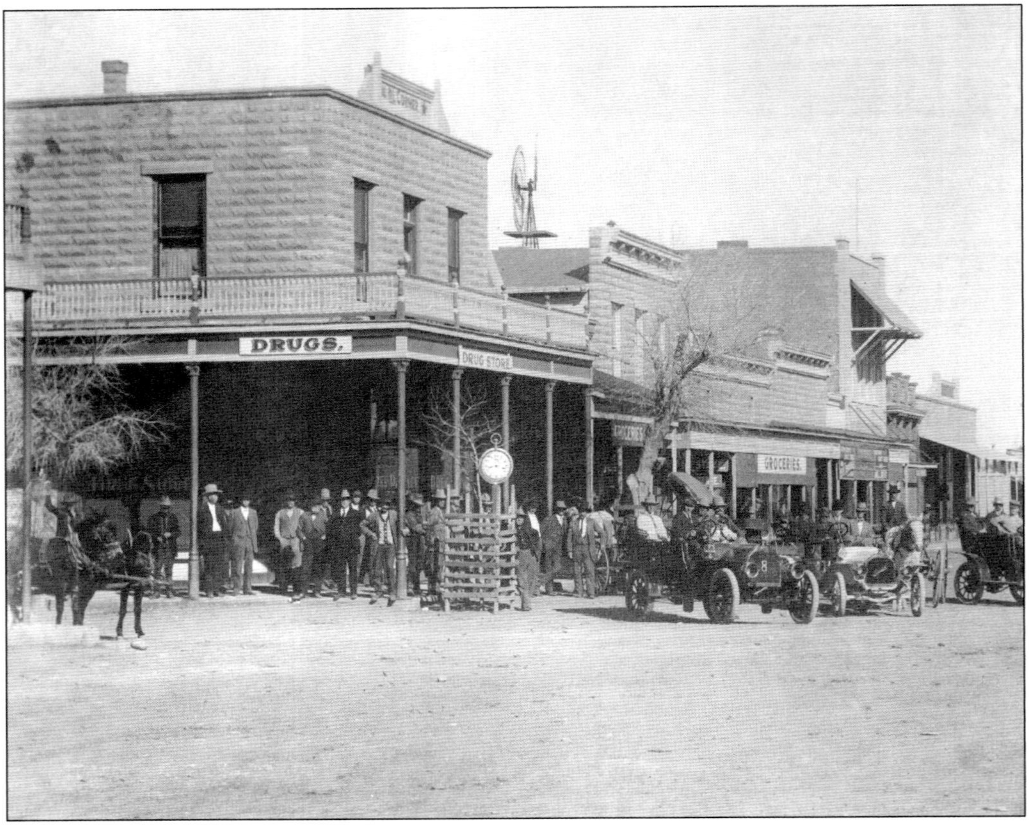

Citizens gather around the corner of Sixth and Front Streets around 1910. On the first floor of the nearest building is the Palace Drug store. This entire block, itself only three years old, would be destroyed by fire the following year. (Courtesy of the Archives of the Big Bend.)

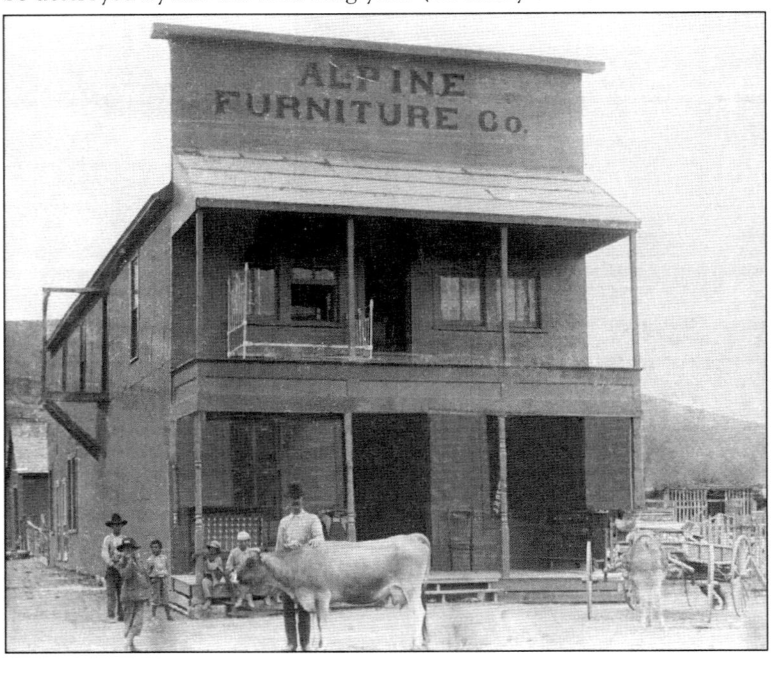

The old Alpine Furniture Company on Murphy Street was constructed around 1902 by N. L. Hulbert. The store passed through several owners and at one time was converted to a rooming house. In 1937, Tomás Valadez bought the property and operated it as a grocery store and meat market. (Courtesy of the Archives of the Big Bend.)

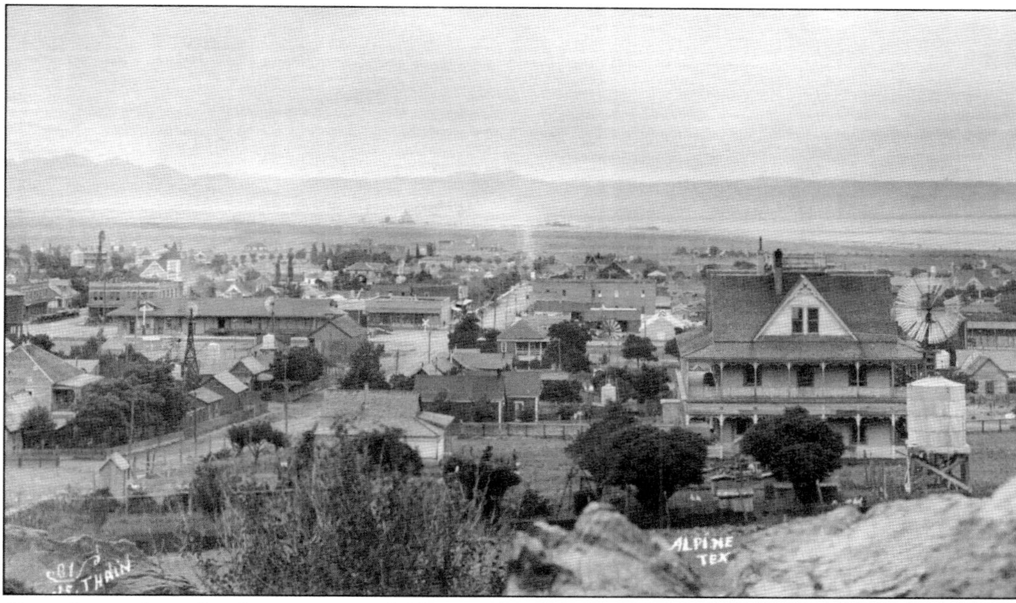

One of a number of early overviews of Alpine taken by photographer John Thain, this photograph looks northwest across the town from A Mountain just east of Fifth Street around 1911. A recent fire had destroyed most of the downtown area, and much of it had yet to be rebuilt. (Courtesy of the Archives of the Big Bend.)

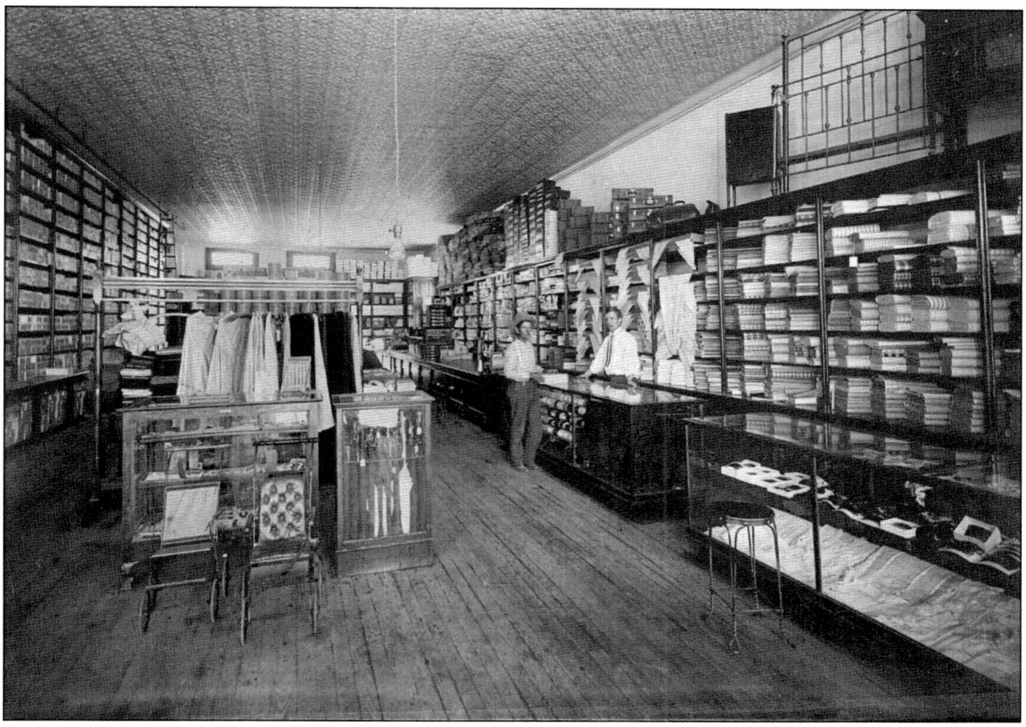

Located on the corner of Fifth Street and Holland Avenue, the merchandise of Mitchell-Gillett Dry Goods was a showcase of organization. Shown here around 1910, the store offered a variety of fabric and ready-to-wear clothing in addition to such things as suitcases, umbrellas, thread, and clothing patterns. (Courtesy of the Archives of the Big Bend.)

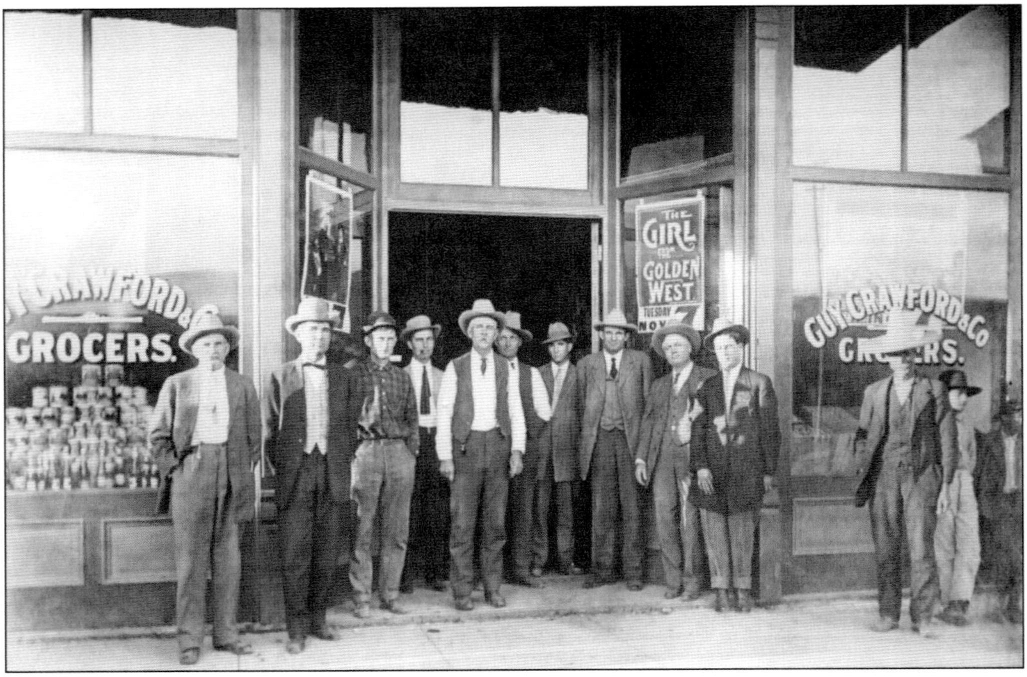

Guy Crawford stands with friends and associates in front of his grocery store around 1910. In the photograph are, from left to right, John Ferguson, W. F. McGaughy, Polk Hinson, unidentified, Guy Crawford, Walter Measday, Felix McGaughy, W. W. Collins, O. L. Shipman, and Frank Crawford. The man and boy at far right are unidentified. (Courtesy of the Archives of the Big Bend.)

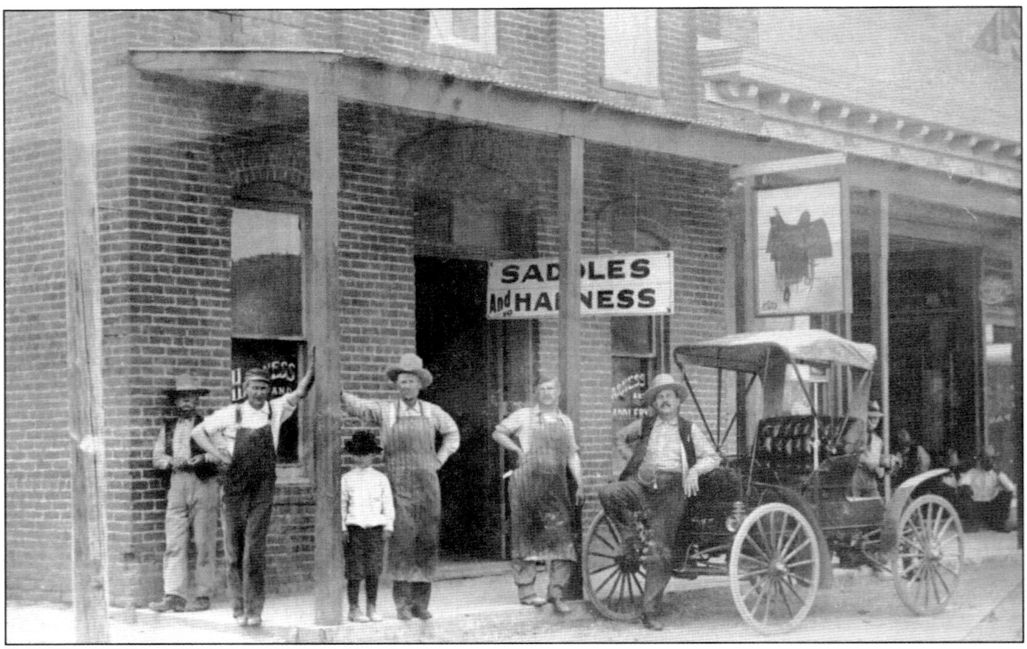

Alpine's Saddle and Harness shop was located for a time in the Hancock building on North Fifth Street, shown here in 1910. Although the man with the horseless carriage had no use for either saddles or harnesses, it seemed of no concern to the proprietors of the shop. (Courtesy of the Archives of the Big Bend.)

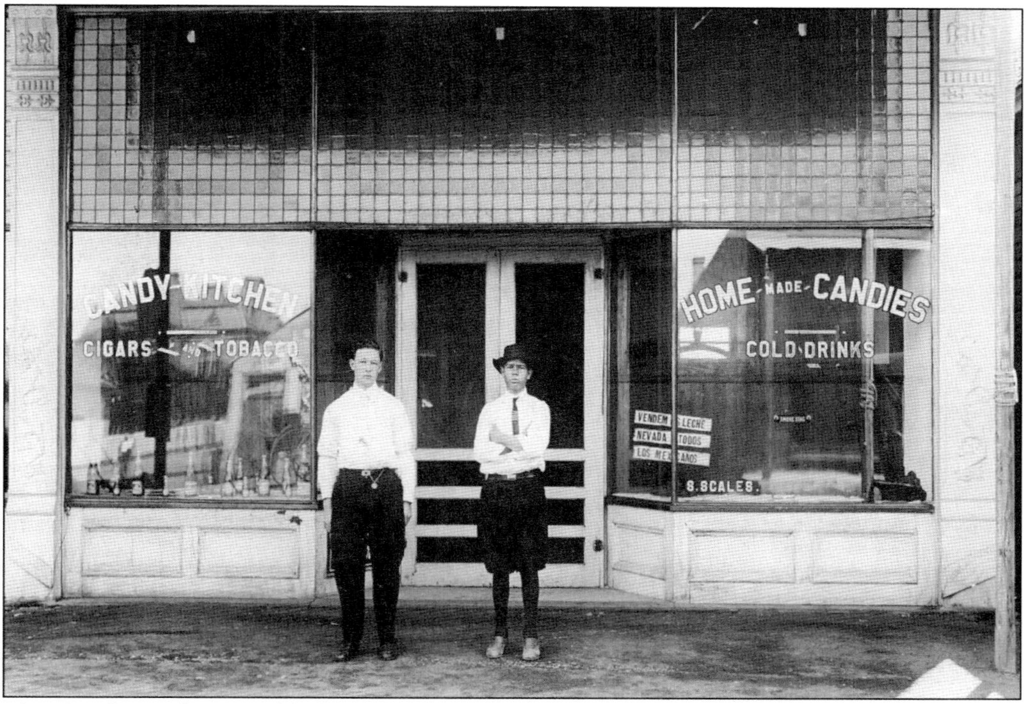

The Candy Kitchen, established in 1911 by Shirley Scales, was an Alpine icon for more than 45 years. Offering homemade candies in addition to popular commercial brands, the business also served homemade ice cream and had a soda fountain with enough seating to accommodate groups of college students. (Courtesy of the Archives of the Big Bend.)

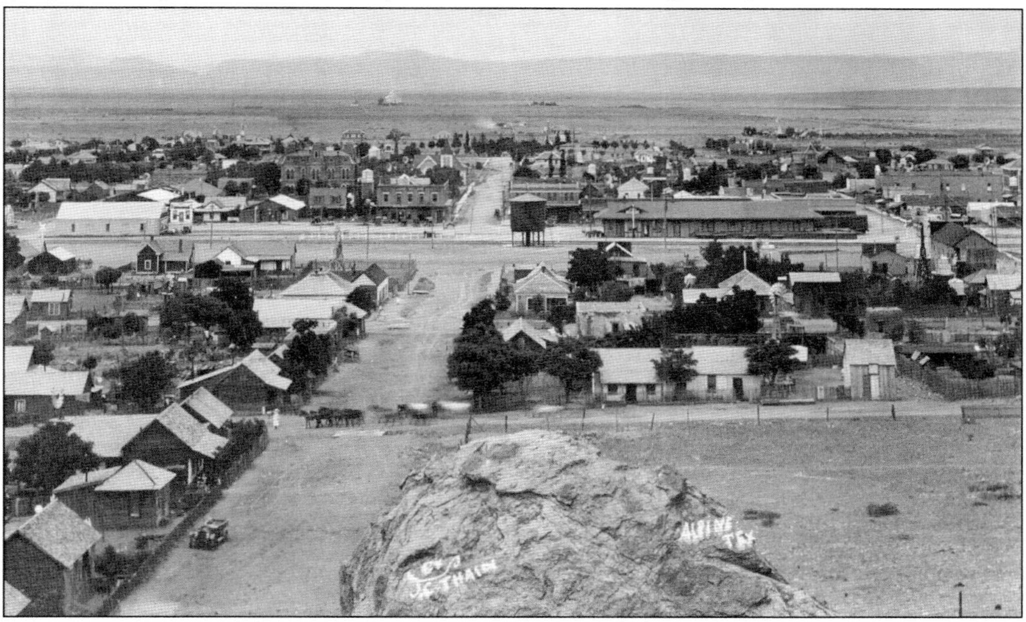

This 1913 photograph looking north down Sixth Street from A Mountain shows a slowly maturing town. At the far end of the street, partially obscured by trees, is the Central School. The depot can be seen just right of the center of the photograph. In the foreground, horses are being herded down Avenue G. (Courtesy of the Archives of the Big Bend.)

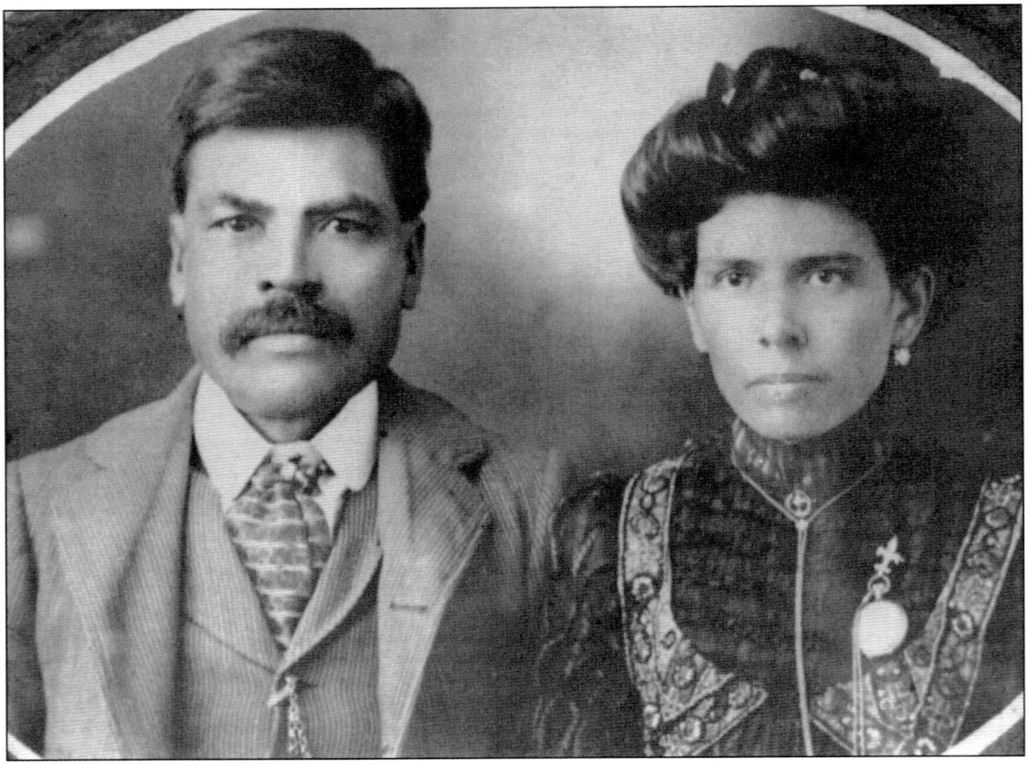

In 1906, Juan and Pilar Ramos moved from Presidio County to Alpine, where he worked as a grocer. Married in 1901, the Ramoses had seven children—Herminio, Jose, Juan, Francisco, Juanita, Alejandra (Ollie), and Minnie. Ramos was also the father of Severo, Jose, and Dolores Ramos. (Courtesy of the Archives of the Big Bend.)

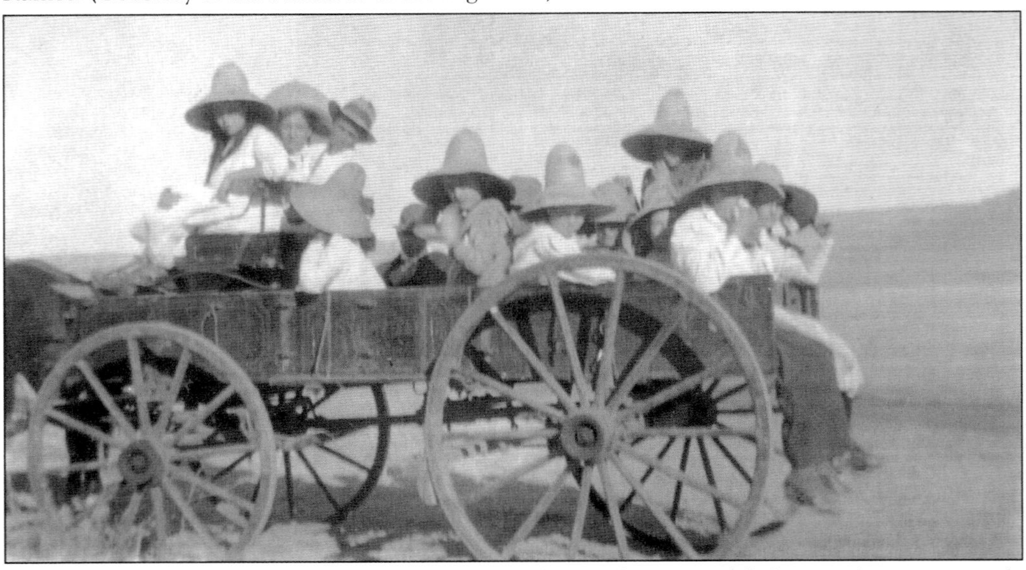

A group of young people with matching headgear takes a ride in a Studebaker ranch wagon outside of Alpine around 1910. At that time, the landscape around town was utterly treeless and shade absent. This, along with the southerly latitude and generally clear skies, made hats essential for protection against the sun. (Courtesy of the Smith collection.)

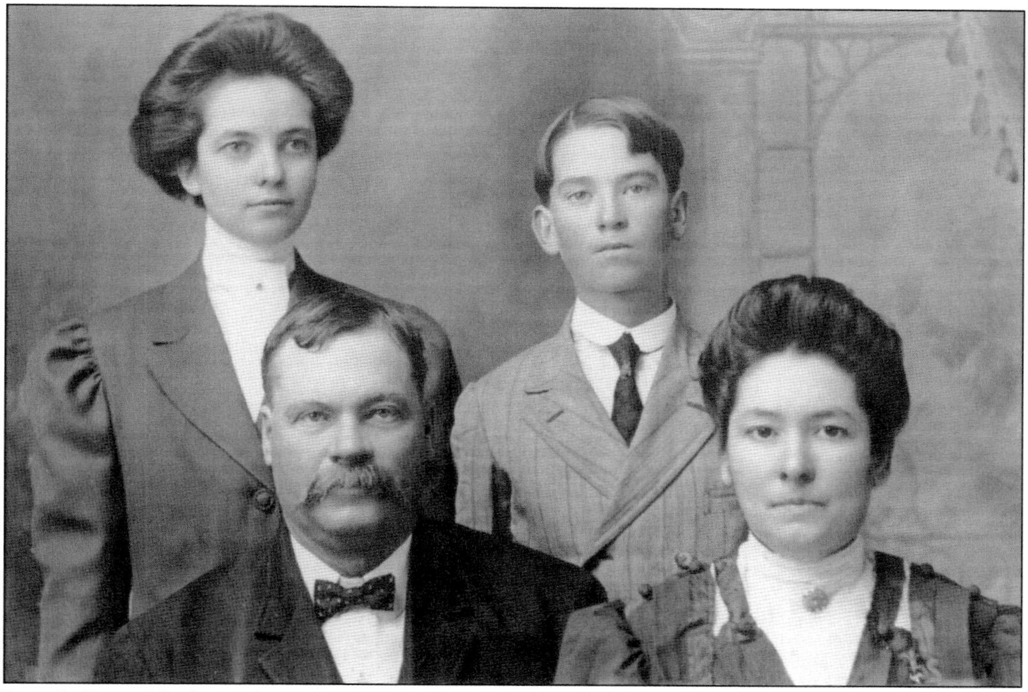

Joseph Daniel Jackson first came to the area as a member of Company B of the Texas Rangers. In 1885, he moved to Alpine, where he would become a prominent cattleman. Jackson was also instrumental in establishing Sul Ross State Teacher's College. This studio portrait includes his wife, Dorcas Ford, and their two children, Una (left) and Ford. (Courtesy of the Museum of the Big Bend.)

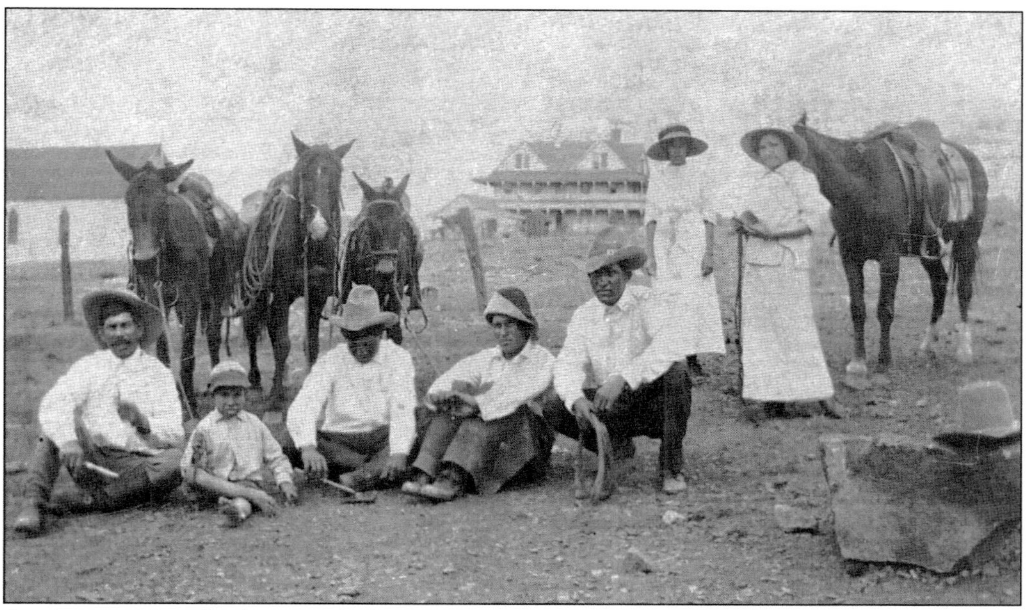

Cowboys and friends relax near the base of A Mountain around 1915. Behind them are the Garnett Hotel (center) and Nuestra Senora de Guadalupe Church (left). The group includes, from left to right, Jose Lopez, Guillermo Lopez, Usebio Lopez, Wally Rodriguez, Francisco Ramirez, Eloisa Ramirez, and Gregoria Sotelo. (Courtesy of the Archives of the Big Bend.)

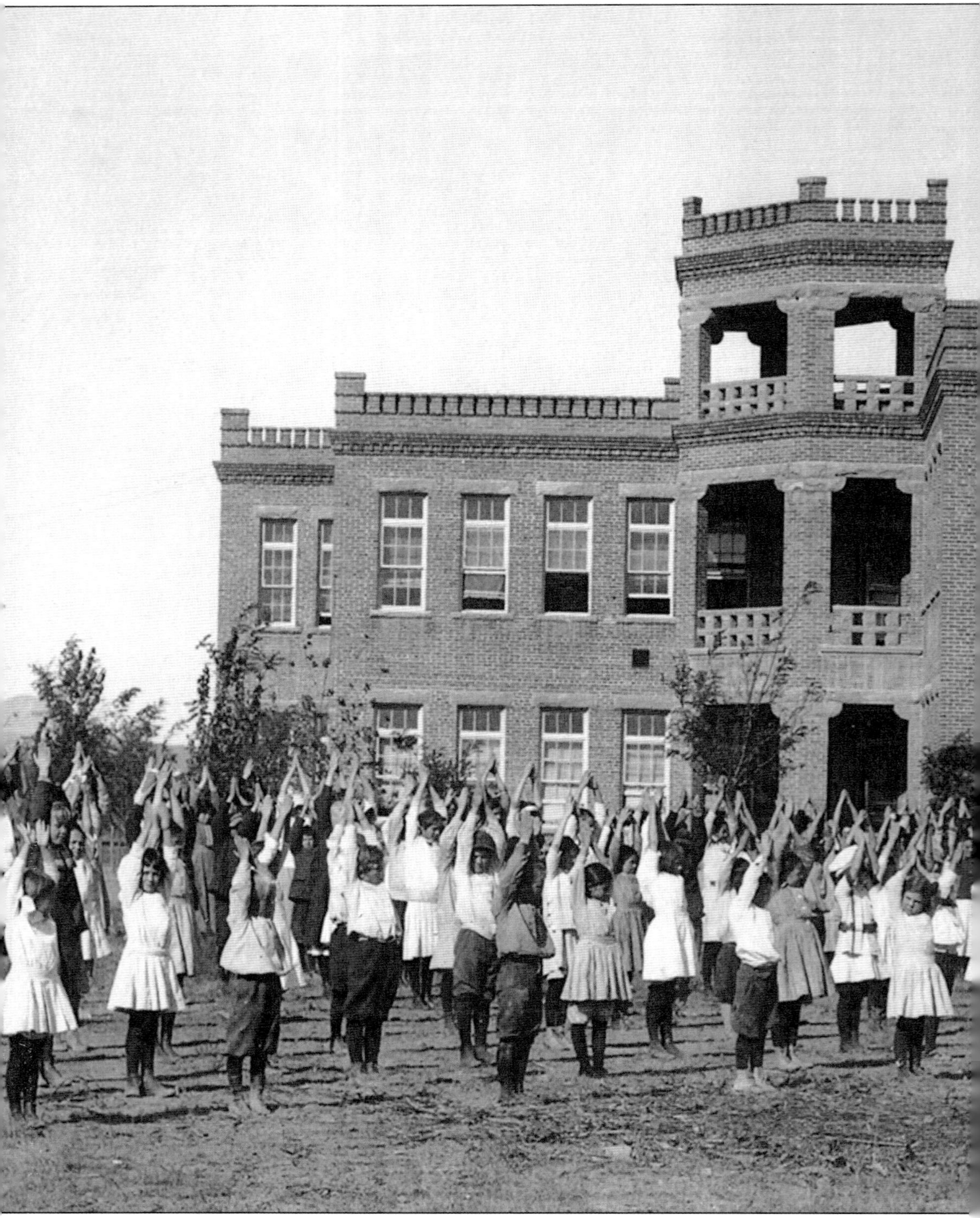

Schoolchildren perform morning calisthenics in front of their new school building that featured a three-story crenellated tower. Built in 1910 at a cost $30,000, this structure was the pride of Alpine and inspired the first Summer Normal, the predecessor to Sul Ross State Teacher's College. Originally used for all grades, the building became the elementary school as new junior

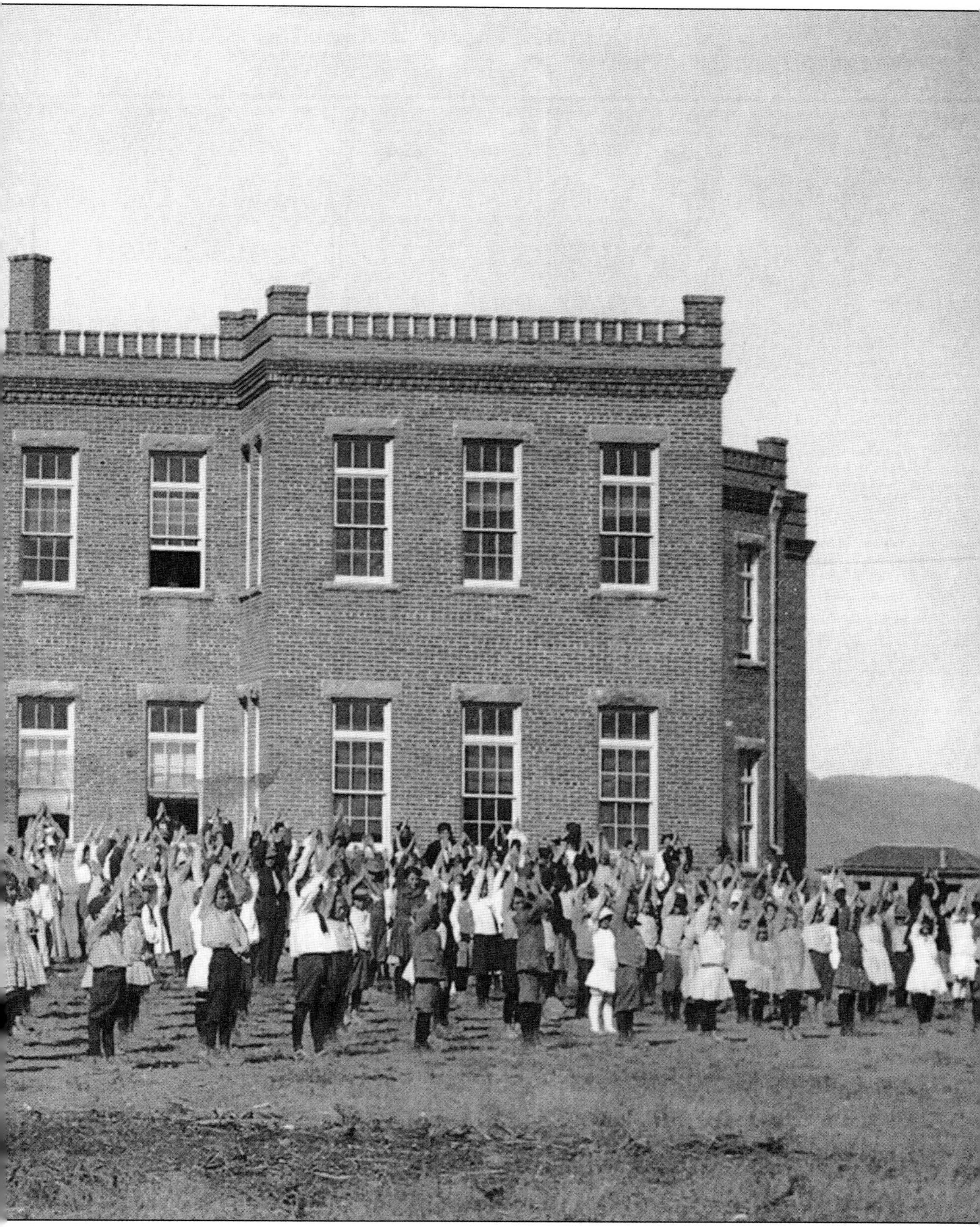

and senior high schools were built. The historic school was demolished in 1971 and replaced with a contemporary single-story brick and glass elementary school. (Courtesy of the Archives of the Big Bend.)

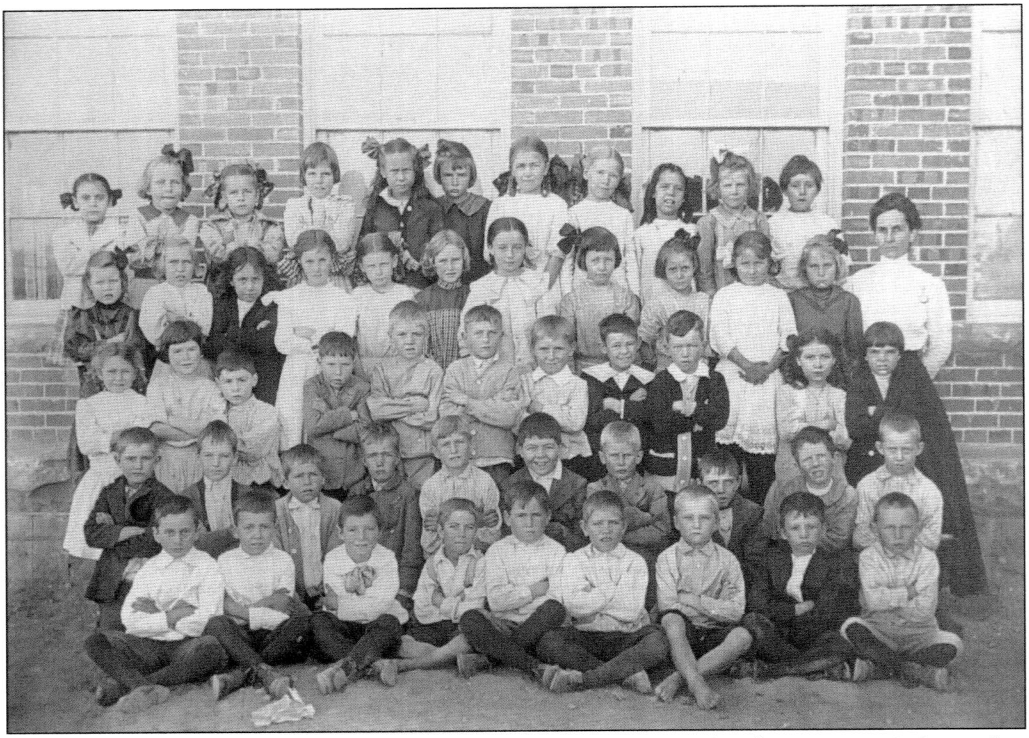

Ade English poses with her first-grade class outside Alpine's new schoolhouse in 1910. Soon after the school opened, class was suspended for a day to allow students to plant trees on the school grounds. At the time, J. Frank Dobie, who would later become Texas's most famous folklorist, served as principal. (Courtesy of the Archives of the Big Bend.)

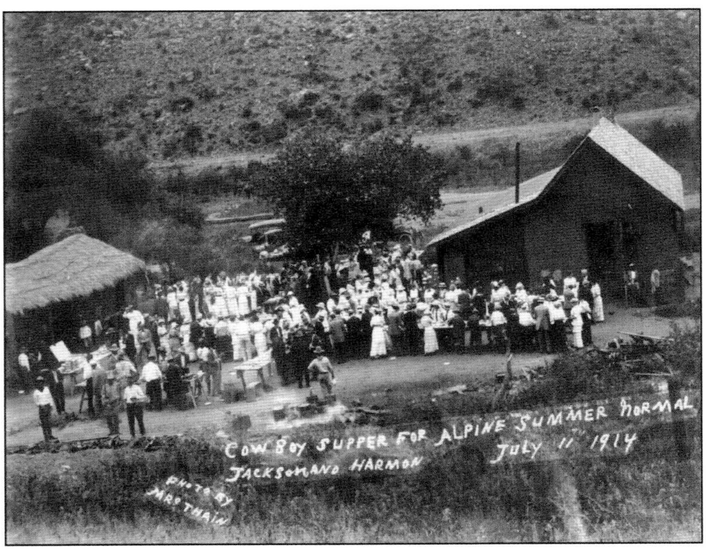

For years, ranching partners J. D. Jackson and Sam Harmon hosted a cowboy supper for the Alpine Summer Normal students and faculty. Both men were enthusiastic supporters of education and helped establish Sul Ross State Normal College. In this 1914 image, Alpine photographer Lizzie Thain captured the students in their Sunday best mingling with the cowboys and cooks. (Courtesy of Smith collection.)

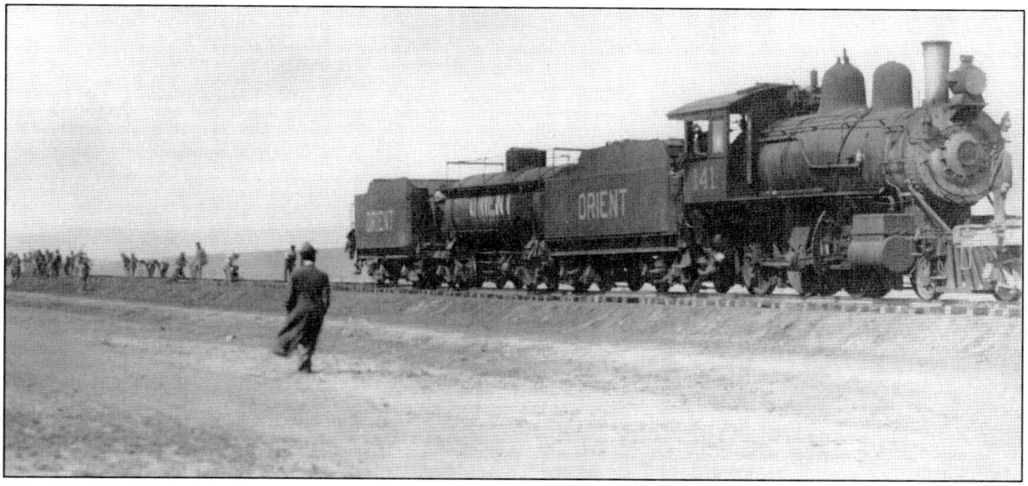

In a much-anticipated event, the first Kansas City, Mexico, and Orient train pulled into Alpine in March 1913. The new railroad further linked Alpine with distant markets and provided a more direct route for shipping cattle to northern feedlots. The *Alpine Avalanche* enthusiastically opined, "There is no reason why Alpine should not be the Denver of Texas." (Courtesy of the Archives of the Big Bend.)

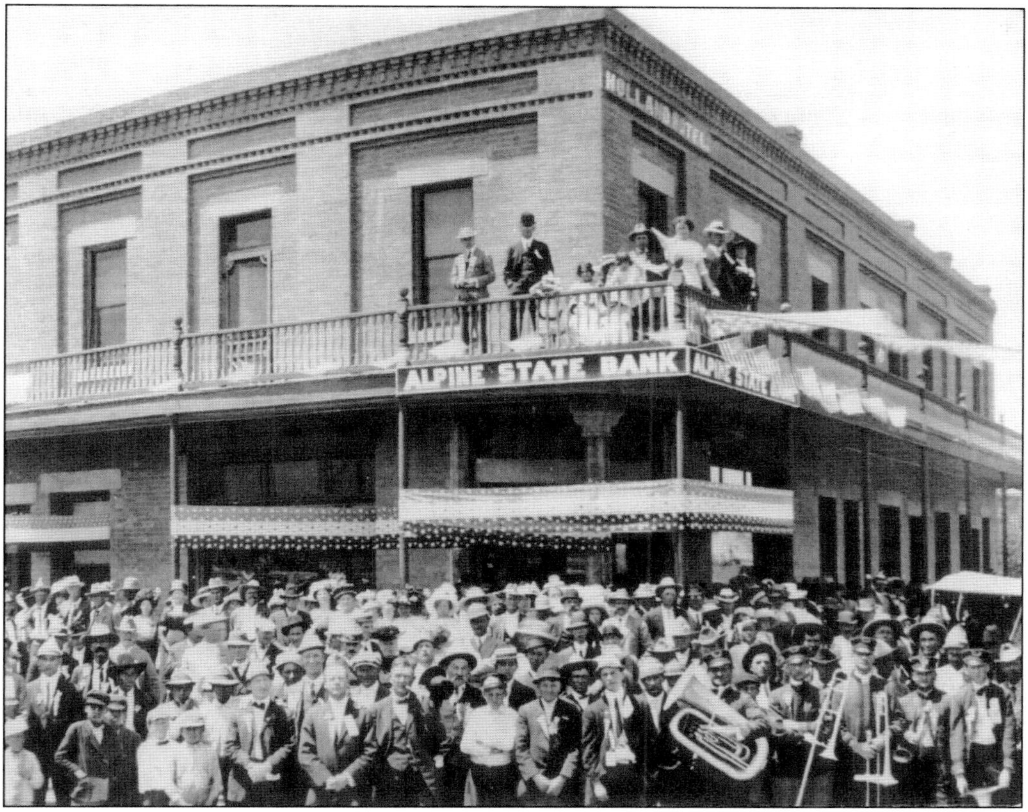

On April 24 and 25, a huge crowd gathered in celebration of the arrival of the Kansas City, Mexico, and Orient Railway. Special trains brought the brass band as well as hundreds of visitors from other towns along the route. Among the festivities were a parade, concerts, a baseball game, and a feast that fed almost 4,000 people. (Courtesy of the Museum of the Big Bend.)

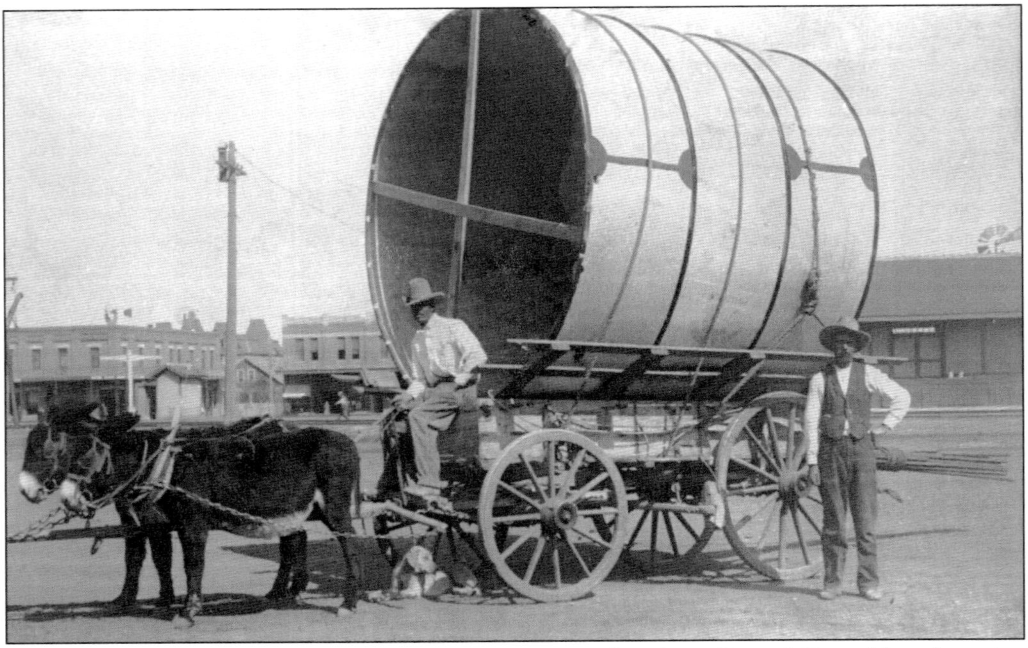

Water tanks were delivered by wagon to customers, most often from Alpine's Dean Manufacturing Company. Standing on the right is freighter Jesus Cobos. Before municipal waterworks were established, most homes in Alpine had their own windmills and storage tanks, many of which still stand today. (Courtesy of the Archives of the Big Bend.)

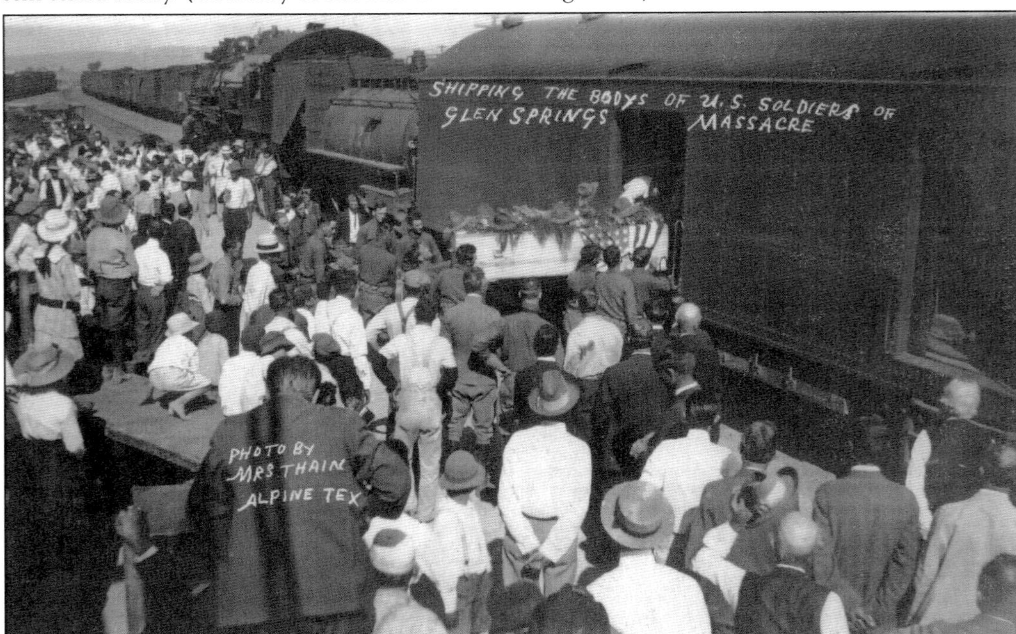

The Glenn Springs Raid in south Brewster County marked the beginning of several raids north of the Rio Grande during the Mexican Revolution. On the night of May 5, 1916, Mexican raiders attacked the village, killing three soldiers from Troop A of the 14th Cavalry and badly wounding others. This photograph shows their caskets being loaded onto the train. (Courtesy of the Museum of the Big Bend.)

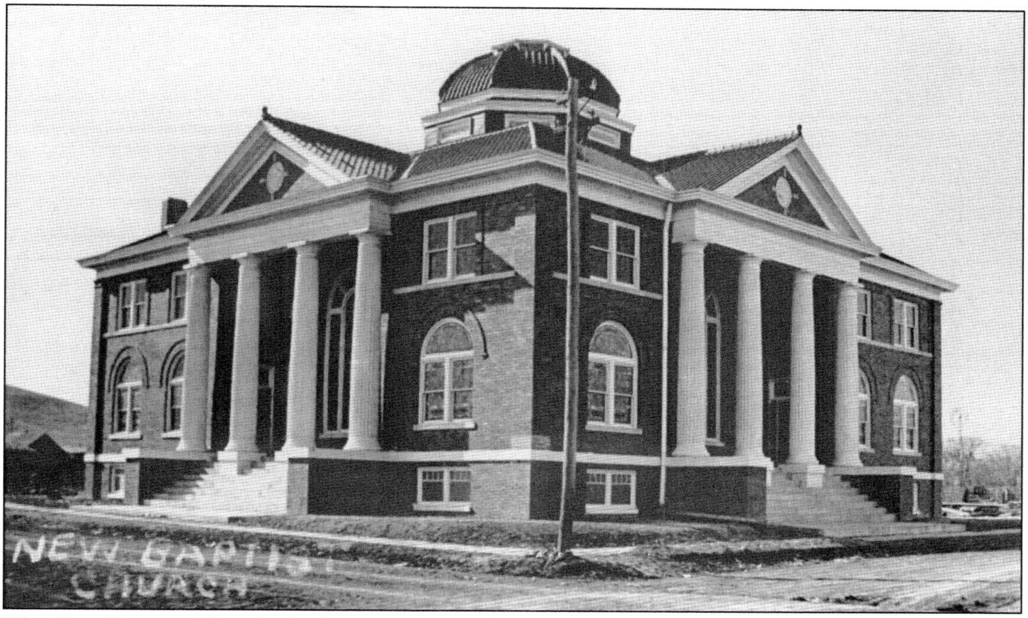

The First Baptist Church, built in 1917, was the earliest example of neoclassical architecture in Alpine. The church was first organized in 1893, and for many years the congregation worshiped in a small adobe church on the same site. This ambitious upgrade seated 700 and had 14 Sunday school rooms and two dressing rooms, among other facilities. (Courtesy of the Archives of the Big Bend.)

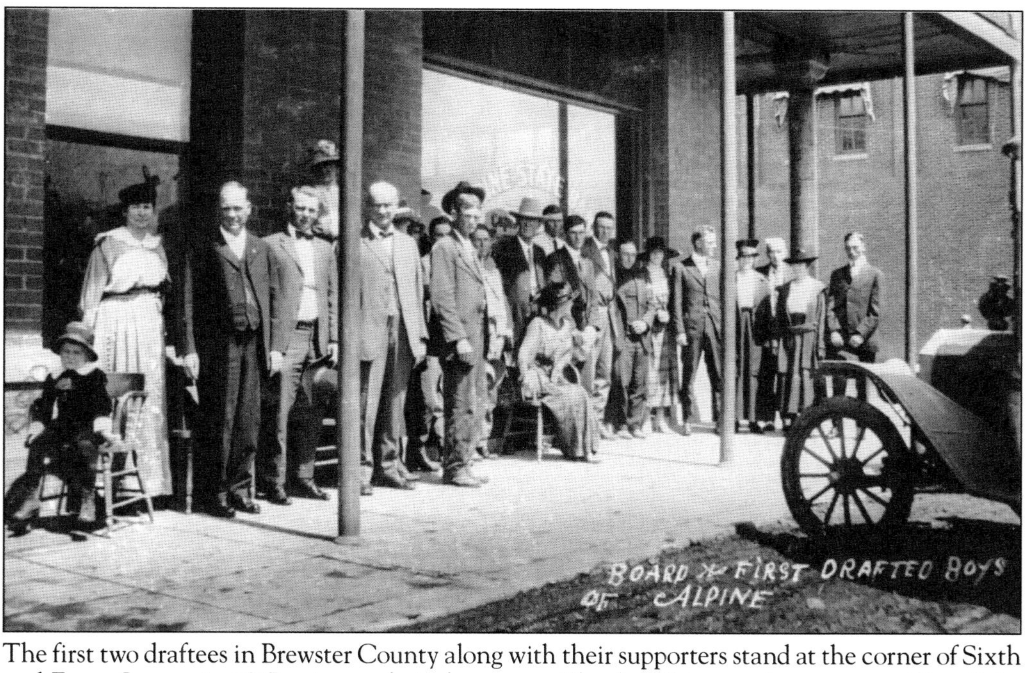

The first two draftees in Brewster County along with their supporters stand at the corner of Sixth and Front Streets in 1917 prior to their departure. Claude White, at the extreme right of the group and Delmar Collins, wearing a white shirt and nearly hidden in the far back row, were to join the U. S. Army at Camp Travis. (Courtesy of the Archives of the Big Bend.)

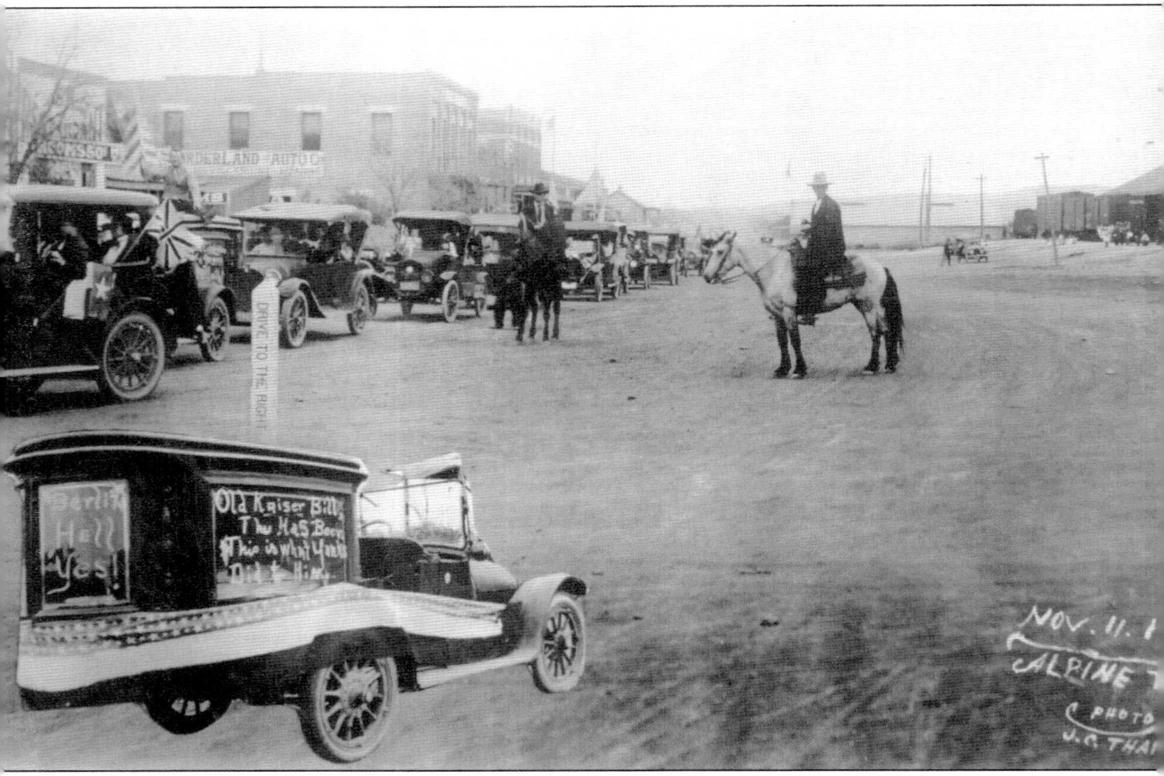

During the first Armistice Day at the end of World War I, Alpine celebrated by burying an effigy of the kaiser—the German emperor—in an abandoned well on a vacant lot. The hearse carrying the kaiser effigy (bottom left) was superimposed on the orginal photograph by photographer John Thain. Although there were four local casualties, all were noncombat. One man, Manuel Espinosa, returned from the war a hero. (Courtesy of the Archives of the Big Bend.)

Three

The Prosperous Years
Alpine's Florescence (1920–1939)

When Sul Ross State Normal College opened its doors in 1920, Alpine finally seemed to have transcended its cowtown roots. Within a matter of years, the town's population would almost double, and the downtown area would gain a number of its most substantial buildings. With its panoramic view of the Davis Mountains, the new stately college on the hill, and a bustling downtown area, Alpine felt a notch above neighboring towns. Over the next decade, the community would enjoy prosperity exceeding all its expectations

The Great Depression and drought of the 1930s were unwelcome intrusions that strained area ranches, some to the breaking point. Foreclosures and rising debt were of epidemic proportions. Then, in 1934, the region experienced its driest year anyone had seen. And though the Drought Relief Office established in Alpine would purchase tens of thousands of cattle from Brewster County ranchers, it was not enough to stave off the drought's impact on the cattle industry.

Fortunately, Sul Ross helped to buffer some of the hardships felt by the town. Even as the market cratered and ranges dried out, the school's enrollment continued to climb. Those employed by the college continued to receive a dependable income. During the same years, the campus enjoyed a major growth spurt, courtesy of various New Deal programs and local relief labor. Consequently, money from the college—both in the form of faculty income and the income of citizens on the relief rolls—continued to circulate through the town.

Although the years of hardship challenged Alpine's resolve, its pride and optimism persevered. The drought finally lifted by the end of the 1930s, and with the record rainfall that arrived in 1941, prosperity returned to the region's ranching industry. The economy, once again, seemed to be on solid ground.

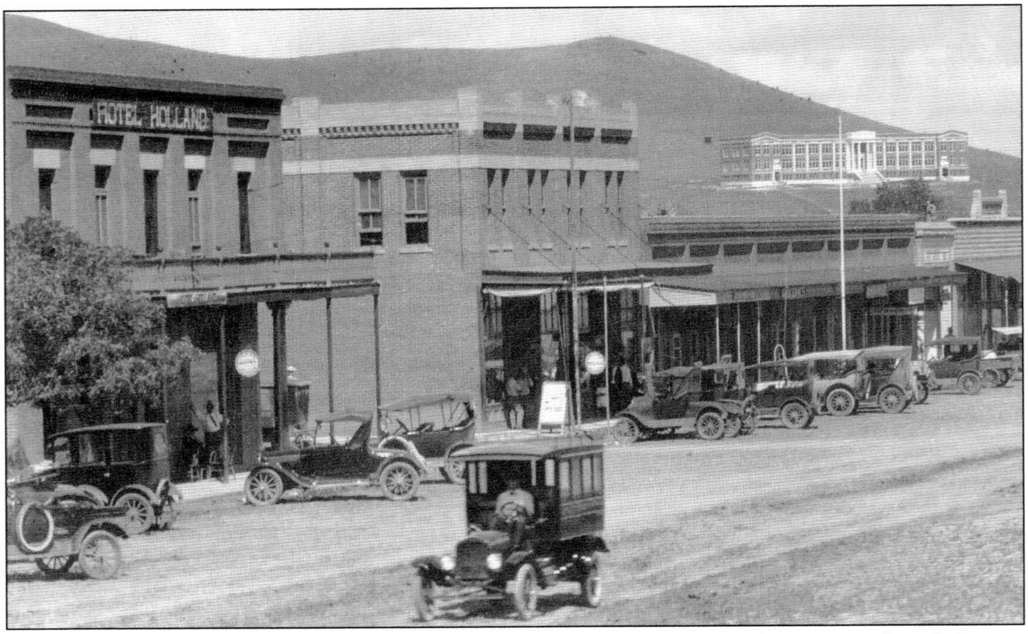

Alpine's Front Street, later Holland Avenue, looking northeast towards the corner of Sixth Street, was a bustling center of activity by 1920. The Holland Hotel, left, and the Lackey-Hord building to its right, are two of very few surviving two-story structures from Alpine's early days. Sul Ross State Teachers College, seen in the background, had just been completed. (Courtesy of the Archives of the Big Bend.)

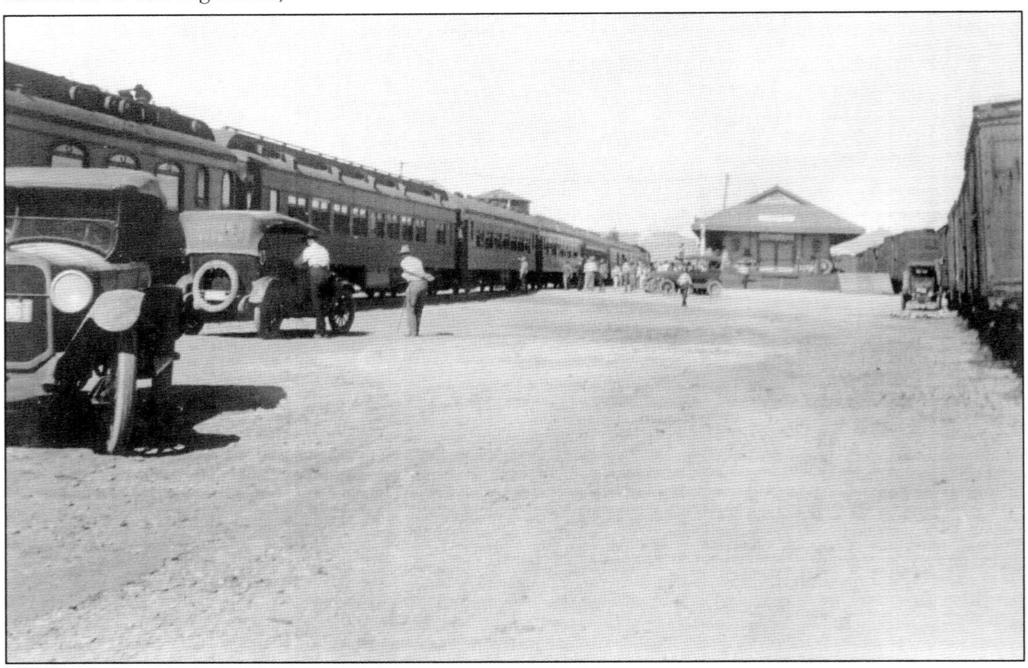

A passenger train pulls into the Alpine depot around 1920. Trains remained the primary form of transportation in and out of the region well into the 1940s. In the early days, the tracks split around the depot, allowing one train to remain stationary while another passed through. (Courtesy of the Roberts collection.)

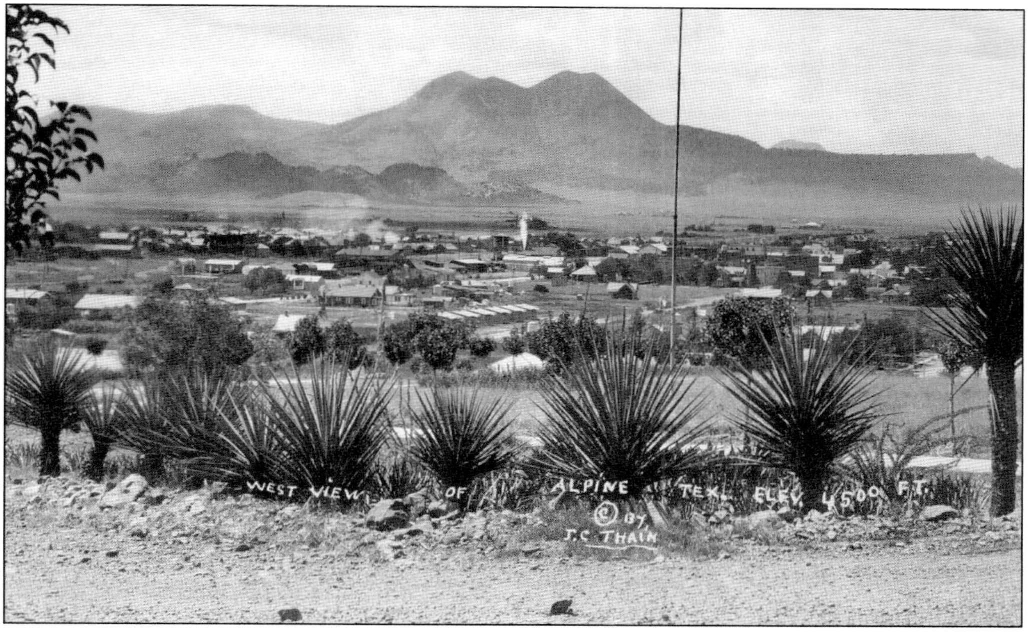

This overview of Alpine by photographer John Thain looks southwest over the town from the flanks of Hancock Hill around 1920. Twin Peaks, known as the Twin Sisters in the early days, can be seen in the background, appearing like protective sentinels over the quiet little town. (Courtesy of the Archives of the Big Bend.)

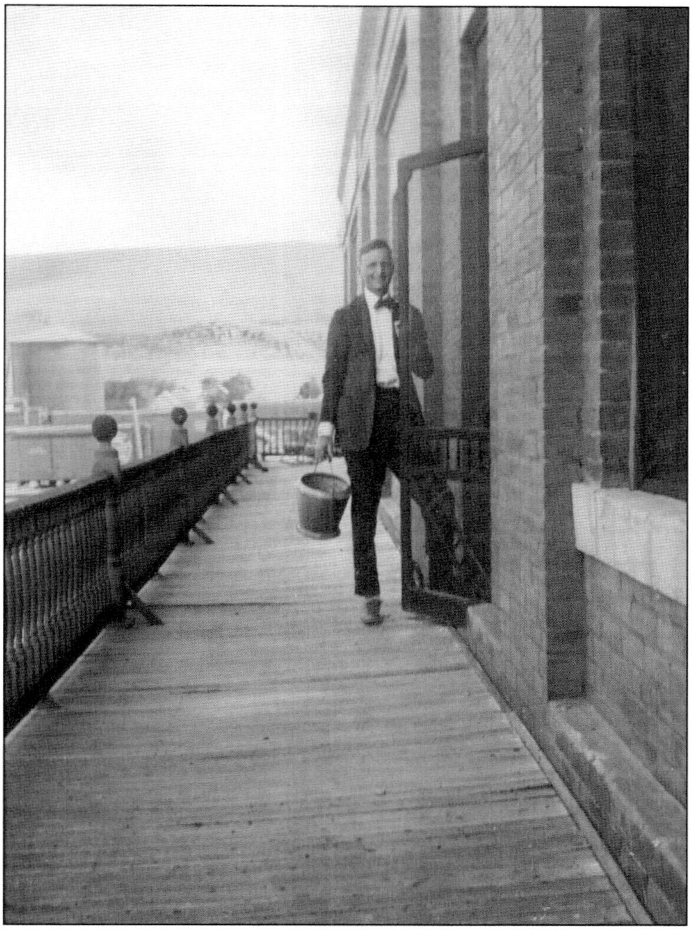

A boarder reenters the Holland Hotel from the balcony around 1920. The Holland was the premier upscale hotel in Alpine for most of the 20th century. In the background is the railroad water tank, and beyond that, A Mountain marks the south end of town. (Courtesy of the Roberts collection.)

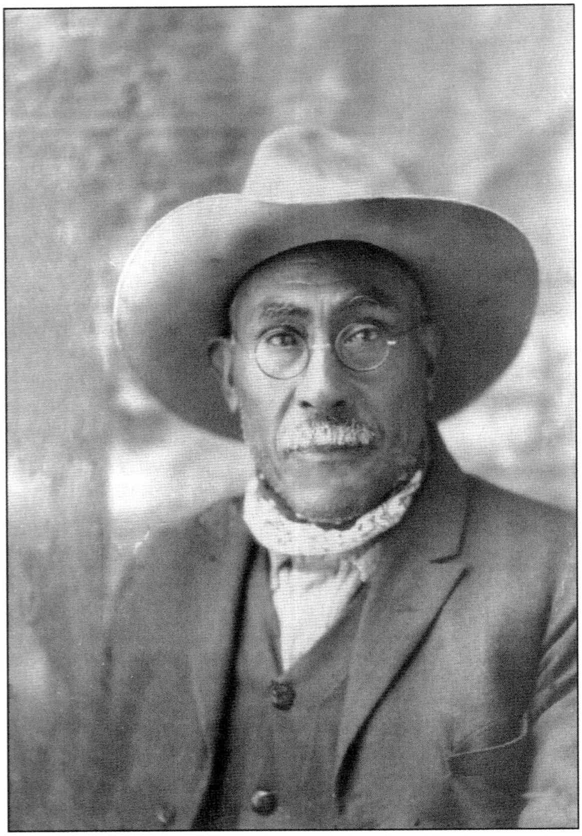

Of Black Seminole ancestry, Monroe Payne came with his wife, Jesusita Vasques, to the Big Bend in 1904. For many years, Payne lived with his family on the Buttrill Ranch on the north side of the Rosillos Mountains 60 miles south of Marathon. Payne's son, Rocky, was a noted cowboy on ranches around Alpine. (Courtesy of the Archives of the Big Bend.)

Teacher Melvin P. Slover stands with his students at the first Hispanic school in Alpine. Built in 1910, the Francisco E. Madero Ward was used until 1936 when the Centennial School was established. Alpine schools remained segregated until 1969. (Courtesy of the Archives of the Big Bend.)

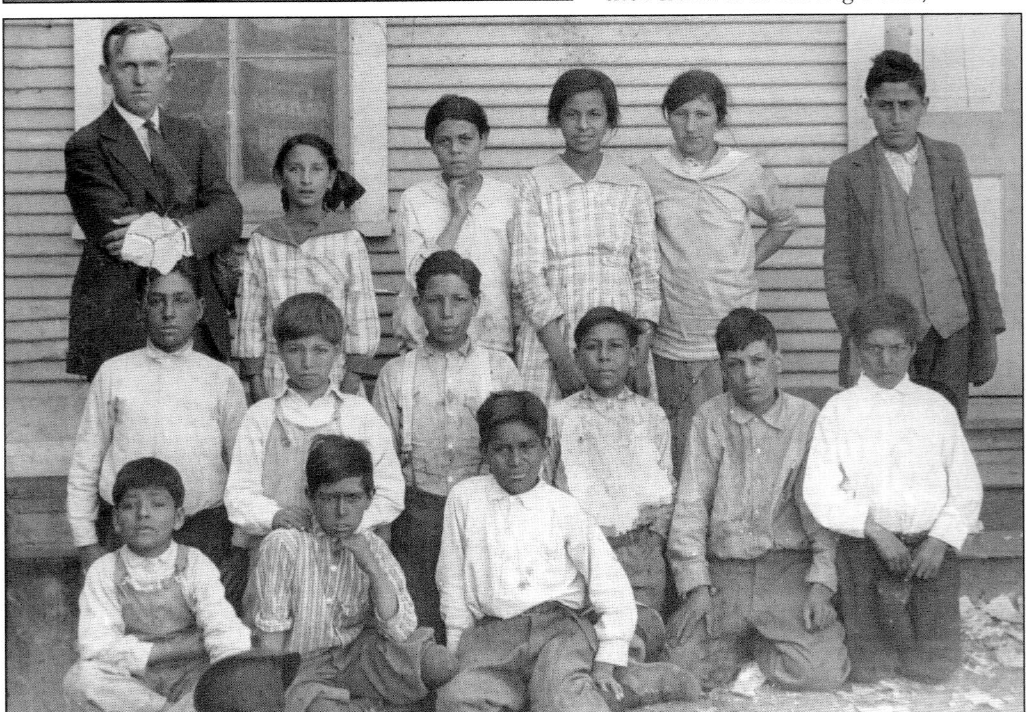

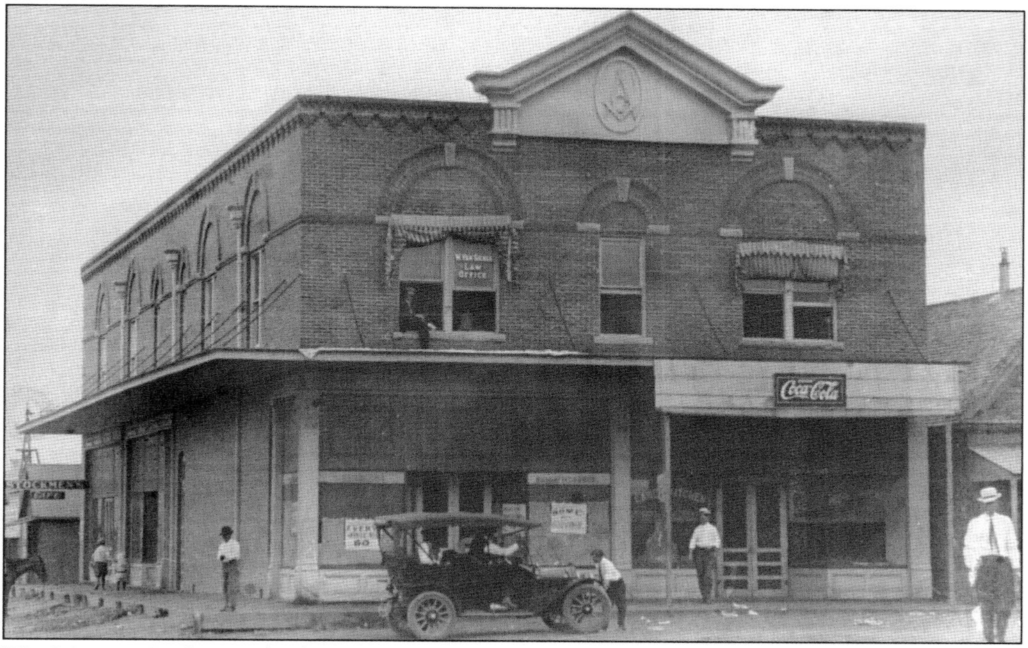

The Masonic Lodge was built in 1912 on the corner of Fifth Street and Avenue E. The law office of Wigfall Van Sickle is upstairs to the left. The downstairs housed the popular Candy Kitchen (right) and the Stockman's Café (left rear). Part of the upstairs served the local Masons until 1975, when a new lodge was built north of town. (Courtesy of the Archives of the Big Bend.)

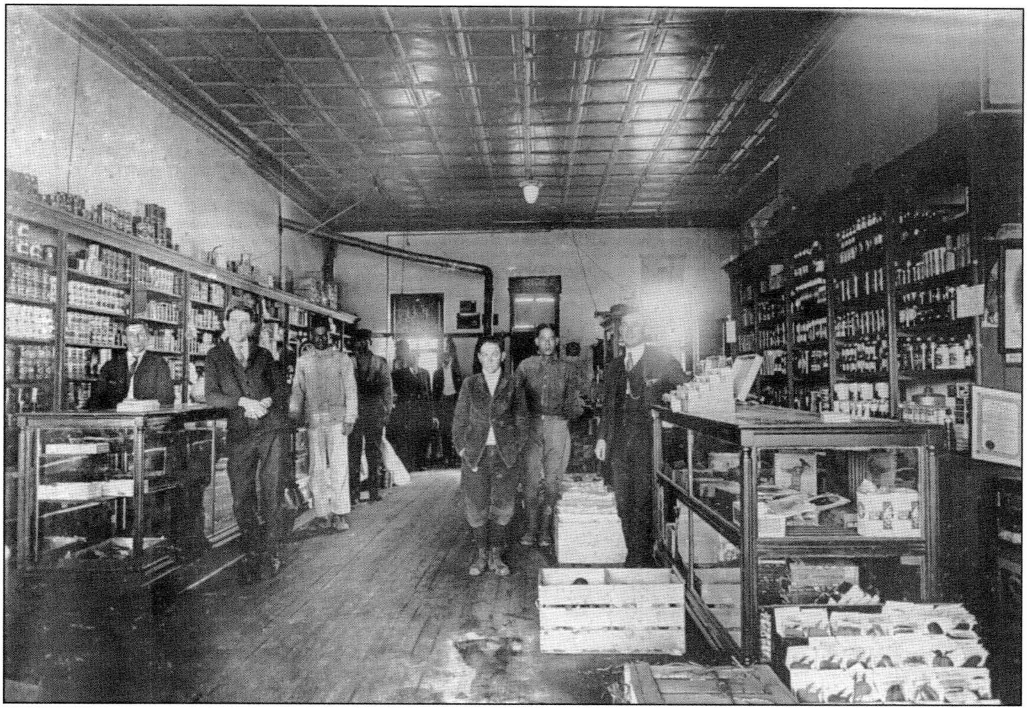

The Williams and Hord grocery, located at 108 North Sixth street, was typical of early grocery stores. In this photograph of the store's interior, partner Erie Williams is second from left, and Clarence Hord is on the far right. (Courtesy of the Archives of the Big Bend.)

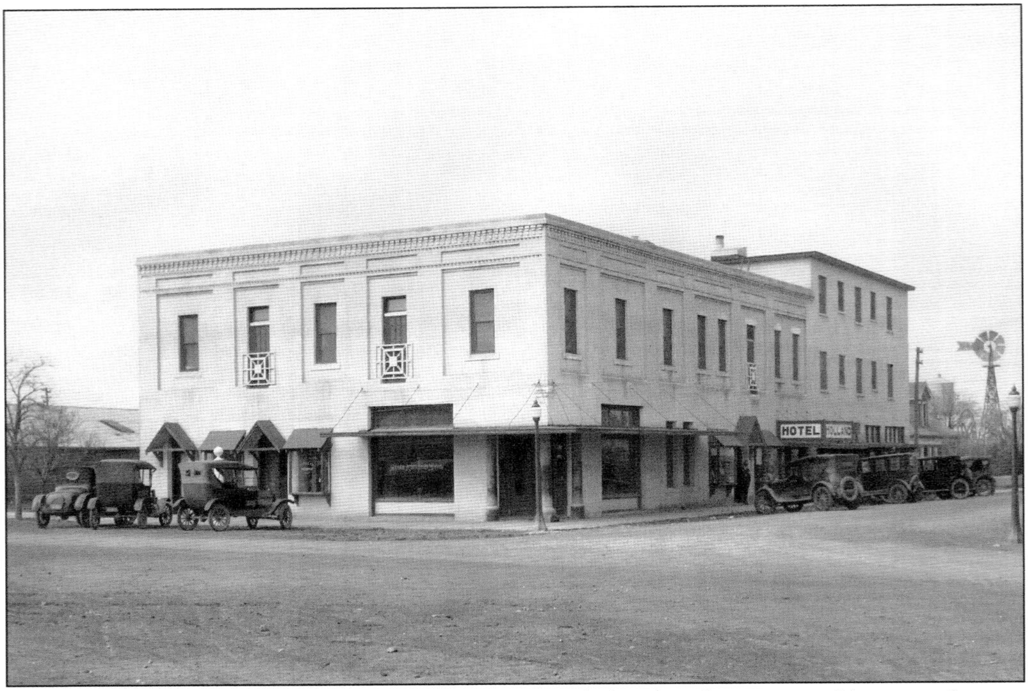

In 1923, the Holland Hotel was remodeled and expanded with a three-story addition to the rear of the building. Steam heat and water were added to each room, and the electrical system was rewired for state-of-the-art accommodations. (Courtesy of the Archives of the Big Bend.)

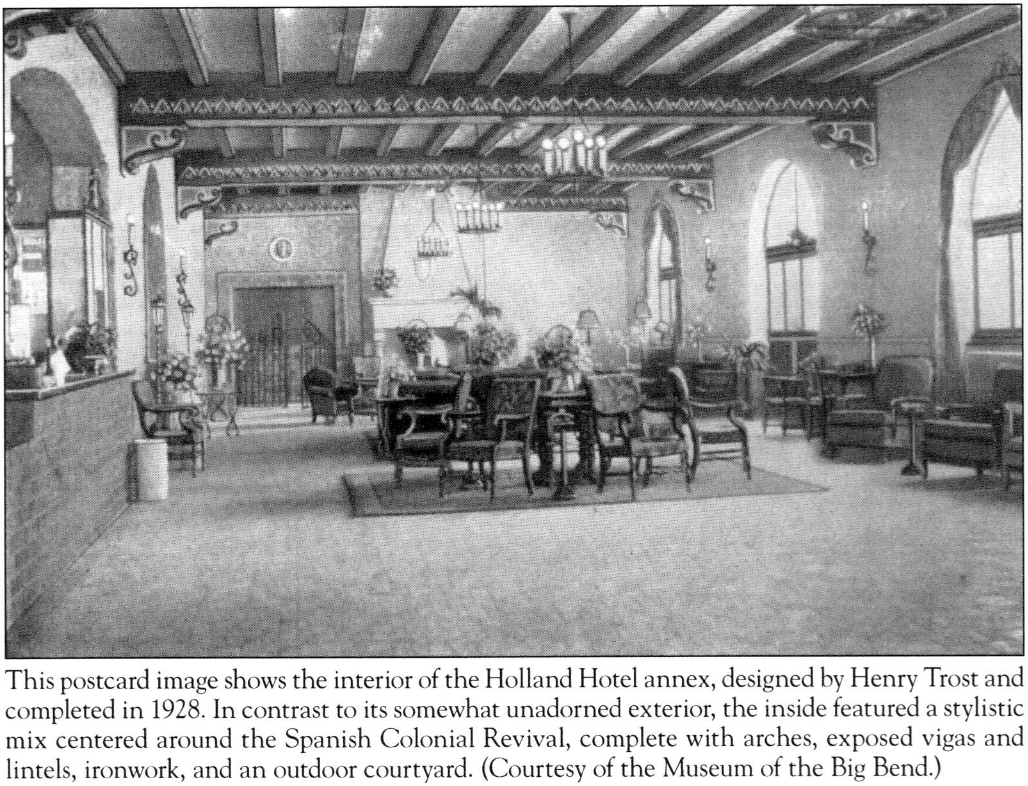

This postcard image shows the interior of the Holland Hotel annex, designed by Henry Trost and completed in 1928. In contrast to its somewhat unadorned exterior, the inside featured a stylistic mix centered around the Spanish Colonial Revival, complete with arches, exposed vigas and lintels, ironwork, and an outdoor courtyard. (Courtesy of the Museum of the Big Bend.)

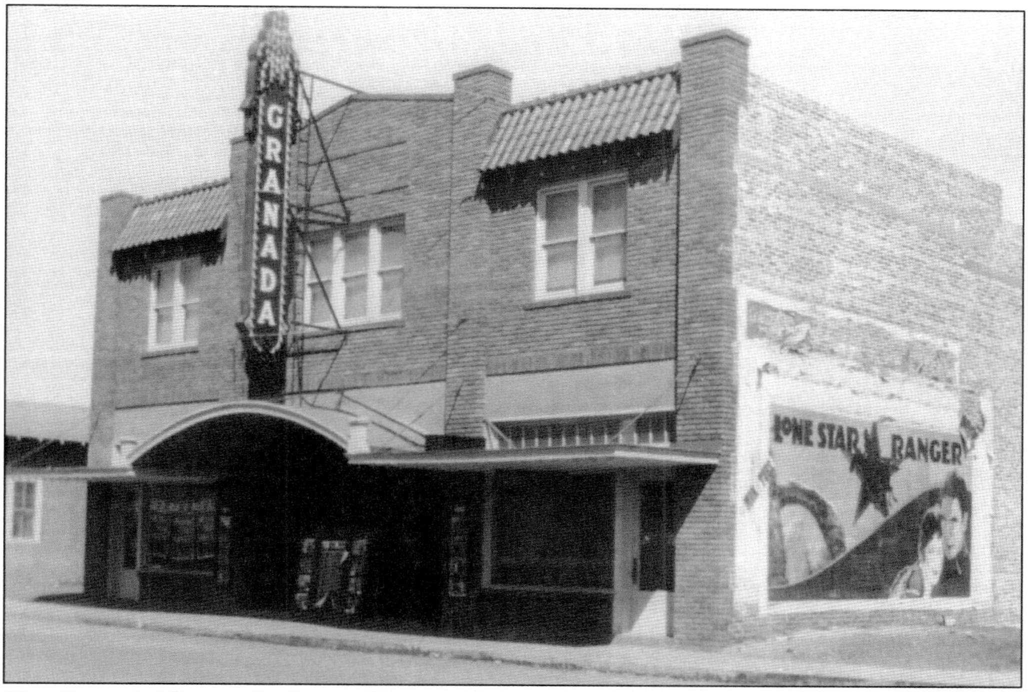

The Granada Theatre, built in 1929, was Alpine's introduction to motion pictures. Eventually closed down and boarded up for decades, in 2009 the Granada was renovated and reopened as a modern performance and event center complete with an upstairs yoga studio. (Courtesy of the Archives of the Big Bend.)

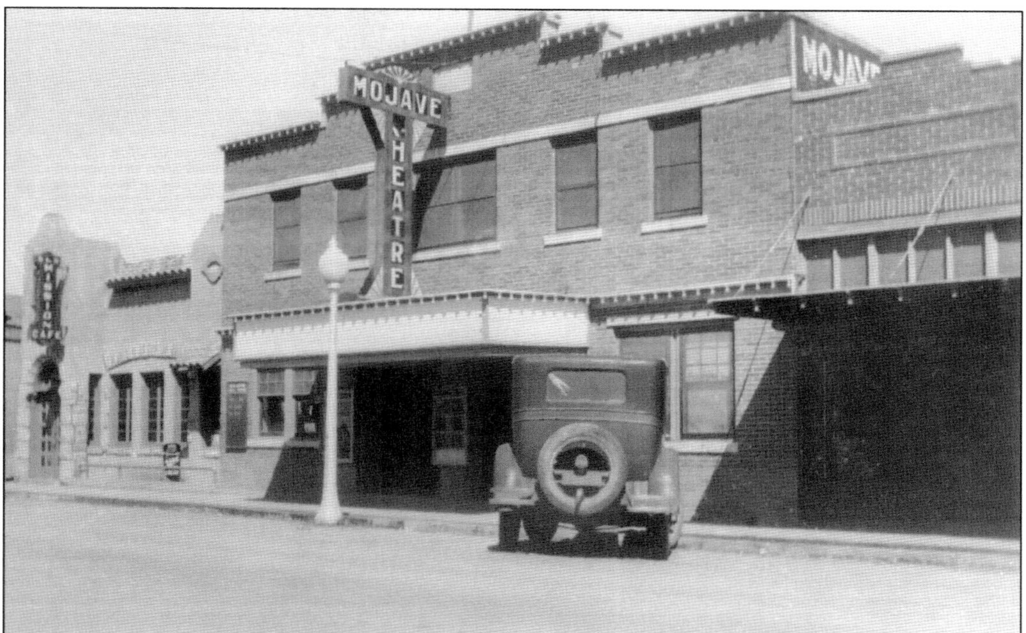

The Mojave Theatre, built by Benjamin Berkeley in 1921, was originally used for traveling shows and vaudeville acts. Although it retains little of its historic character, today the Rangra is Alpine's only movie venue. (Courtesy of the Archives of the Big Bend.)

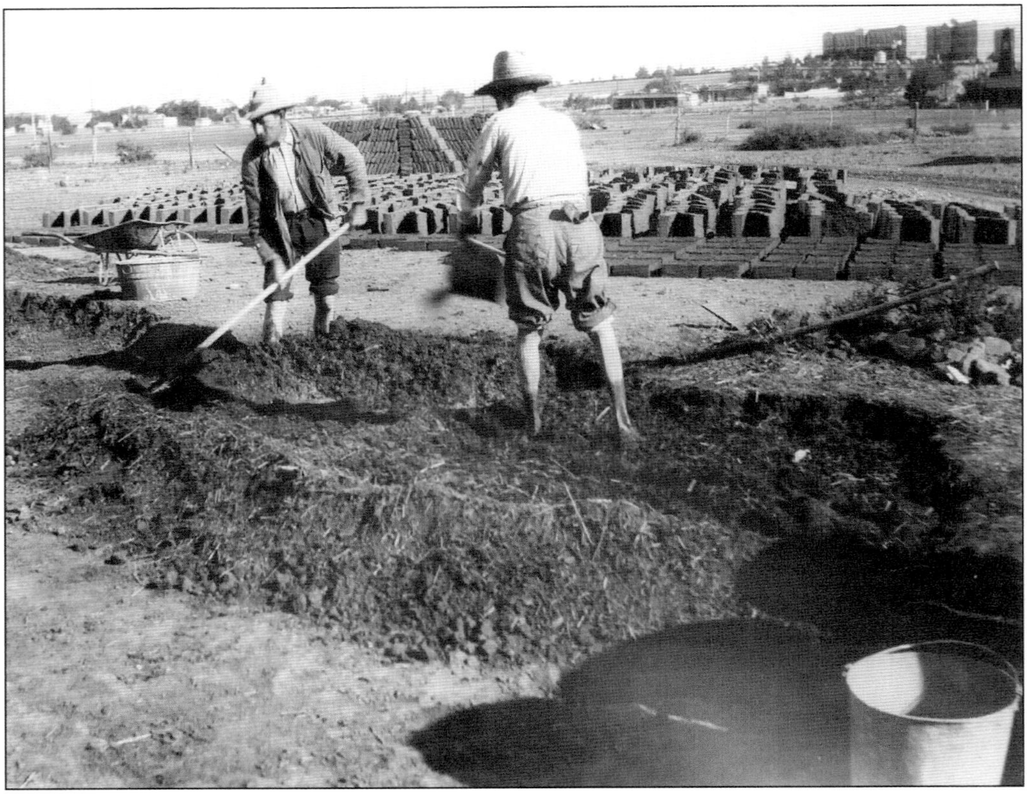

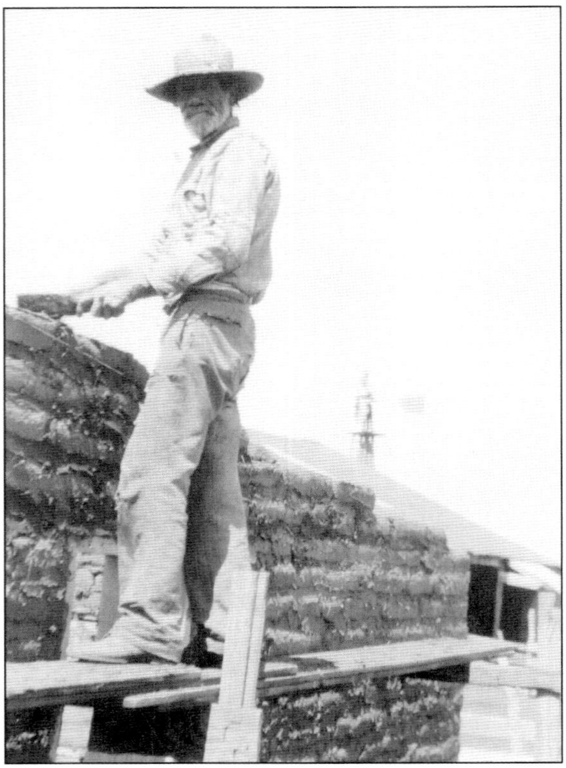

Two adoberos, or adobe makers, are shown making adobe bricks the traditional way around 1930. The adobe was mixed by foot and hoe before being poured into a wooden form. After the form was pulled, the brick was allowed to air-dry before being stacked, ready for use. (Courtesy of the Archives of the Big Bend.)

Manuel Fierro, an early adobe mason, is shown here mortaring in a course of adobe bricks. The adobe bricks used in Alpine were typically of a larger than average size (4 by 12 by 18 inches), and laid with the long axis to form the thickness of the walls, providing much greater thermal mass. (Courtesy of the Archives of the Big Bend.)

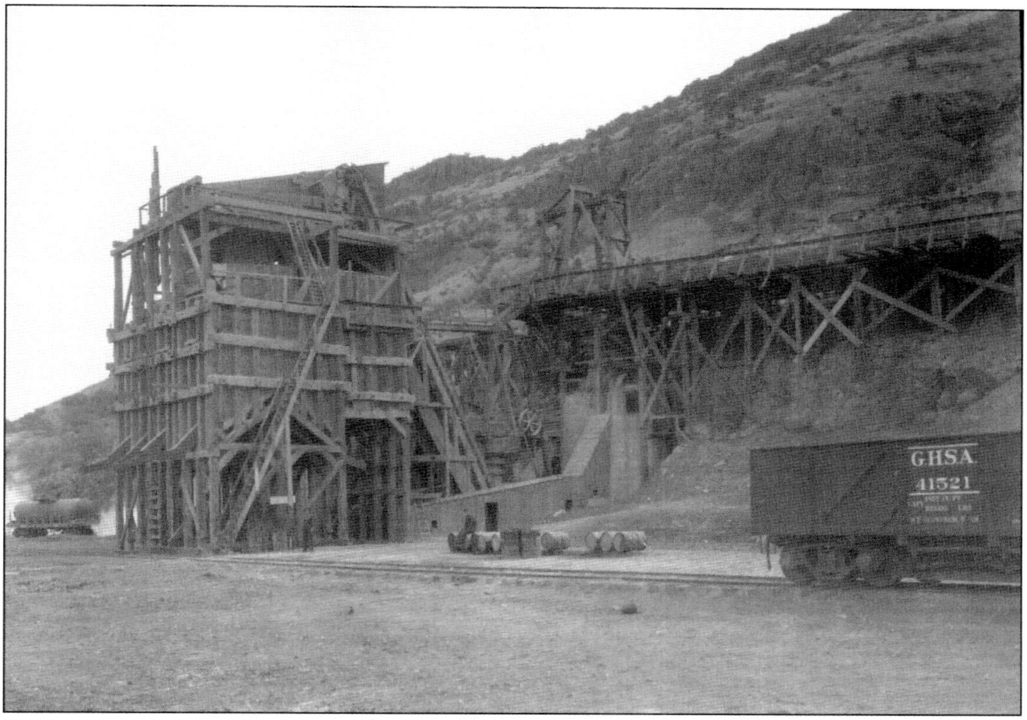

Toronto Mountain, located 6 miles west of Alpine, was chosen in 1920 as a quarry site for ballasts for the Southern Pacific Railroad. This photograph shows the massively timbered rock crusher to the left that filled as many as 35 carloads a day. (Courtesy of the Marfa and Presidio County Museum.)

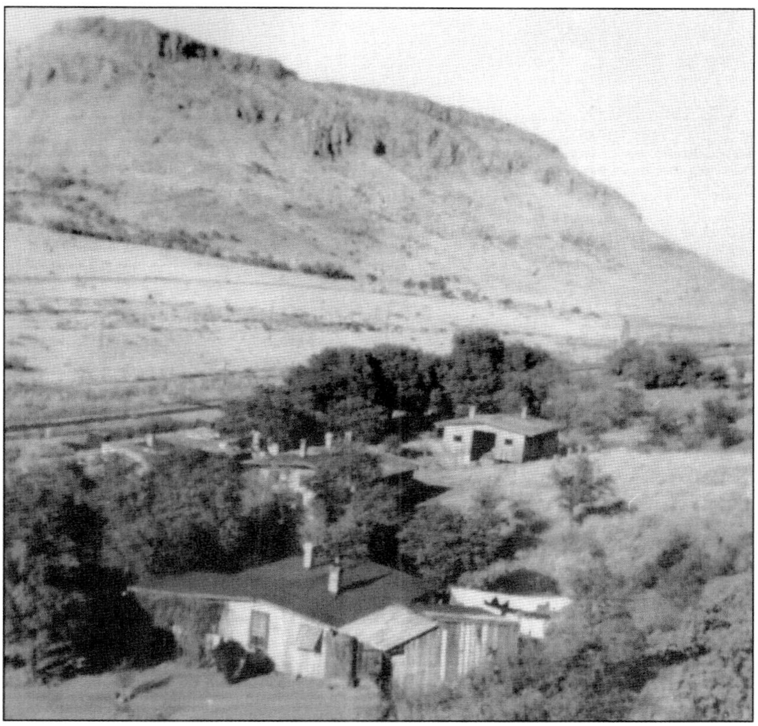

Toronto was established as a siding on the Southern Pacific Railroad 5 miles west of Alpine in 1882. By the 1920s, Toronto had about 100 inhabitants who maintained a 10-mile section of track and operated the rock crusher. In the 1930s, the railroad began using another type of rock as ballast, signaling the end of this small community. (Courtesy of the Archives of the Big Bend.)

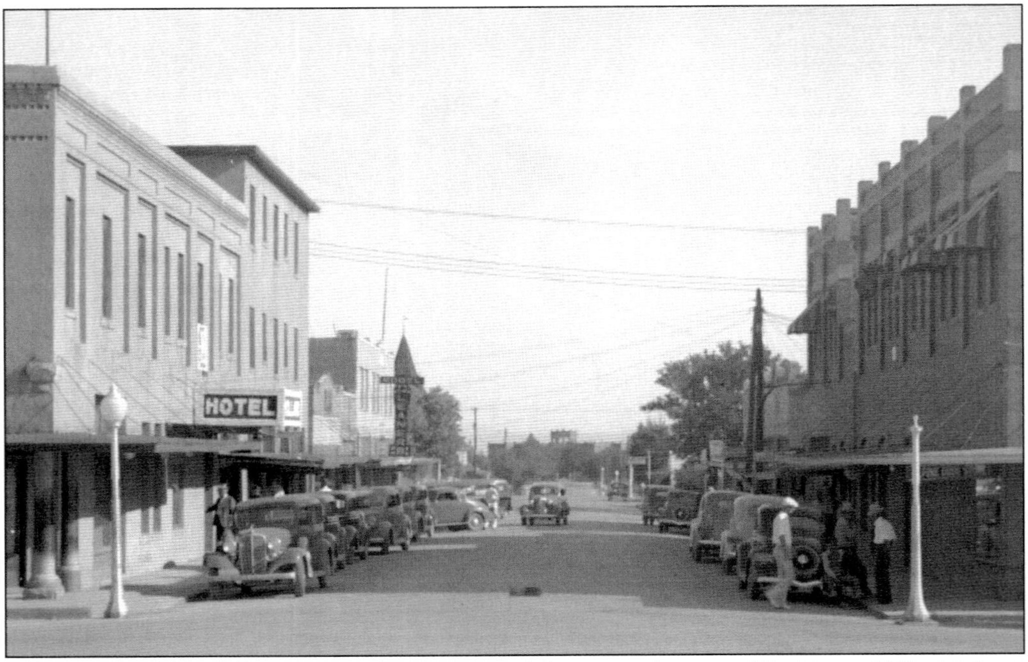

The view down Sixth Street around 1935 featured the turreted tower of the Central Ward School at the end of the block. The prominent Model Cleaners sign can be seen just behind the Holland Hotel. The Alpine Drug store was located in the Lackey-Hord building on the right. (Courtesy of the Archives of the Big Bend.)

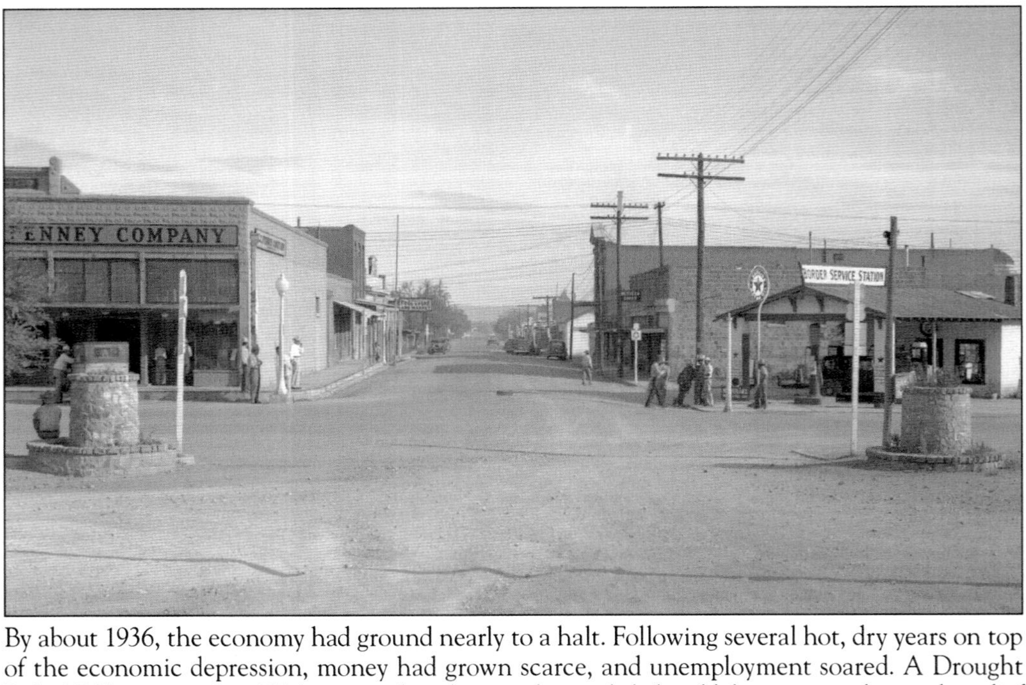

By about 1936, the economy had ground nearly to a halt. Following several hot, dry years on top of the economic depression, money had grown scarce, and unemployment soared. A Drought Relief Office opened in 1934 to provide aid to ranchers, while local laborers signed onto the relief rolls. (Courtesy of the Archives of the Big Bend.)

The Carroll Vaughn Chiropractic Offices and Clinic were located on North Sixth Street. Dr. Vaughn arrived in 1935 and ran this clinic for several years before moving to Austin. Chiropractic services in Alpine date back to the mid-1920s and continue to the present day. (Courtesy of the Archives of the Big Bend.)

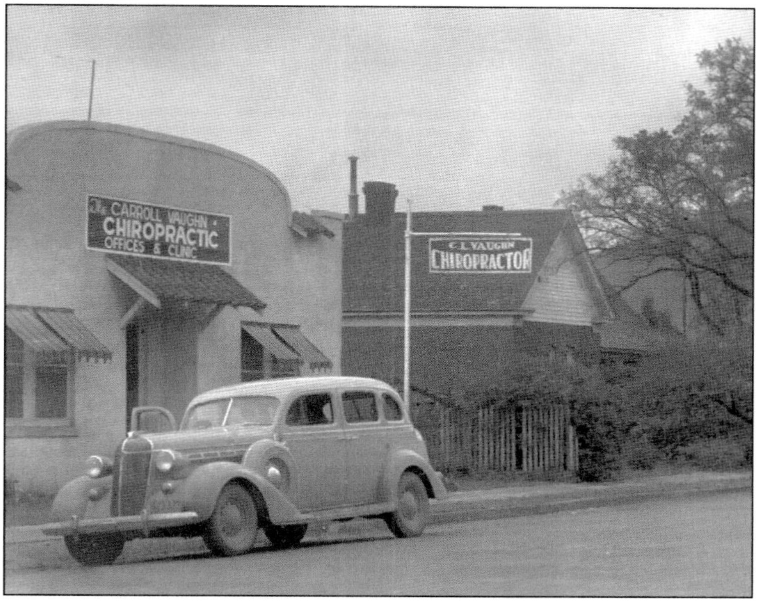

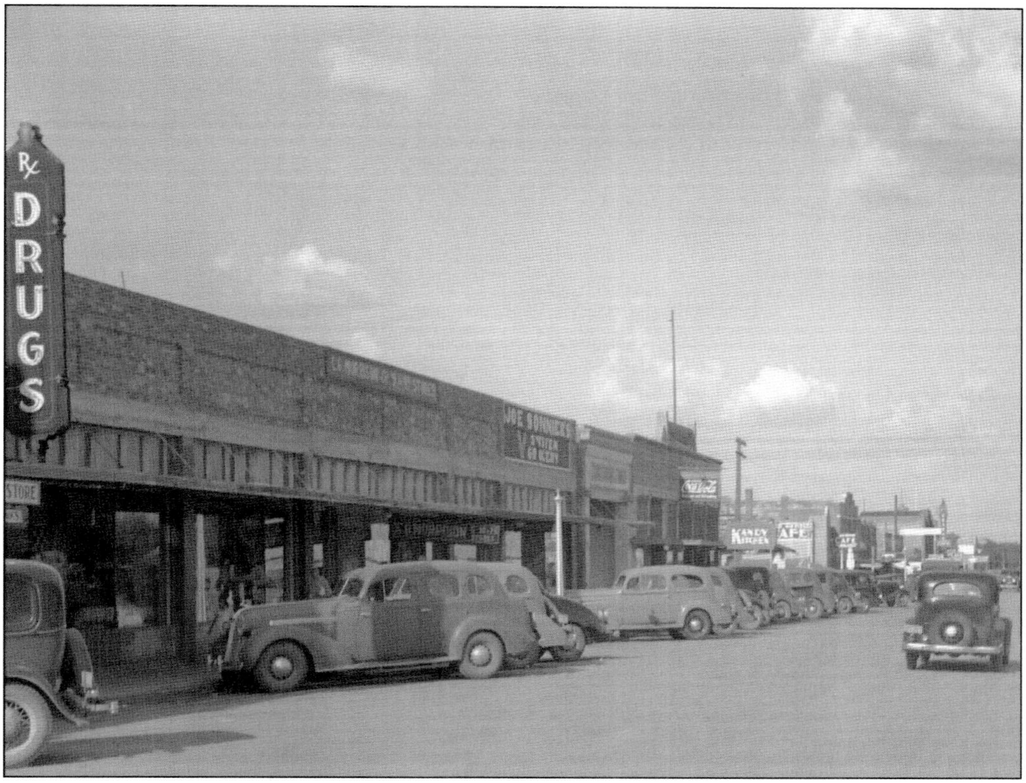

This view looking east down Front Street in the late 1930s shows a bustling business district: from left to right, the drugstore, C. G. Morrisons five-and-dime, Joe Sonnier's V System Grocery, the old First National Bank, and the Kandy Kitchen with "fountain service." (Courtesy of the Archives of the Big Bend.)

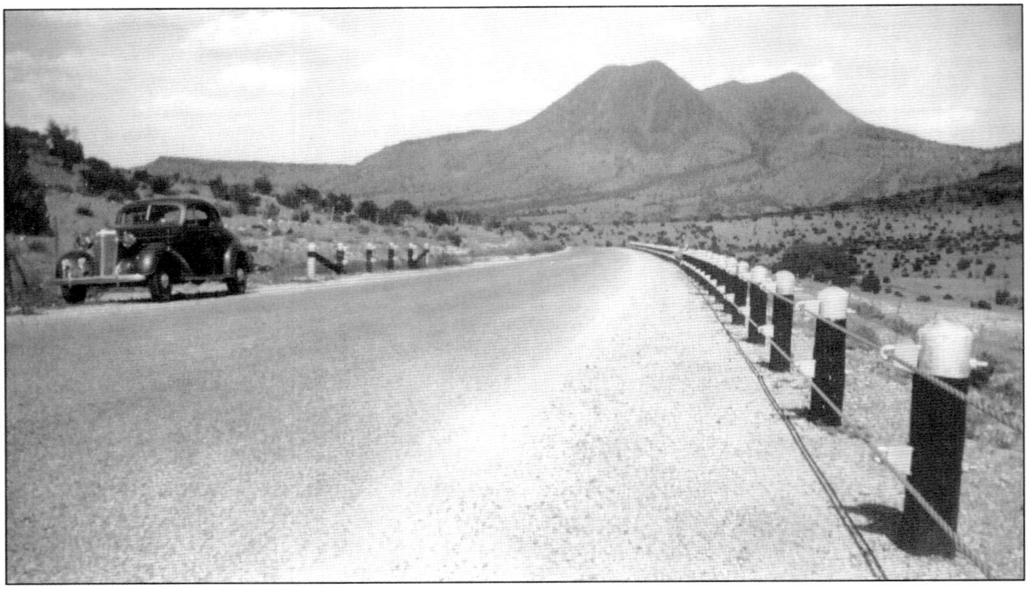

This stretch of Highway 90 built in the mid-1930s through Paisano Pass was, until 1949 (when the precursor to Interstate 10 was established), one of the major transcontinental thoroughfares across the southern part of the United States. Known as the Border Highway, it became the focus of a local association formed to promote travel and tourism through the area. (Courtesy of the Ivey collection.)

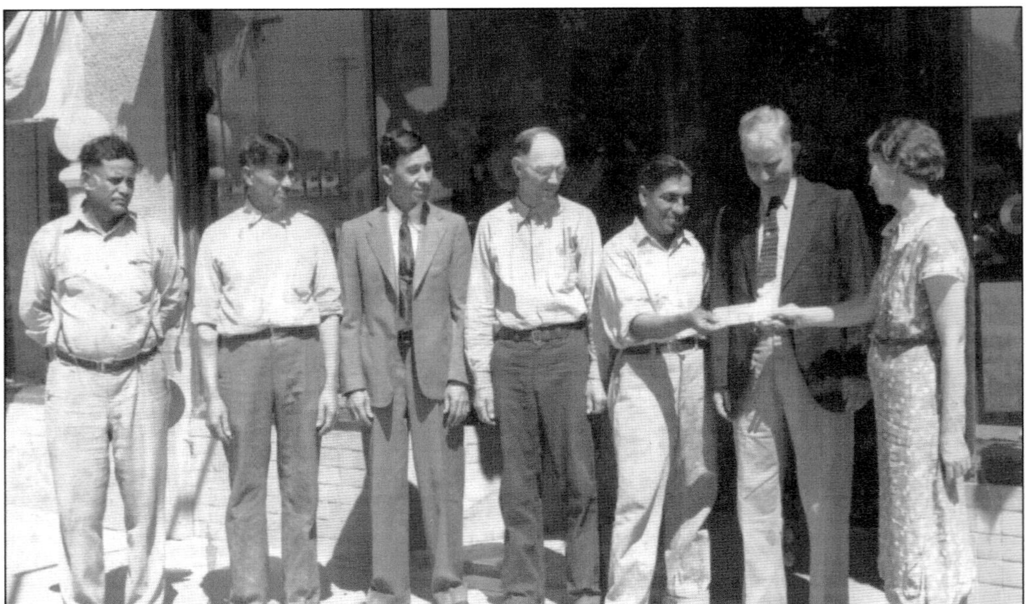

Hispanic businessmen in Alpine hand a check to Berta Clark Lassiter of the chamber of commerce in 1937. They are, from left to right, Tomás Valadez, Juan Portillo, Juan Sotello, Clemente Uranga, Apolinar Garcia, and Jose Gallego. (Courtesy of the Valadez collection.)

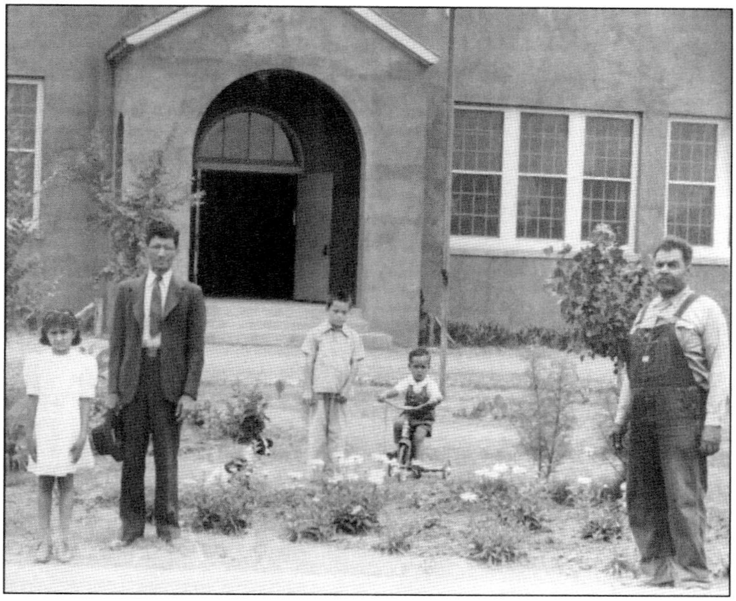

Custodian Don Aurelio Olazaba (right) and several unidentified individuals stand in front of the Centennial School in 1941. The structure was built of adobe bricks by the Works Progress Administration in 1936. Named in celebration of the 100th anniversary of Texas's independence from Mexico, it served as the school for Hispanic students during segregation. (Courtesy of the Archives of the Big Bend.)

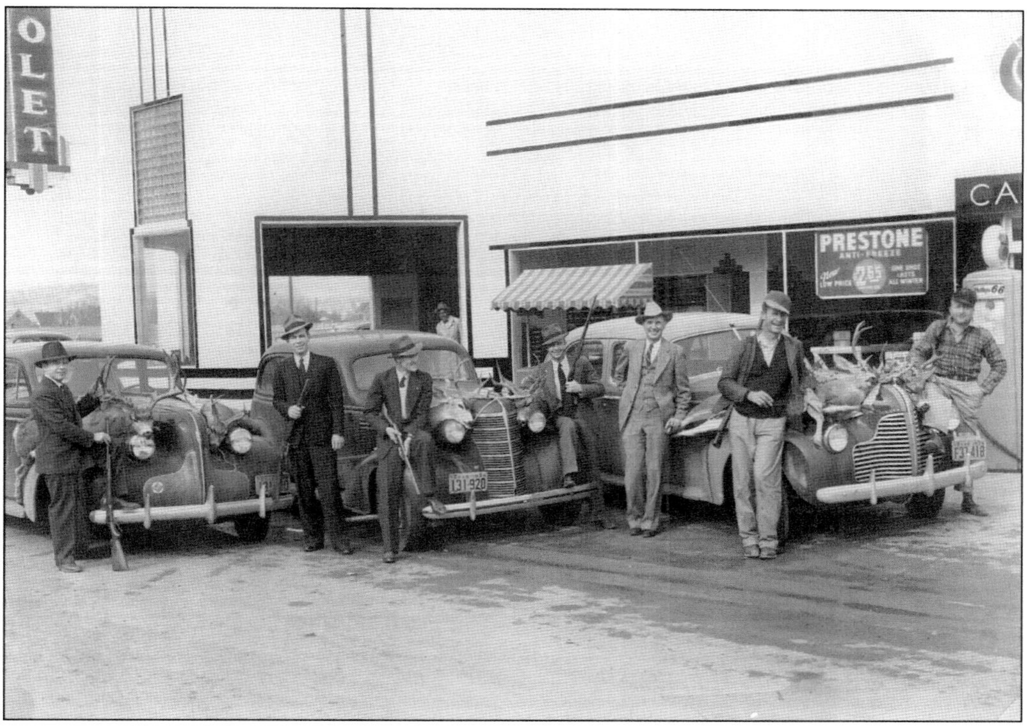

Jim Casner (far right) and unidentified friends pose in front of the Casner Motor Company at the corner of Seventh Street and Holland Avenue following a successful deer hunt. Completed in 1924, the state-of-the-art facility featured a showroom, filling station, tire service, auto repair shop, and a ladies "comfort station." (Courtesy of the Terry collection.)

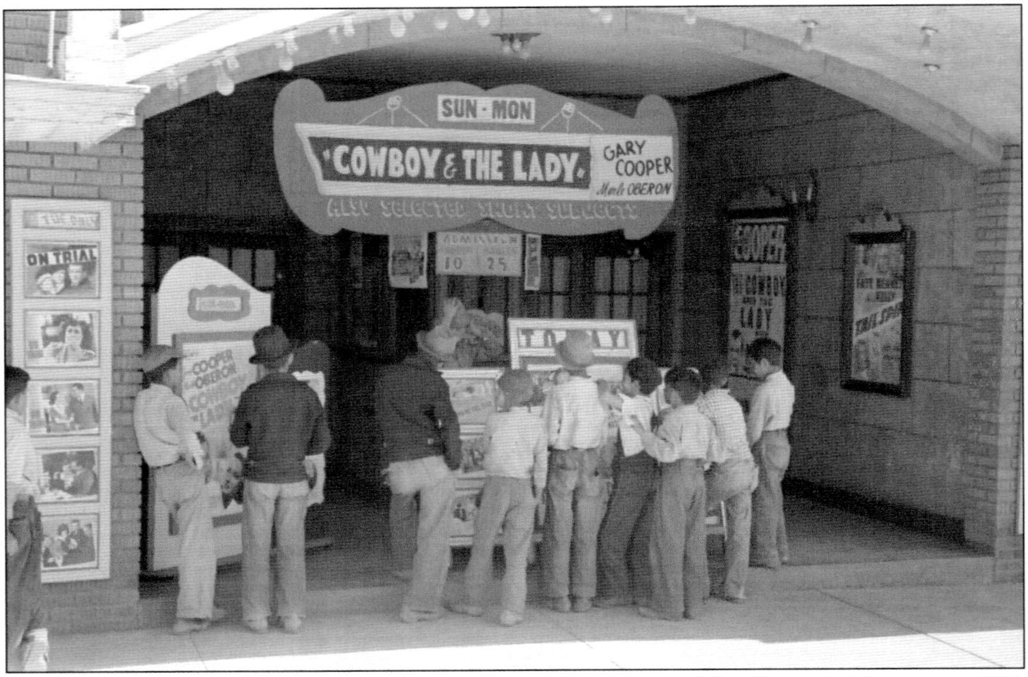

Alpine children crowd around the latest movie posters in front of the Granada Theatre in 1939. During the 1930s, movies offered a welcome diversion from the troubles brought by drought and the Great Depression. (Courtesy of the Library of Congress.)

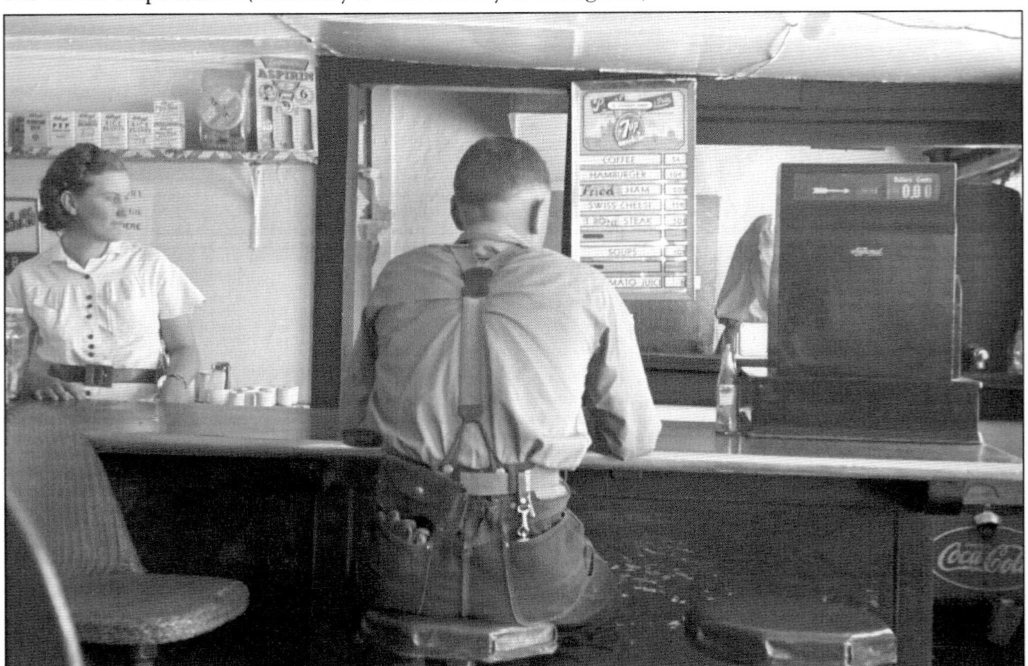

A waitress looks on as a diner waits for his meal in an Alpine hamburger stand in 1939. This is one of several Alpine photographs taken by Russell Lee during his work with the Farm Security Administration—a program designed to portray the hardships faced by rural America during the Great Depression. (Courtesy of the Library of Congress.)

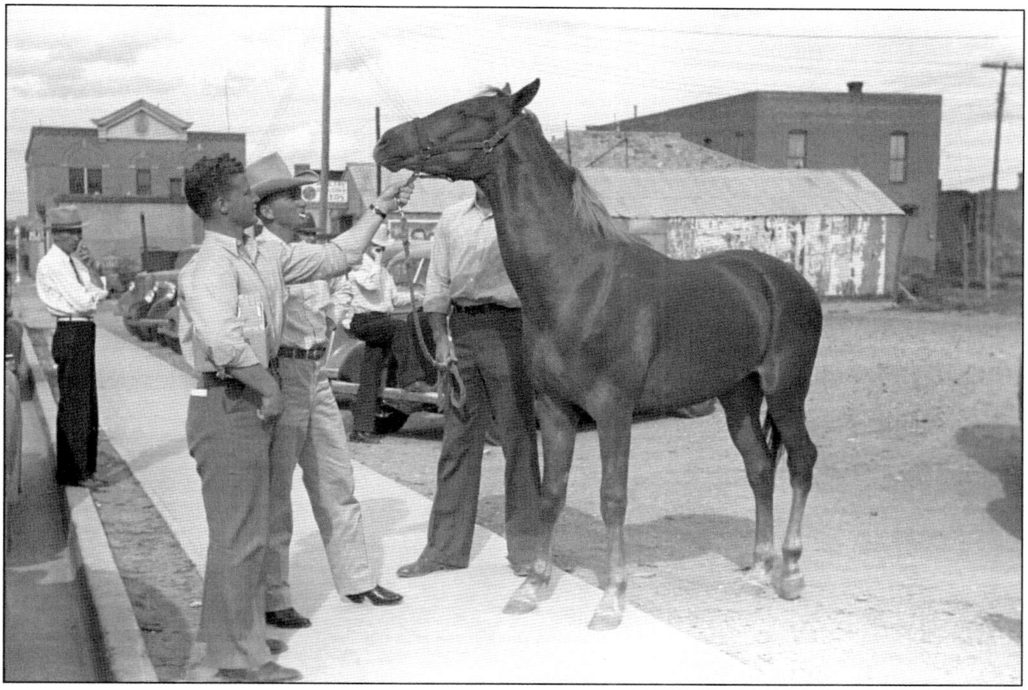

A man examines a horse for sale on Avenue E between Fifth and Sixth Streets in 1939. The two-story building in the upper right of the photograph is the Hancock Building; to the upper left is the Masonic Building. (Courtesy of the Library of Congress.)

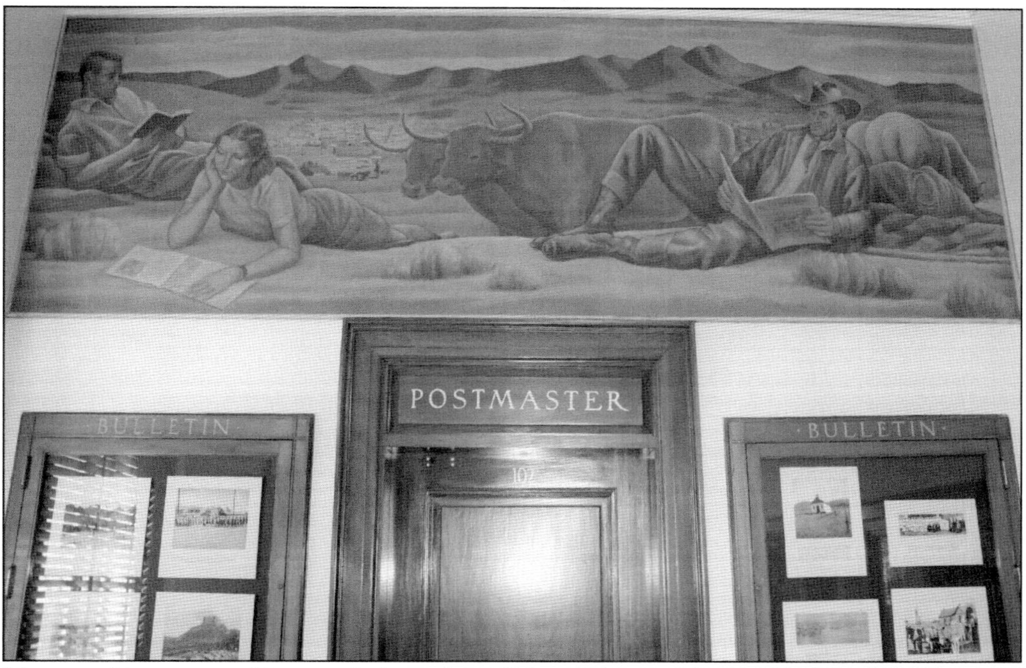

The new Alpine post office was dedicated in 1939, and this mural was added the following year. *View of Alpine* was painted by Spanish muralist José Moya del Pino, employed by the New Deal Public Works of Art Project. An award-winning artist, Moya in 1925 had been appointed director of the Spanish Artistic Mission to the United States, where he remained. (Photograph by author.)

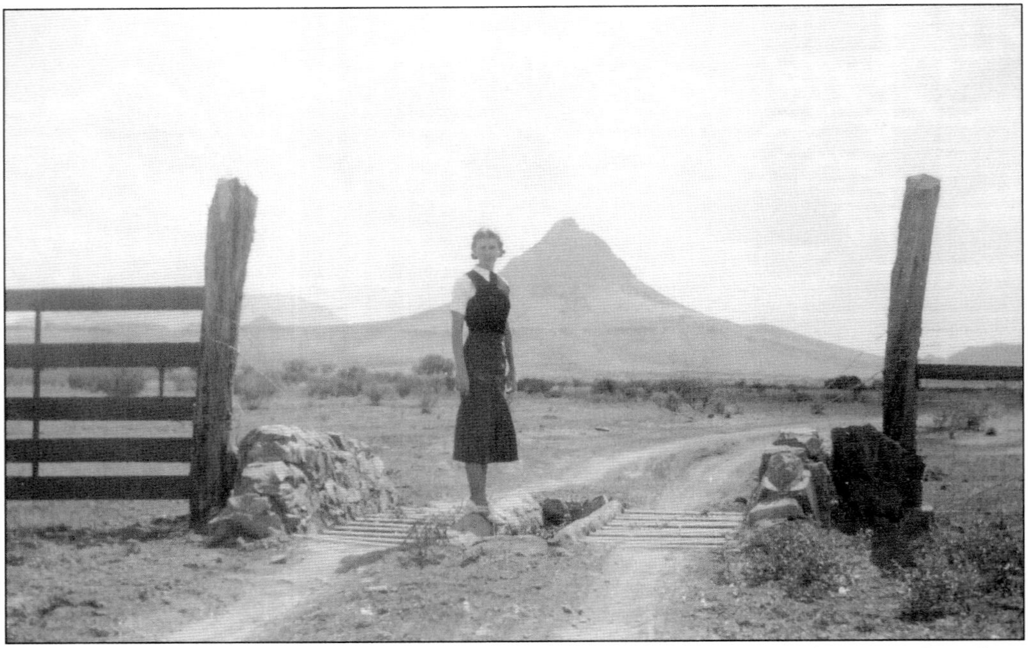

Katherine Carr (who later married Rex Ivey Jr.) stands at the entrance to the Tippit Ranch in the 1930s, with Mitre Peak prominent in the background. One of the most distinctive landmarks in the area, the peak was so named because it resembled the traditional ceremonial headdress of Catholic bishops. (Courtesy of the Ivey collection.)

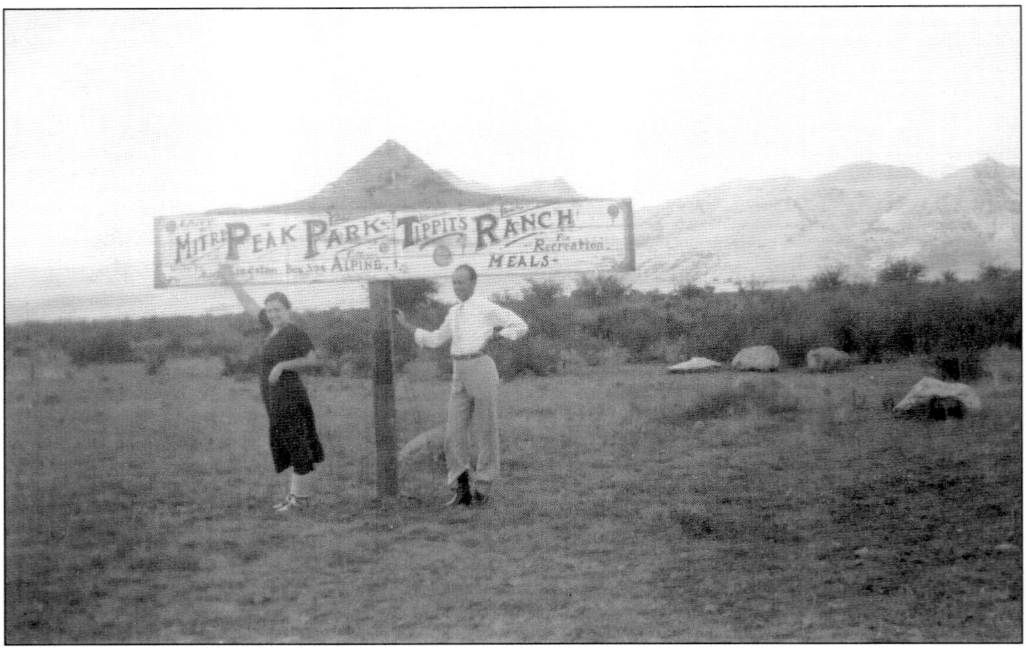

The Tippit Ranch was a popular gathering place for Sul Ross faculty and students and was a favored retreat for out-of-town guests. For years, it had the only swimming pool in the area, in addition to an orchard and cabins for rent. The top of prominent Mitre Peak was a frequent destination for visitors until climbing was discouraged after a girl died in a fall there. (Courtesy of the Ivey collection.)

Four

Riding High
Ranching the Highlands

Ranching in the Alpine area started at least as early as 1880, when Lawrence Haley and George Crosson drove 3,000 head of sheep into Alpine valley. But after the railroad arrived, livestock were driven into the area by the thousands. The better grassed and watered country around Alpine filled quickly. And for most of two decades, ranches were flush with livestock. Between 1898 and 1910, the cattle industry was stronger than it would ever be again.

The passage of the Eight-Section Act created a second land rush as new homesteaders filed in to take up the maximum allowable acreage. But after the required three years, most sold their land and left. The drought of 1910 ushered the last of them out of the area but also allowed those who remained to expand their holdings—in many cases to hundreds of thousands of acres.

Droughts continued to plague ranching, none more than those of the 1930s and the 1950s. But for many, the intervening wet years were enough to carry them through and allowed a great many to flourish. Ample precipitation during the 1940s and especially from 1966 to 1992 helped to renew grasslands and return vitality to area ranches.

Although the cattle industry will never regain the prominence it held in the earlier part of the century, ranching remains a large part of the regional identity and grounds Alpine in a tradition that has been a vital part of its past.

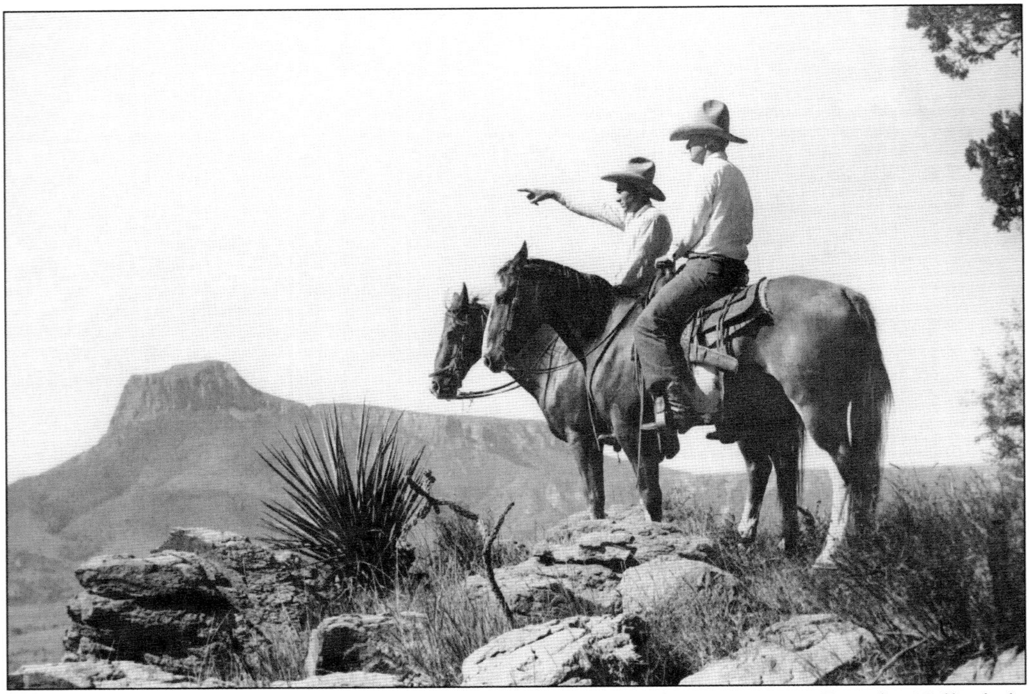

Cowboys Dom Adams and Pete Crawford overlook Cathedral Mountain on Rancho Valle de la Cienega around 1928. Adams arrived in Alpine in a covered wagon in 1911 from Polk County, Texas, ranched in the Christmas Mountains, and worked as a cowhand for Jackson and Harmon before settling in Alpine. Crawford managed the ranch. (Courtesy of the Archives of the Big Bend.)

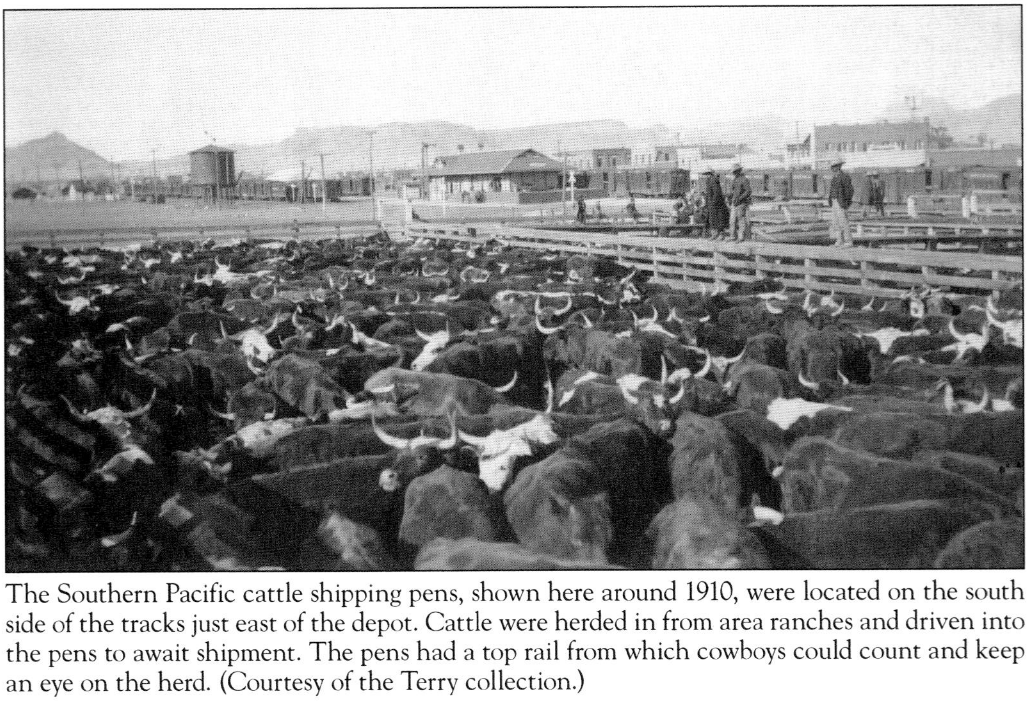

The Southern Pacific cattle shipping pens, shown here around 1910, were located on the south side of the tracks just east of the depot. Cattle were herded in from area ranches and driven into the pens to await shipment. The pens had a top rail from which cowboys could count and keep an eye on the herd. (Courtesy of the Terry collection.)

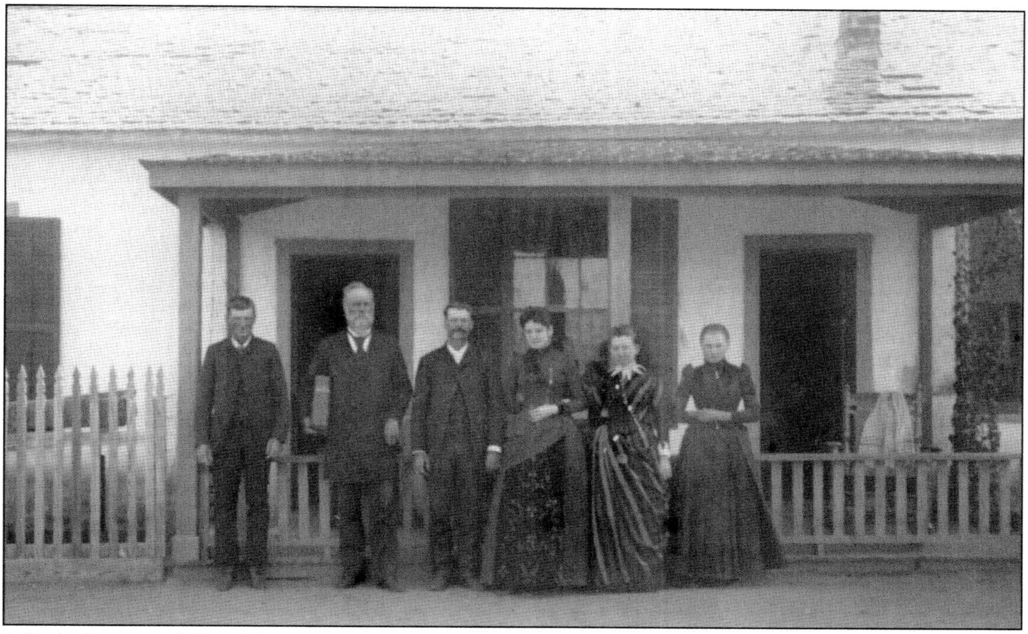

J. D. Jackson and Sam Harmon were prominent early Big Bend ranching partners. From 1889 to 1935, the Jackson and Harmon Cattle Company was among the largest and best-known outfits in the Big Bend, at one time running more than 15,000 head of cattle. Standing in this 1890 photograph are, from left to right, Sam Harmon, R. M. Gano, J. D. Jackson, Dorcas Ford Jackson, Mrs. Pink Taylor, and an unidentified woman. (Courtesy of the Archives of the Big Bend.)

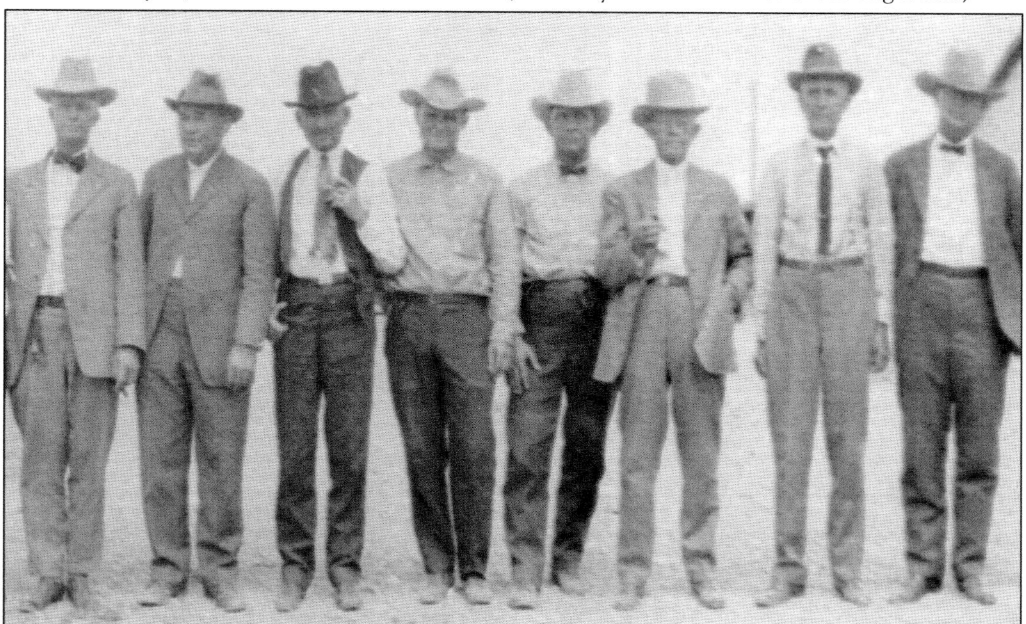

The Highland Hereford Breeders Association was organized in 1918 to promote the region's high quality Hereford cattle. Shown here in a select portion of a larger group photograph of the founding members are prominent Alpine and Marfa area cattlemen. They are, from left to right, Homer Colquitt, J. C. Bird, Herbert L. Kokernot Sr., Charlie Pruett, Crawford Mitchell, W. P. Fisher, Archie Murrey, and H. B. Holmes. (Courtesy of the Archives of the Big Bend.)

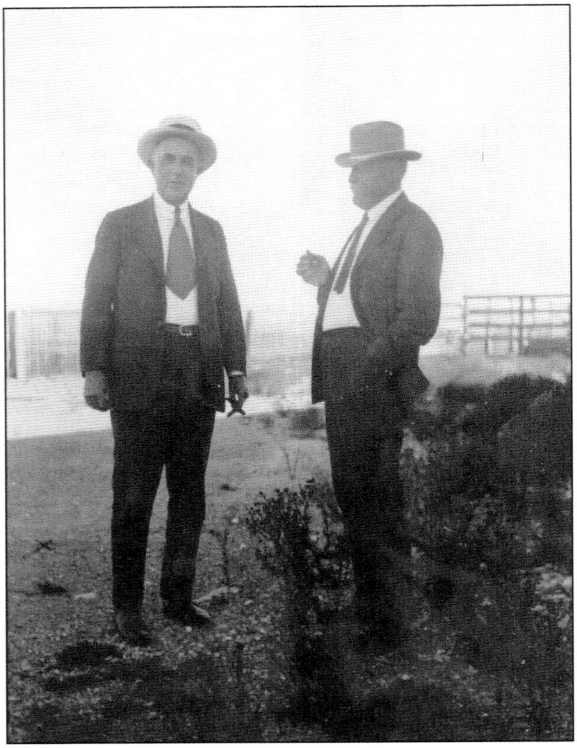

Alfred Gage (left) and cattle buyer John Molesworth talk business on the Gage Ranch around 1920. Gage, a native of Vermont, moved to the Big Bend in 1882 to manage his half-brother's ranching operation. By 1913, he was able to buy out the other stockholders in the Alpine Cattle Company, amassing a cattle-raising empire. (Courtesy of the Roberts collection.)

Gage (second from right) is shown here with his employees and representatives from the Peyton Packing Company. From left to right are Oscar Roberts, Jim Roberts, Ed Tarrant, unidentified Peyton representative, Alfred Gage, and unidentified Peyton representative. In the early days, there was an unspoken dress code, with white shirts, ties, and fedoras distinguishing the ranch owners and businessmen from the cowboys. (Courtesy of the Roberts collection.)

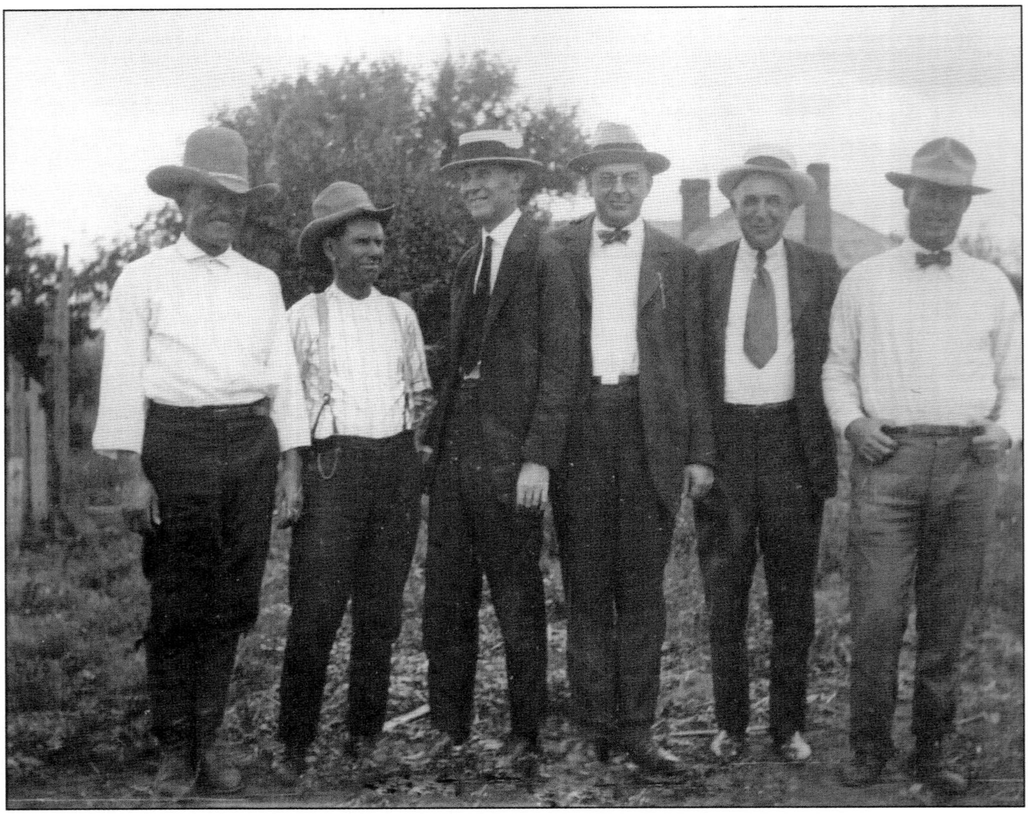

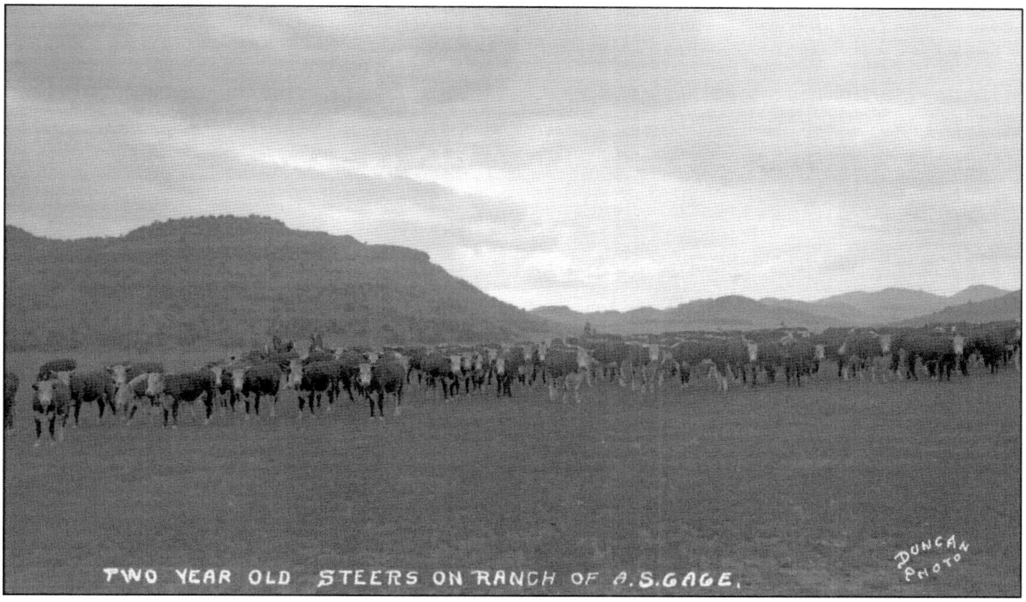

At one time, the Gage Ranch ran 10,000 cattle on more than 500,000 acres. Spanning country from Marathon to Marfa, the ranch encompassed some of the finest grazing land in the region. The better quality Highland grasslands around Alpine contrasted sharply with the poorer rangeland in the southern Big Bend. (Courtesy of the Marfa and Presidio County Museum.)

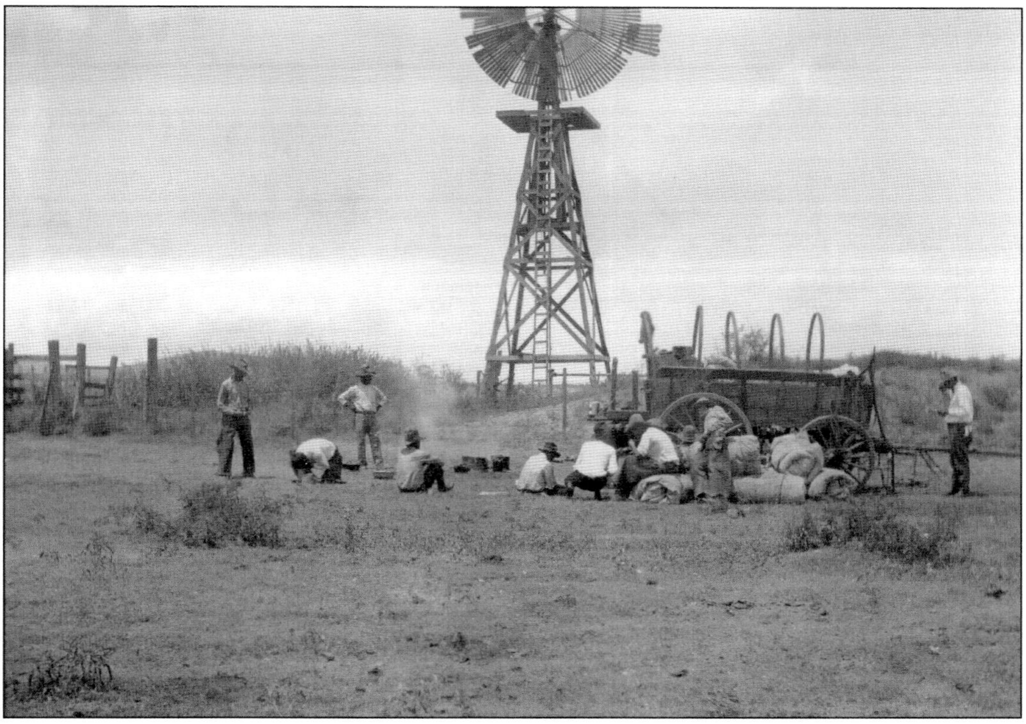
Cowboys relax and wash up before mealtime around the chuckwagon on the Gage Ranch. Behind them towers a Railroad Eclipse windmill, the largest of the wooden-wheeled Eclipse line, designed to pump vast quantities of water for steam locomotives or large numbers of cattle. (Courtesy of the Roberts collection.)

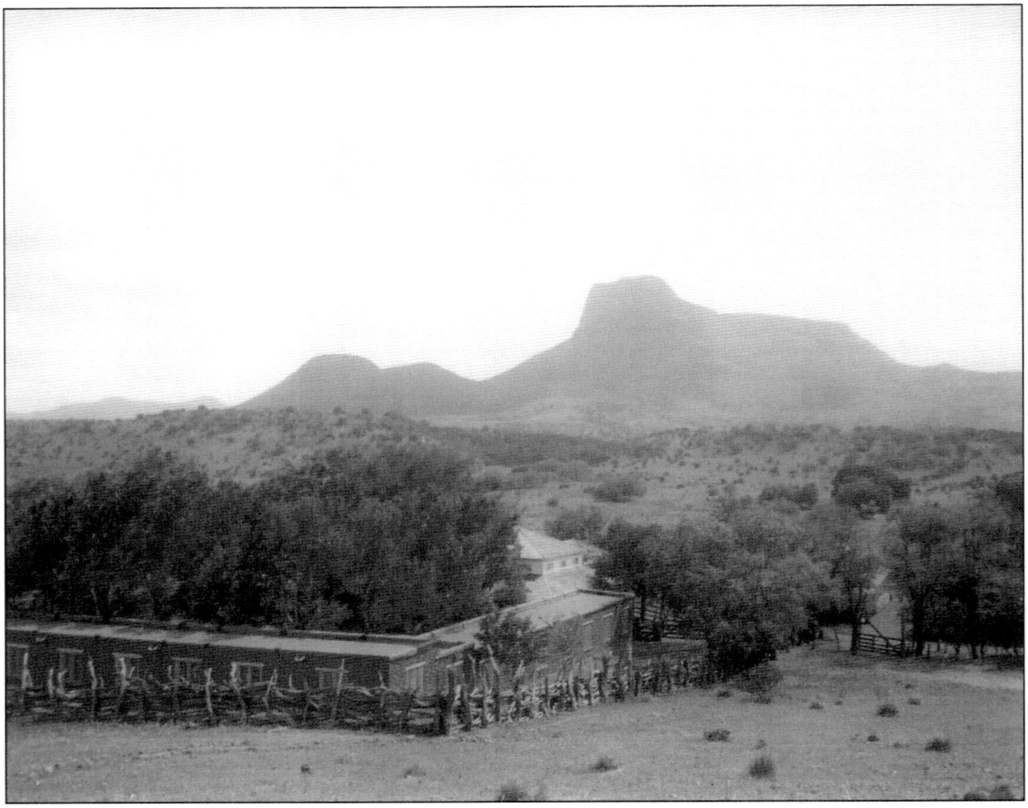

The ranch house and lodge beyond at Rancho Valle de la Cienega are shown against the backdrop of Cathedral Mountain. Lawrence Haley started the ranch in the early 1880s and willed it to his foreman of many years, George Brown. It was operated during the late 1920s and 1930s as a guest ranch. (Courtesy of the Museum of the Big Bend.)

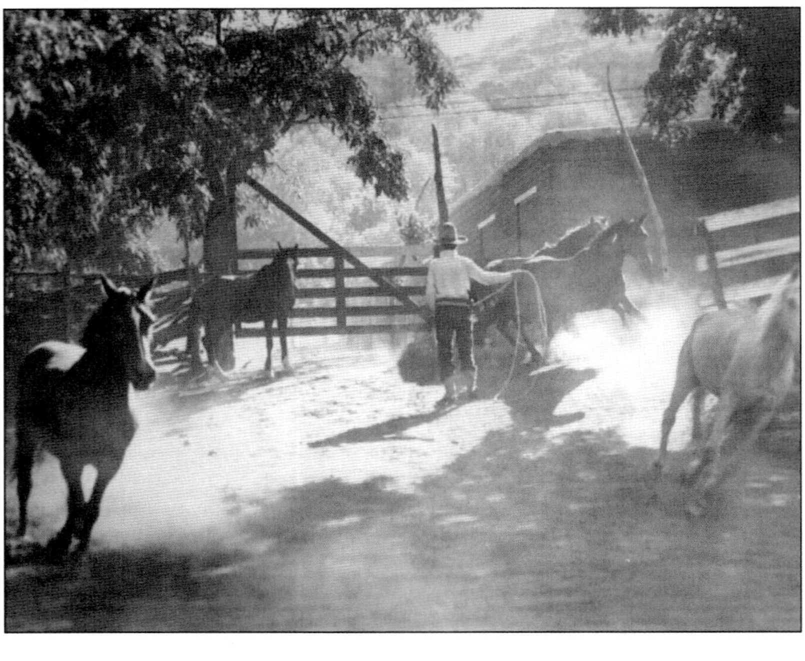

Pete Crawford prepares to rope a horse in the corrals at Rancho Valle de la Cienega in 1924. A special throw was used, called a houlihan, designed to drop down gently around the horse's neck with just a single, fluid backward swing. (Courtesy of the Museum of the Big Bend.)

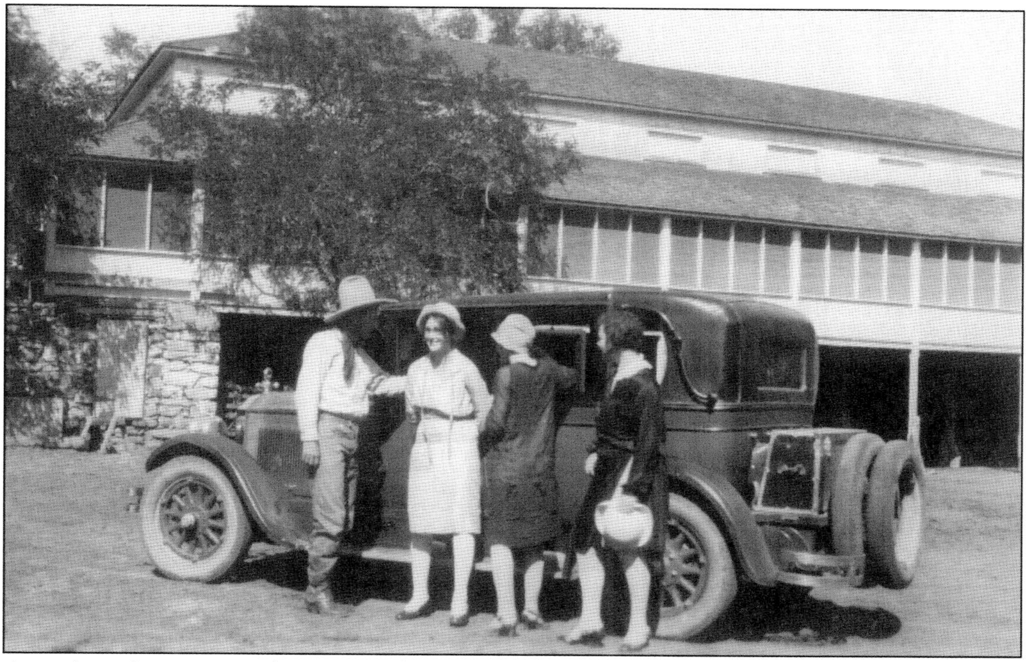

A cowboy charms several new arrivals at Rancho Valle de la Cienega around 1930. The ranch had the distinction of being the first guest ranch in the region and one of the earliest in the state. It was a popular weekend destination for students at Sul Ross State Teacher's College. (Courtesy of the Ivey collection.)

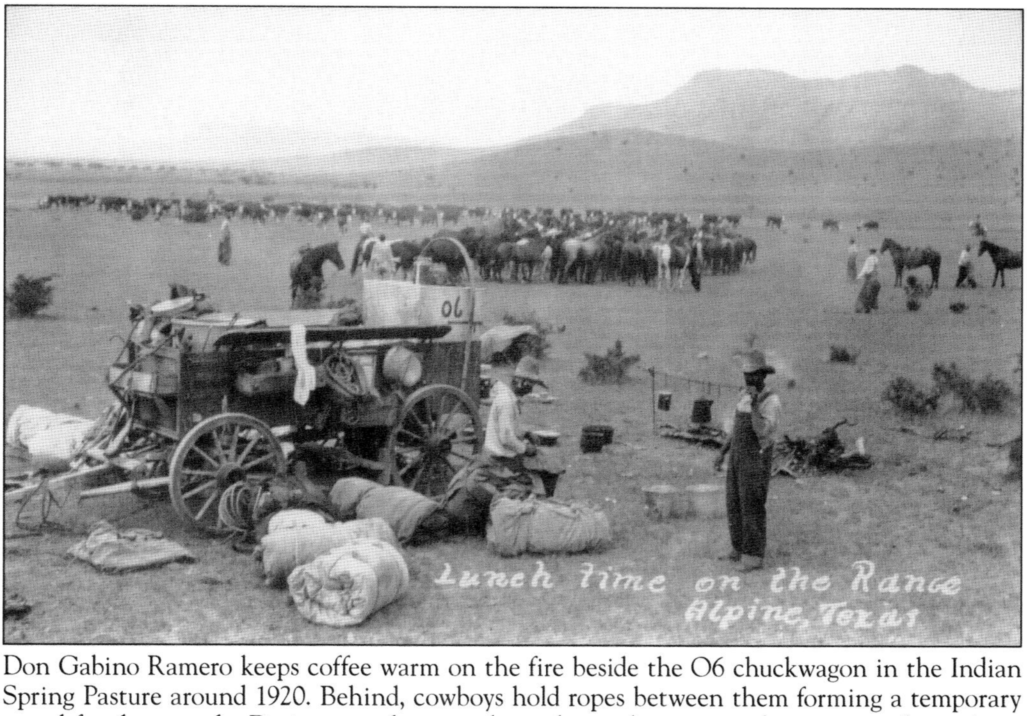

Don Gabino Ramero keeps coffee warm on the fire beside the O6 chuckwagon in the Indian Spring Pasture around 1920. Behind, cowboys hold ropes between them forming a temporary corral for the remuda. During roundups, cowboys changed mounts at least once a day to keep their horses fresh. (Courtesy of the Ivey collection.)

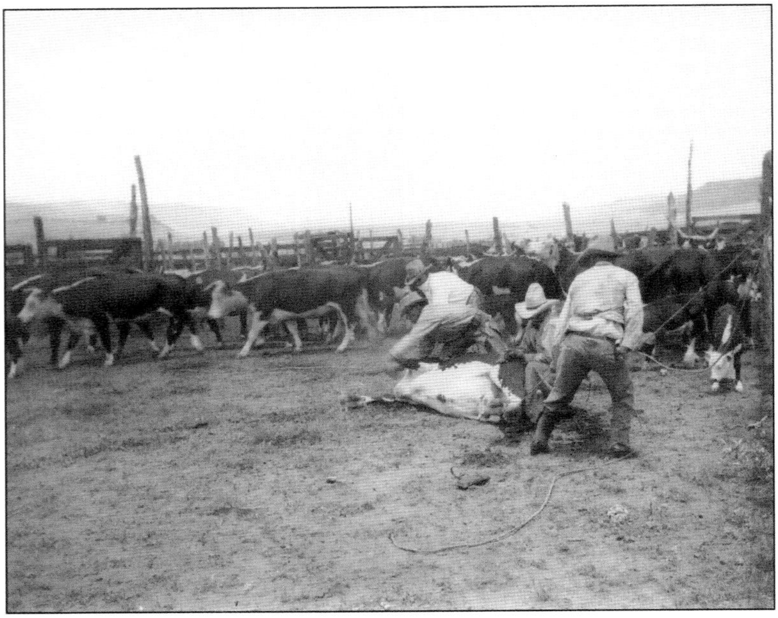

To hold a full-grown cow took both skill and brute force—as well as many men—as shown here on the O6 Ranch in 1935. One pins down the head, another bends the foreleg, another pulls on the tail, and a fourth holds a rope that binds the cow's heels and that has been looped around a corral post for leverage. (Courtesy of the Museum of the Big Bend.)

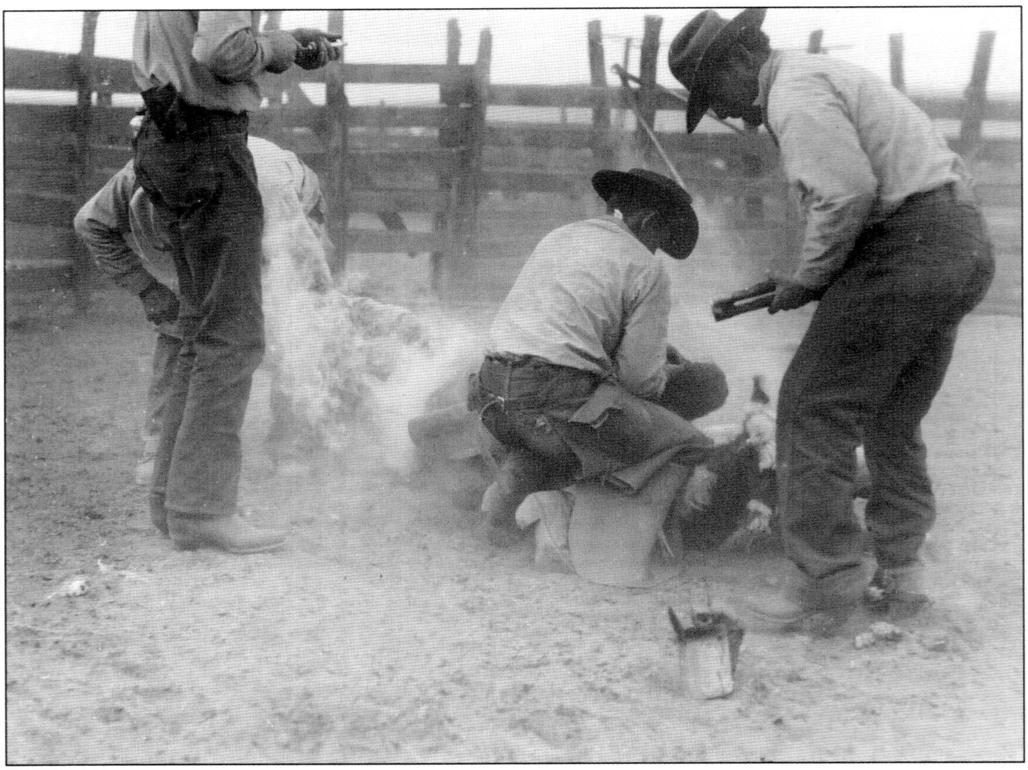

Cowboys brand, dehorn, and vaccinate on the O6 Ranch in the late 1940s. From left to right are Don Nicasio Ramirez, J. E. Gray Jr., Tommy Rodriguez, and Alfredo Muñoz. (Courtesy of the Gray collection.)

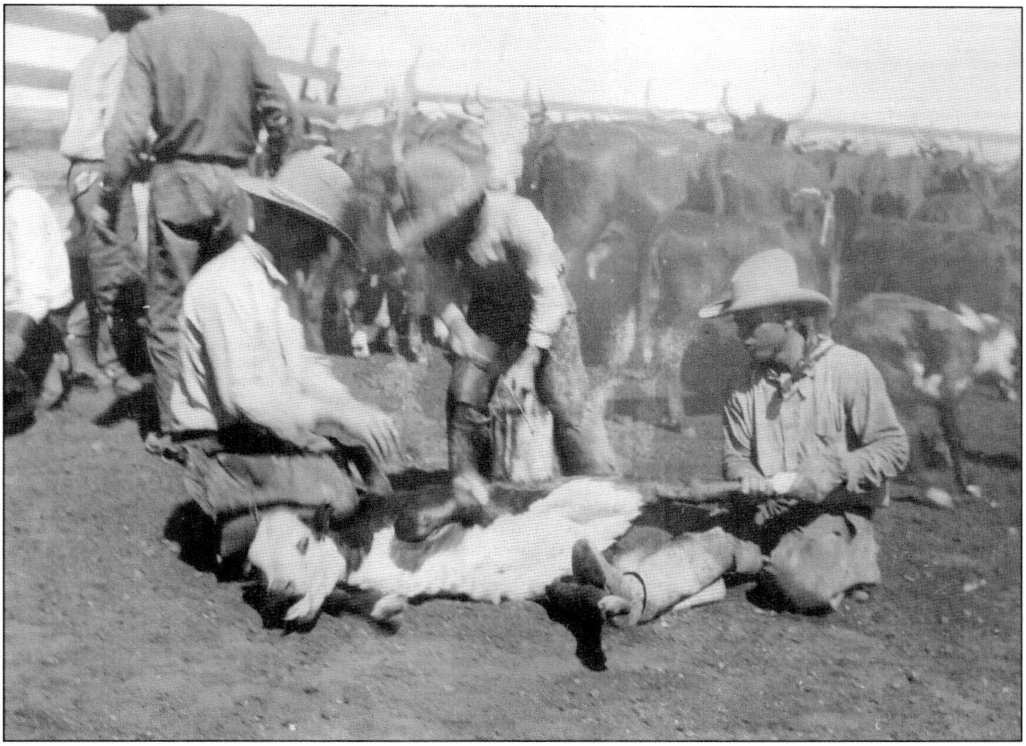

Cowboys began working at a young age and were often put to tasks requiring less skill but more sweat, such as flanking and holding calves, as shown here on the Gage Ranch around 1920. (Courtesy of the Roberts collection.)

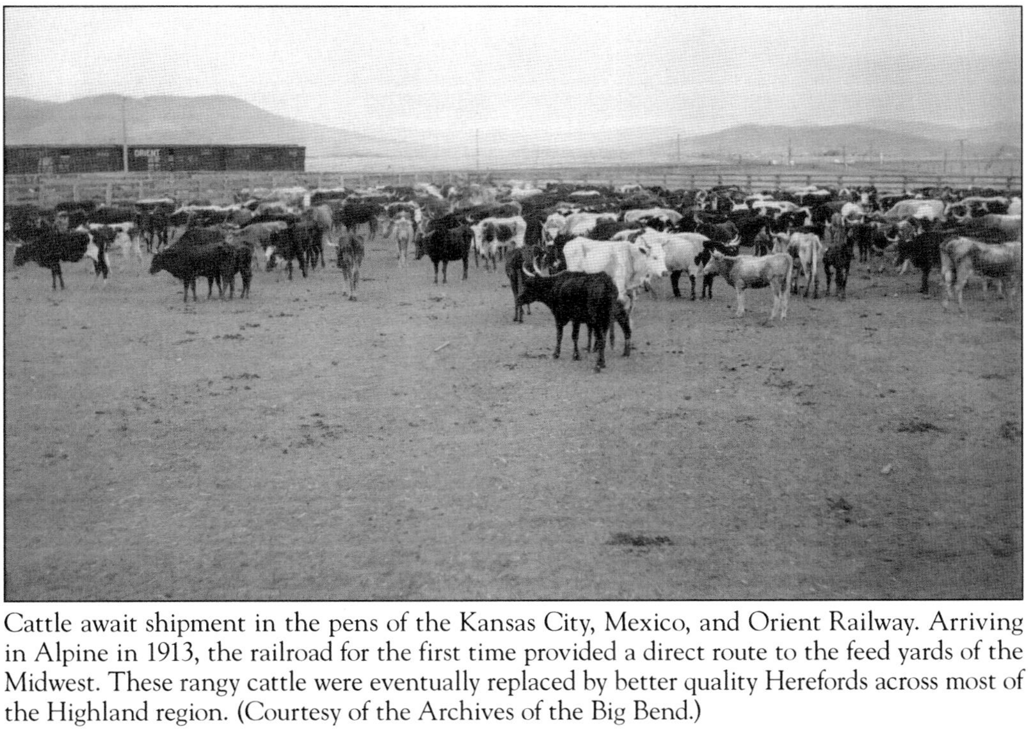

Cattle await shipment in the pens of the Kansas City, Mexico, and Orient Railway. Arriving in Alpine in 1913, the railroad for the first time provided a direct route to the feed yards of the Midwest. These rangy cattle were eventually replaced by better quality Herefords across most of the Highland region. (Courtesy of the Archives of the Big Bend.)

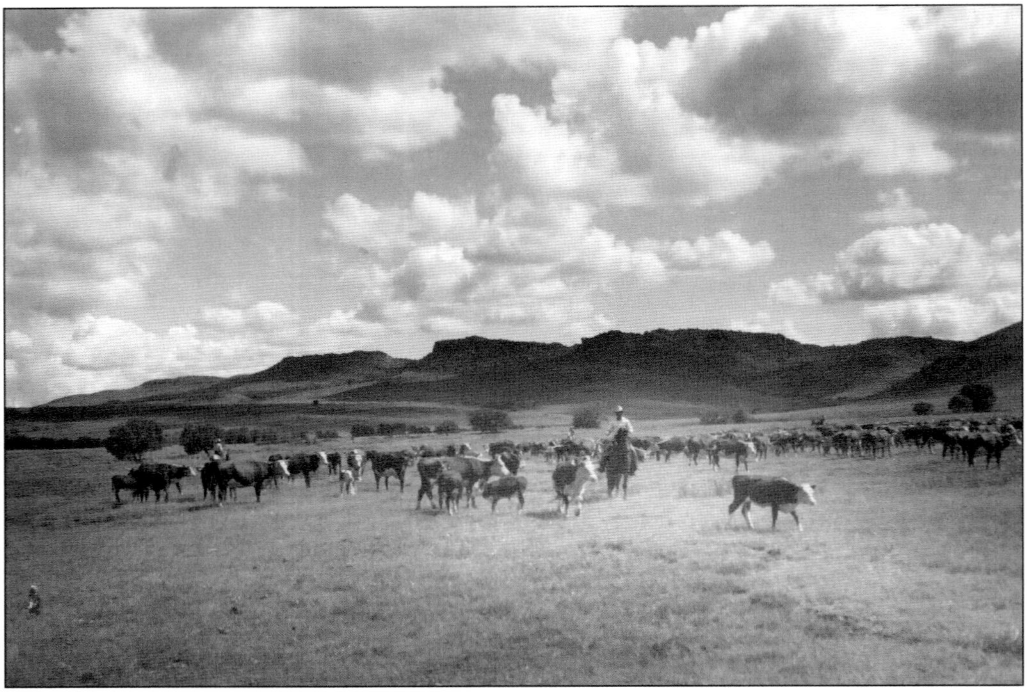

Clive Acton separates cattle on the O6 Ranch in the Cienega Pasture in 1936. The ranch was started by Herbert Kokernot Sr. in the early 1910s by buying up quality grazing land in the Davis Mountains and Alpine Valley. (Courtesy of the Museum of the Big Bend).

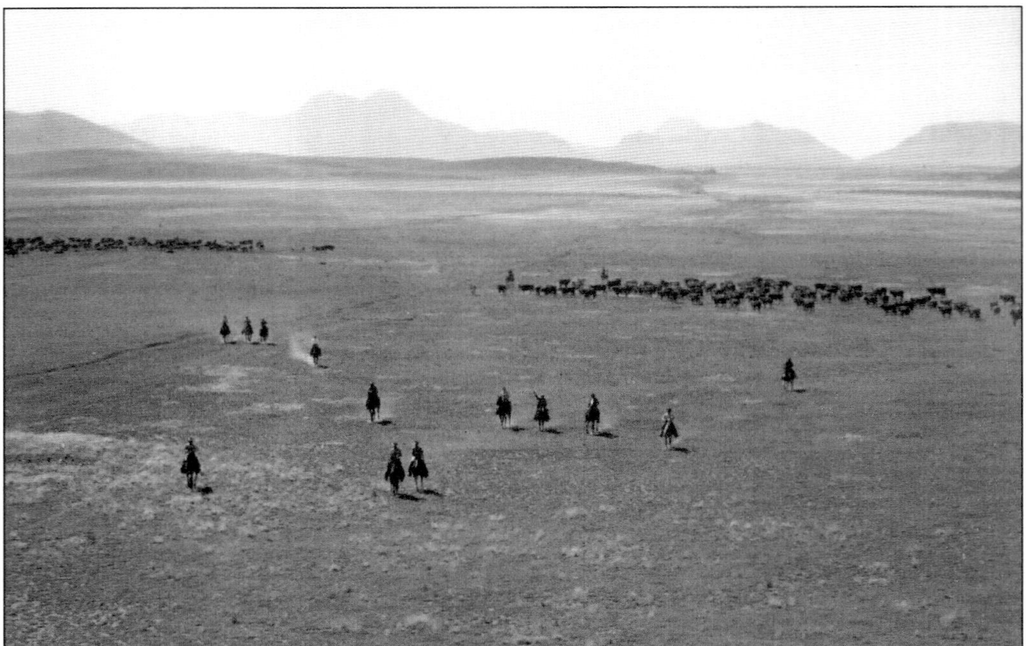

Cowboys ride to lunch while others hold separate herds on the O6 pasture north of Alpine. Among the men are top hand Nicasio Ramirez and wagon boss Ted Gray. In the background is Twin Peaks. Well-known regional photographer W. D. Smithers captured this image from a low-flying plane around 1946. (Courtesy of the Museum of the Big Bend).

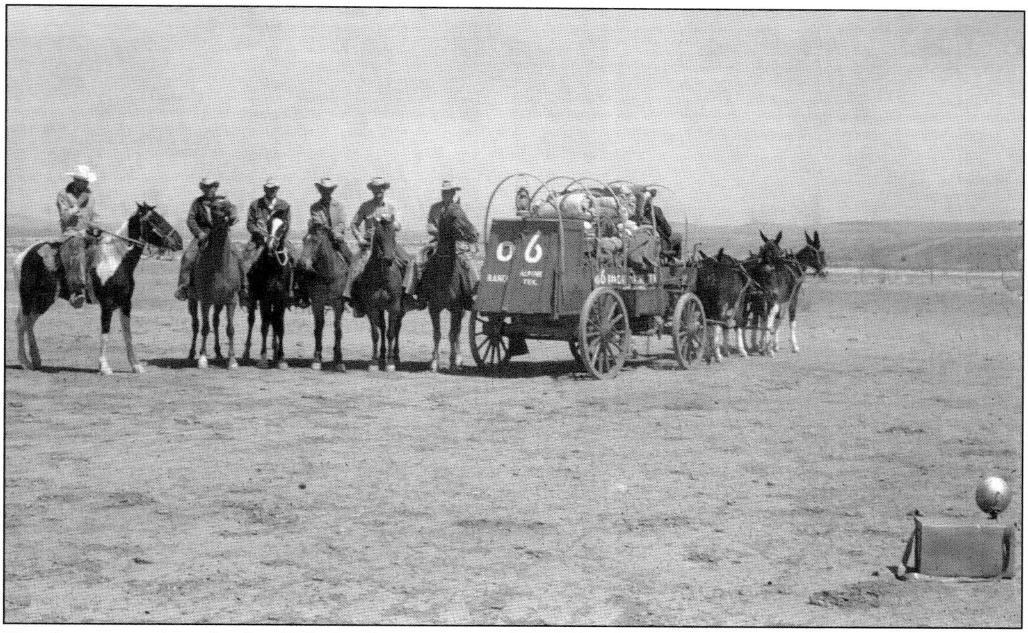

Cowboys pose beside the O6 chuckwagon in 1960. The O6 was one of the last holdouts of the old ways of operating. Frugality as much as a sense of tradition kept the historical methods of ranching alive. (Courtesy of the Hunter collection.)

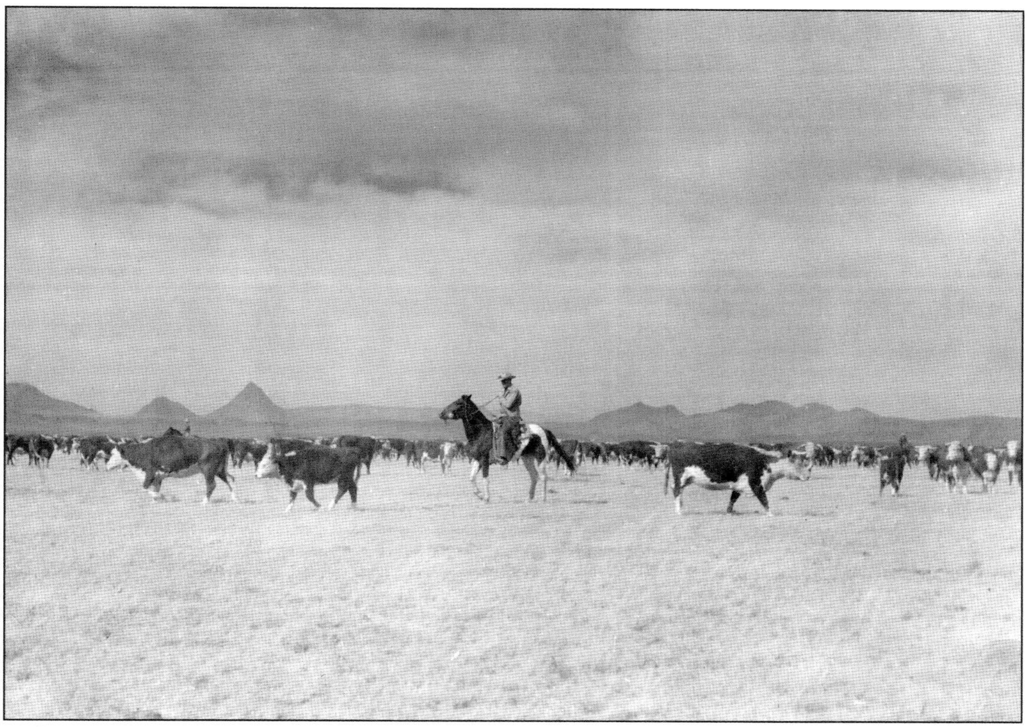

Ted Gray rides a paint named Tony during a roundup in the O6 pasture around 1945. In the background are Mitre Peak and the Davis Mountains. Gray started working on the O6 in late 1930s and within a matter of years had risen to a position as ranch manager. (Courtesy of the Gray collection.)

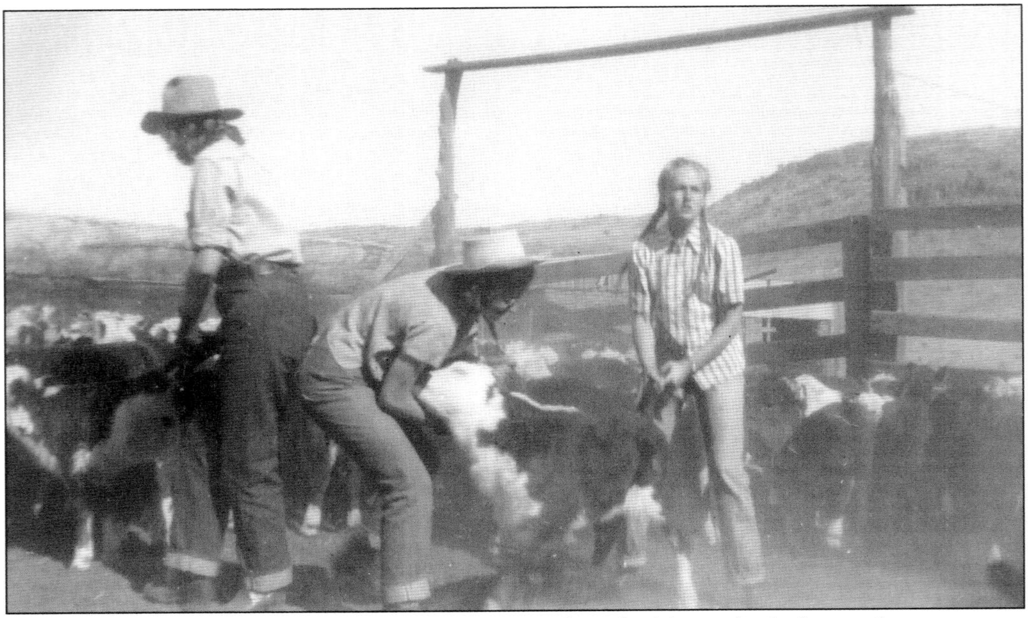

During World War II, when most of the area's cowboys had been drafted into the war, many ranches had to find other sources of labor. Here Celia Smith (right) and a friend prepare to flank a calf during branding on a ranch outside Alpine. (Courtesy of the Smith collection).

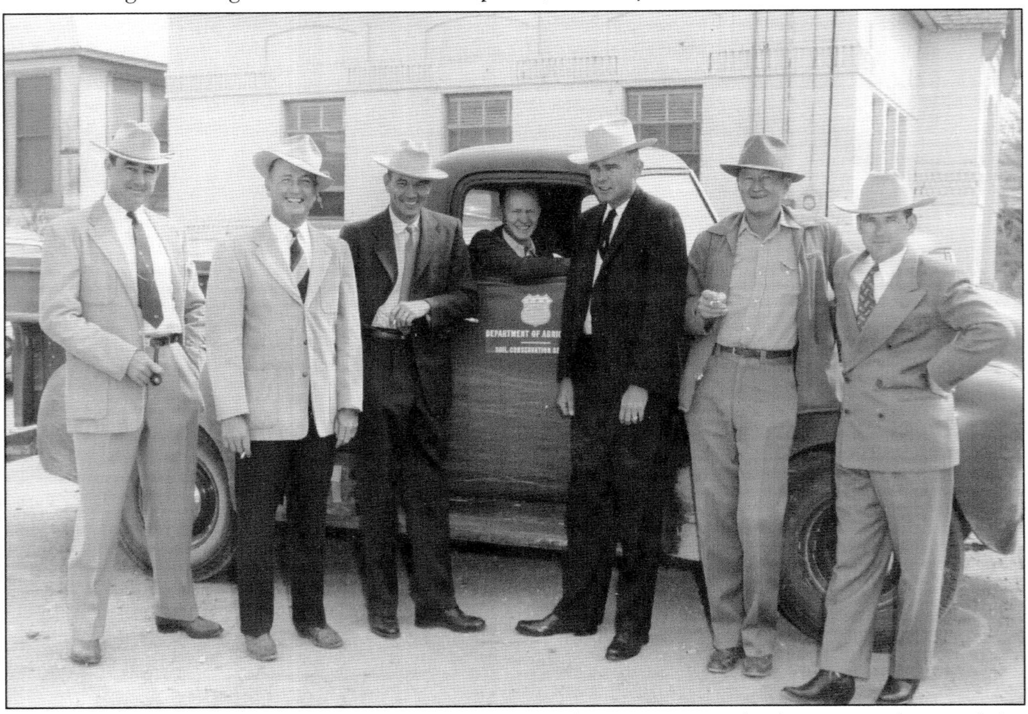

The Big Bend Soil Conservation District, organized in 1948, was the largest, and one of the most active, in the state. The board of supervisors, shown here around 1950, stand in front of their headquarters at the old Alpine Schoolhouse. They are, from left to right, George Mills, Jimmy Pate, Lamar Kay, Billy Sullivan, Neville Haynes, C. F. Cox, and Bill Sohl. (Courtesy of the Natural Resource Conservation Service.)

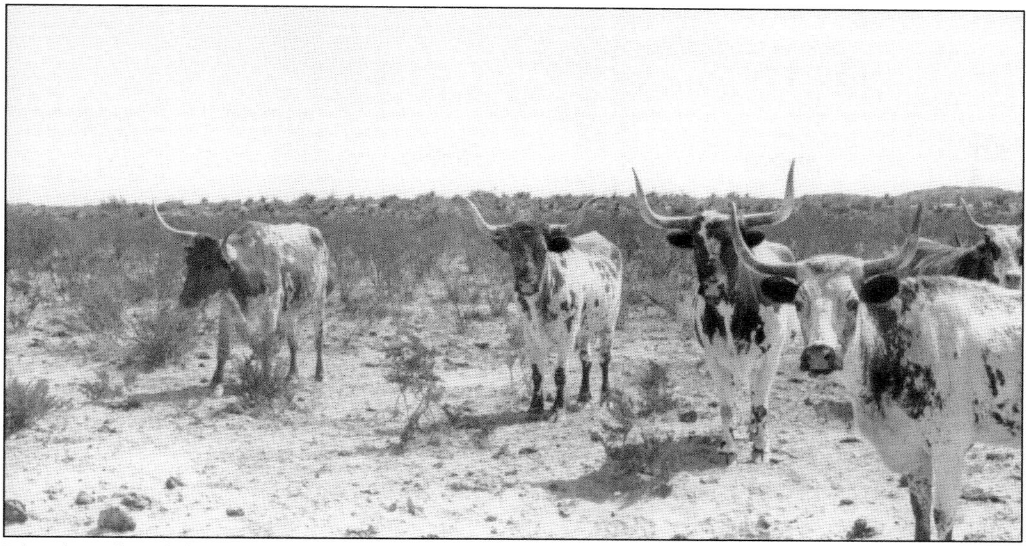

The drought of the 1950s was the longest and by many estimates the worst in history. Between 1950 and 1954, Brewster County ranchers were forced to reduce their herds almost by half. Some ranches began running rangy longhorns, such as those shown here, that were better able to utilize diminishing forage. (Courtesy of the Natural Resource Conservation Service.)

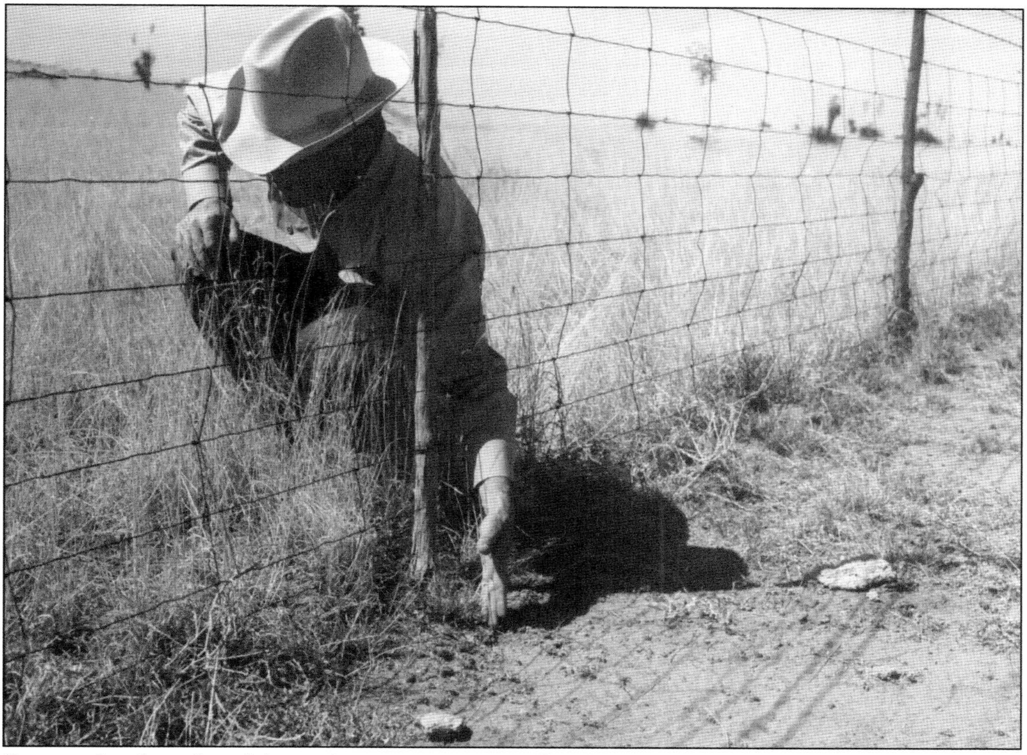

During the drought of the 1950s, area ranges suffered the effects of intense heat and limited moisture. Here Jim Brunner of the Soil Conservation Service points to dead clumps of grass where overgrazing and drought had taken their toll. The stark difference in grass cover on either side of the fence is the result of varying grazing pressure. (Courtesy of the Natural Resource Conservation Service.)

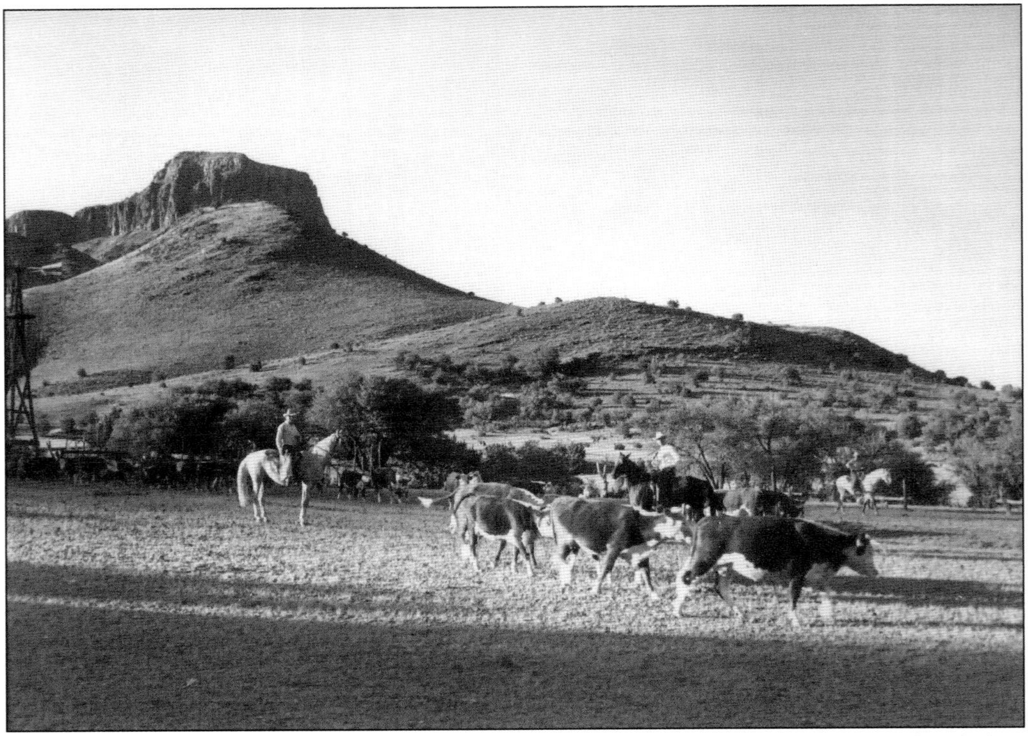

King Terry Sr. (left) and King Terry Jr. work cattle on their ranch in 1951. The Terry family first came to the region in 1905, acquiring ranchland northeast of Alpine before moving the operation southwest of town where they remained. (Courtesy of the Terry collection.)

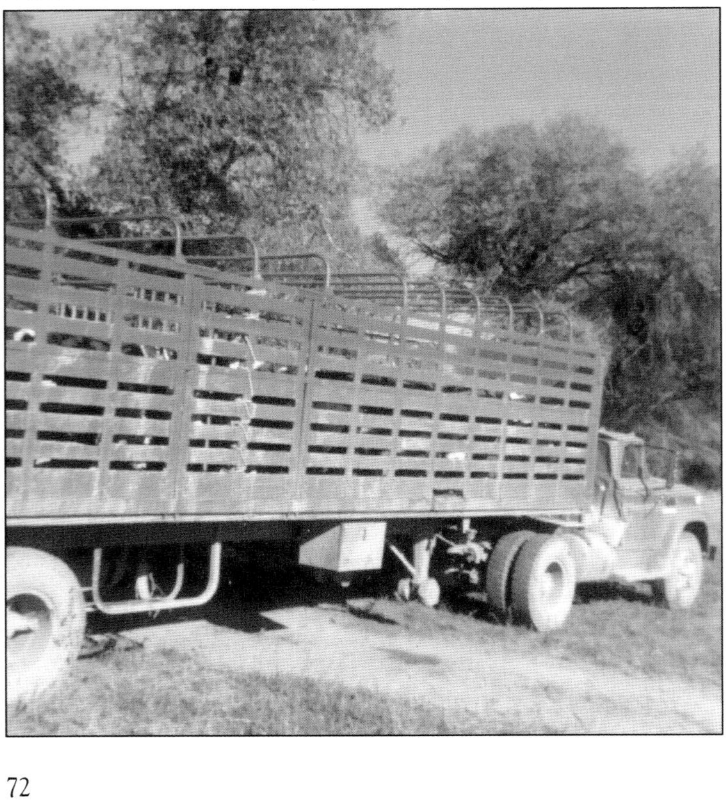

By the 1950s, trucks had largely replaced railroad cars for shipping cattle to market. Many factors—including more powerful vehicles, decreased distance to stockyards, and the cost and hassle of dealing with the railroads—ended the era of driving the herds to railroad shipping pens. (Courtesy of the Terry collection.)

Five

Coming Together
Social Events and Organizations

From its earliest days, Alpine has had a strong network of social organizations and been quick to seize just about any reason for a celebration. Churches and religious organizations have been among the most prominent and long-standing, starting with Alpine's first church service held in the waiting room of the Southern Pacific depot in 1883. For many years thereafter, all the town's denominations shared the First Methodist Church built in 1889. By 1910, the town could boast a total of five churches.

In terms of scale and popularity, the Paisano Baptist Encampment, established in 1921, was in a league of its own. Fashioned after the Bloys Camp Meeting that had met annually in the Davis Mountains since 1890, Paisano was designed to bring people from the far-flung ranches of the Big Bend together to worship and often hosted hundreds.

Although the Catholic church was central to the lives of much of the Hispanic population, in the early days, mutual aid societies—a sort of early community-based insurance policy—also served a vital function in helping families in need. In 1908, the Amor al Trabajo y Union was established, and a clubhouse (later the Apache Bar) was built on Ninth Street and Avenue G. Two years later, the Sociedad Mutualista Mexicana was founded, one purpose of which was to improve the status of women.

National Holidays, most notably the Fourth of July and Cinco de Mayo, have long been a part of the town's history. Alpine has hosted annual festive Fourth of July gatherings since the first townwide celebration in 1888, and Cinco de Mayo has been celebrated since at least the beginning of the 20th century. Similarly, Alpine's historic sporting events—most notably baseball and rodeo—have sometimes drawn nearly every resident. For sheer turnout, however, nothing in the early days matched the Soldier's Welcome Home Day in 1919 or the celebration of the arrival of the Kansas City, Mexico, and Orient Railway in 1913—an event so large that it briefly caused the town's population to double.

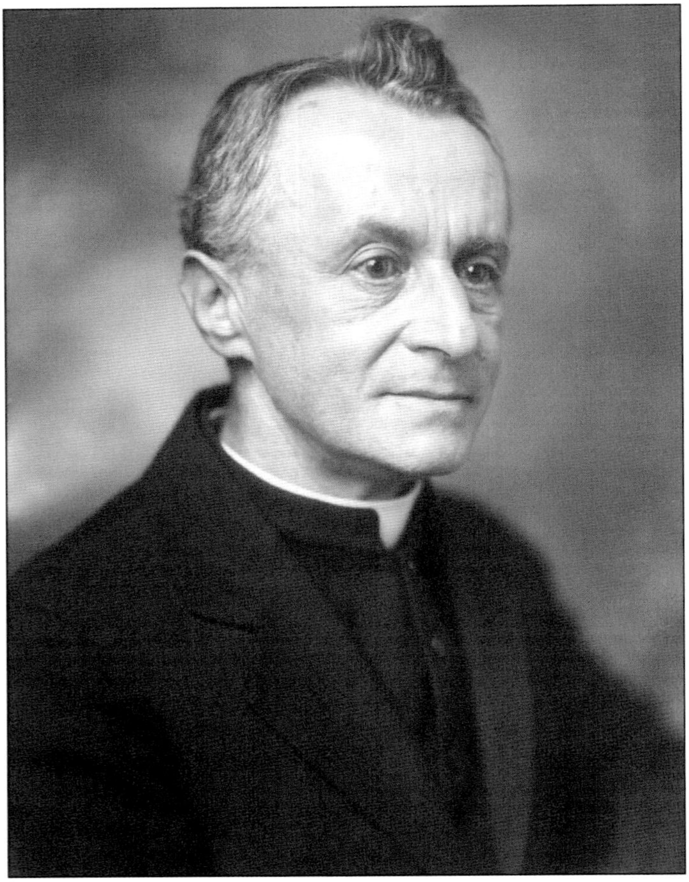

Fr. Brocardus Ecker lived in Fort Davis but presided over services across the entire Big Bend region for some 40 years. Starting in 1892, he held regular monthly Catholic services in Alpine. After 1902, services were held in Nuestra Señora de Guadalupe on the northern flank of A Mountain. (Courtesy of the Archives of the Big Bend.)

The Bloys Camp meeting was founded by William Benjamin Bloys, a Presbyterian missionary serving in Fort Davis. In 1890, Bloys came up with the idea for an annual meeting at Skillman's Grove in the Davis Mountains. The annual five-day gathering, which is still a yearly event, was as much a social event as a religious one. (Courtesy of the Archives of the Big Bend.)

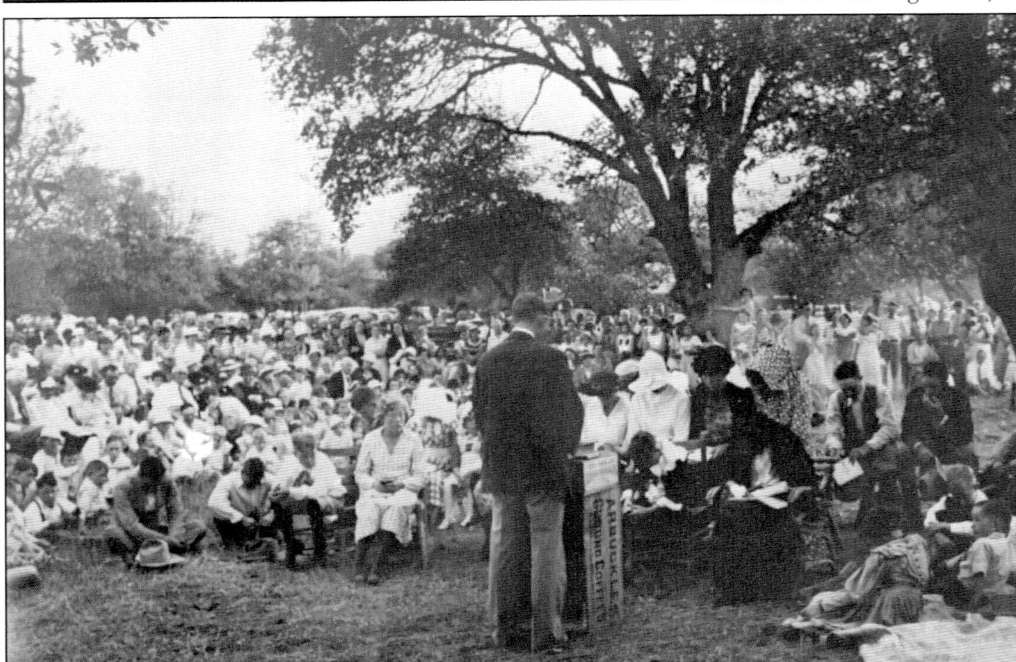

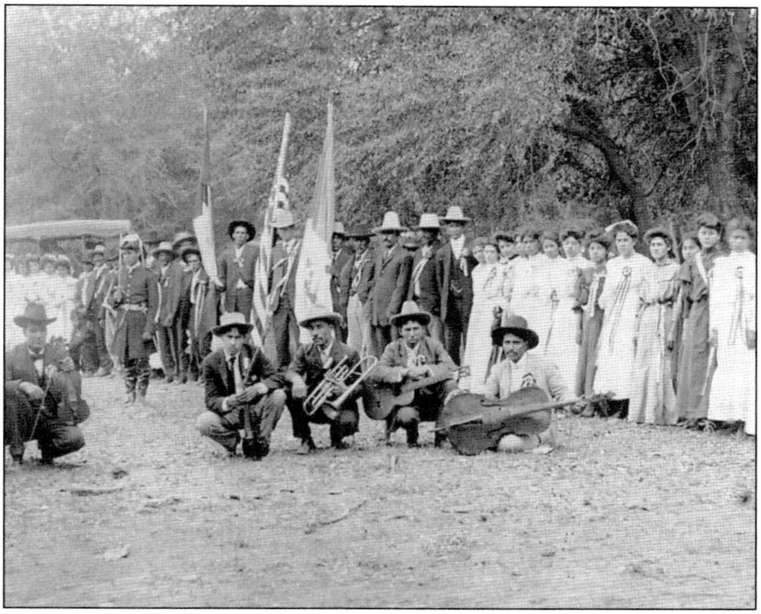

Men and women gather near Paisano Peak in 1907 to celebrate Cinco de Mayo. Although the date actually marks the Mexican Army's unlikely victory over the French at the Battle of Puebla in 1862, in the United States the event has become a more general celebration of Mexican heritage and pride. (Courtesy of the Archives of the Big Bend.)

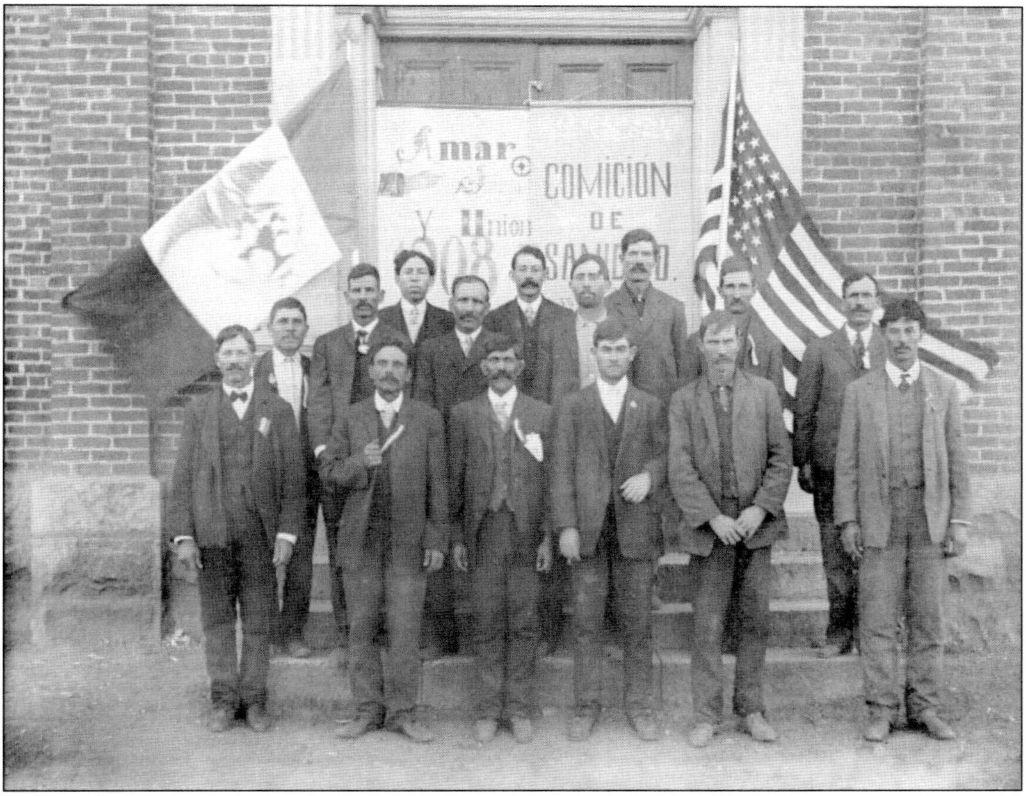

Members of the newly established mutual aid society Amor al Trabajo y Union celebrate Mexican Independence Day in 1908. They are, from left to right, (first row) Jesus Chavez, Pedro Ramirez, Panchito Avila, Donaciano Cobos, Joe Gallego, Salvador Samaripa; (second row) Juan Vega, Pedro Leyva, Pilar Hernandez, Roque Elizal, unidentified, John Gallego, Jesus Cobos, George Cobos, and unidentified. (Courtesy of the Archives of the Big Bend.)

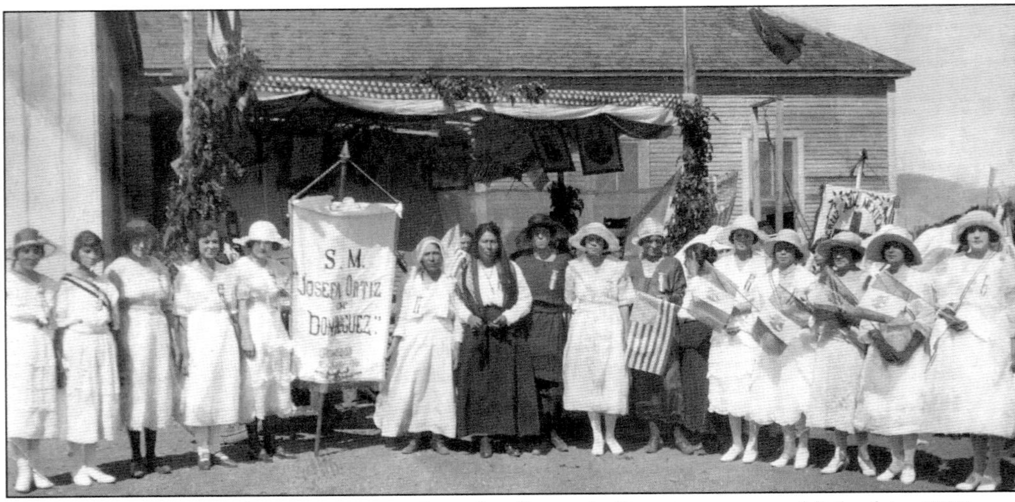

The Sociedad Mutualista Mexicana, Josepha Ortiz de Dominguez, established in 1910, was dedicated both to helping members during hard times and to improving the status of women in the community. Such mutual aid societies were organized across the Southwest to provide a support structure within Hispanic communities. (Courtesy of the Archives of the Big Bend.)

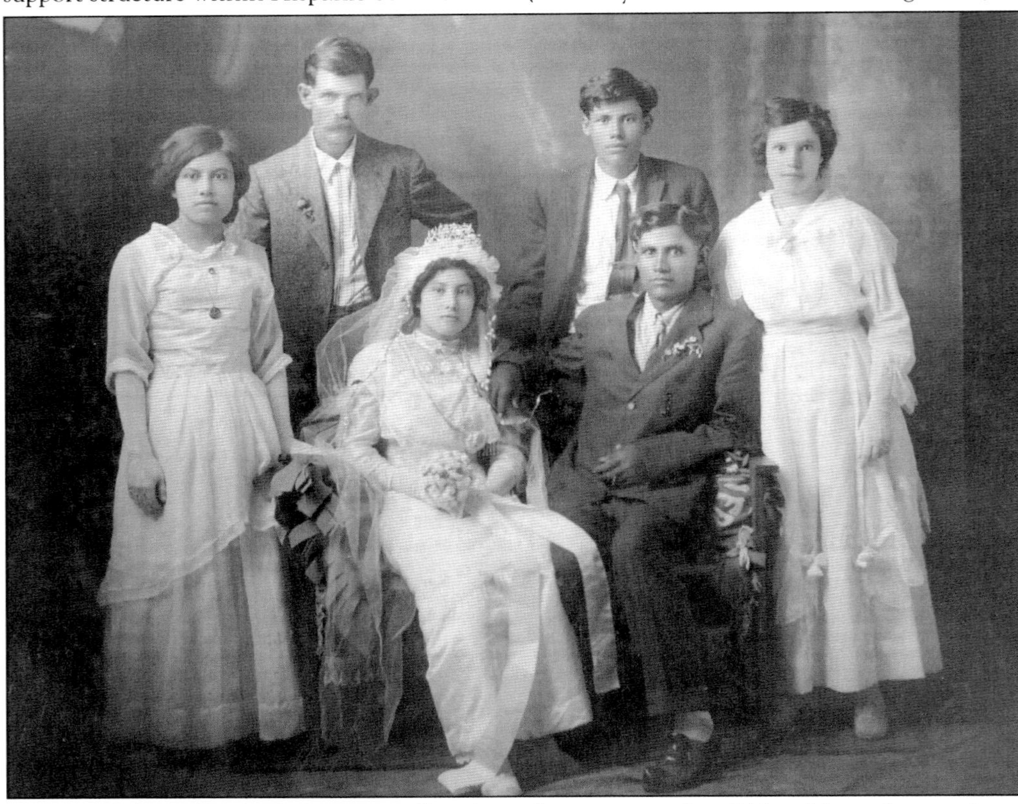

Tomás Valadez and his bride, Juanita Gallego (seated), were married in 1916 in Alpine. In attendance are, from left to right, Estefana Fierro-Uranga, Dario Cobos, Luis Valadez, Ester Sotelo-Martinez. Born in Ojinaga, Chihuahua in 1886, Valadez came to Alpine in 1903. In 1937 he purchased the Alpine Furniture Company building at the corner of South Fifth Street and Murphy Avenue and converted it to Valadez Grocery and Meat Market. (Courtesy of the Valadez collection.)

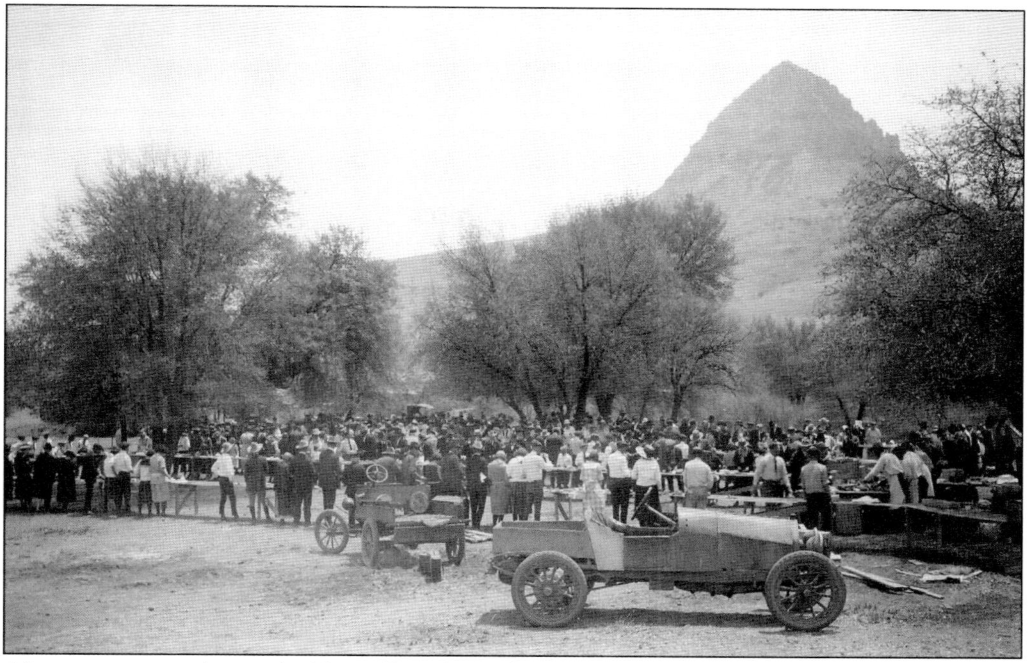

Alpine citizens gather at the Tippit Ranch northwest of Alpine for a picnic around 1920. In the back is Mitre Peak, a prominent local landmark. The car in the foreground is a heavily modified 1915 Buick that has been fashioned to resemble a roadster. (Courtesy of the Marfa and Presidio County Museum.)

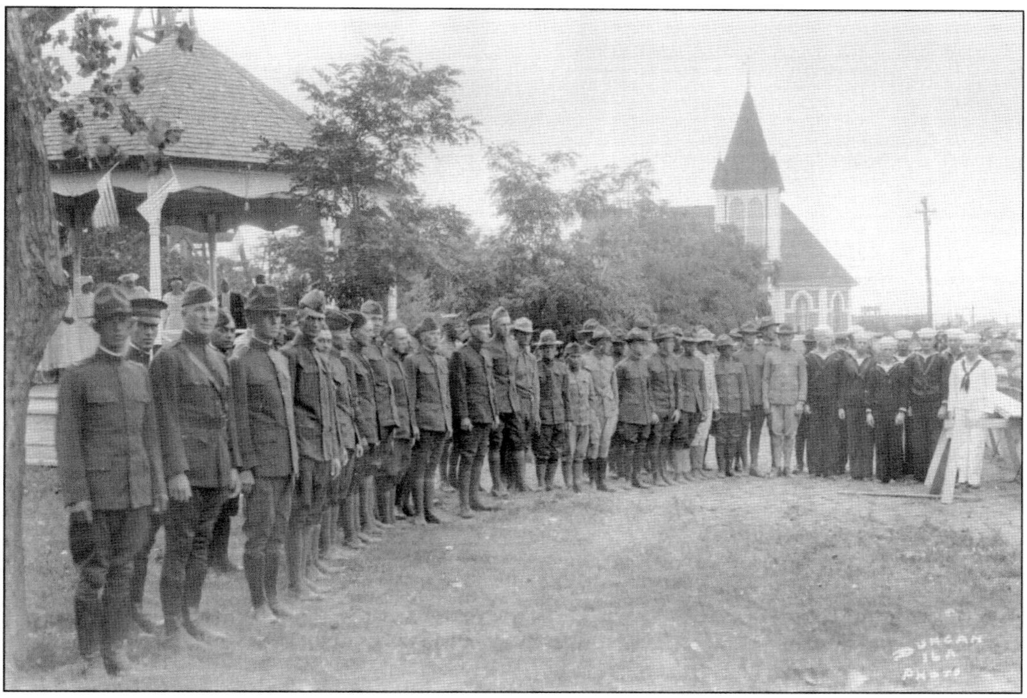

World War I veterans assemble during the Soldier's Welcome Home Day celebration in July 1919. The day included a parade, a band concert, a free barbeque, horse races, and a baseball game, among other events. (Courtesy of the Archives of the Big Bend.)

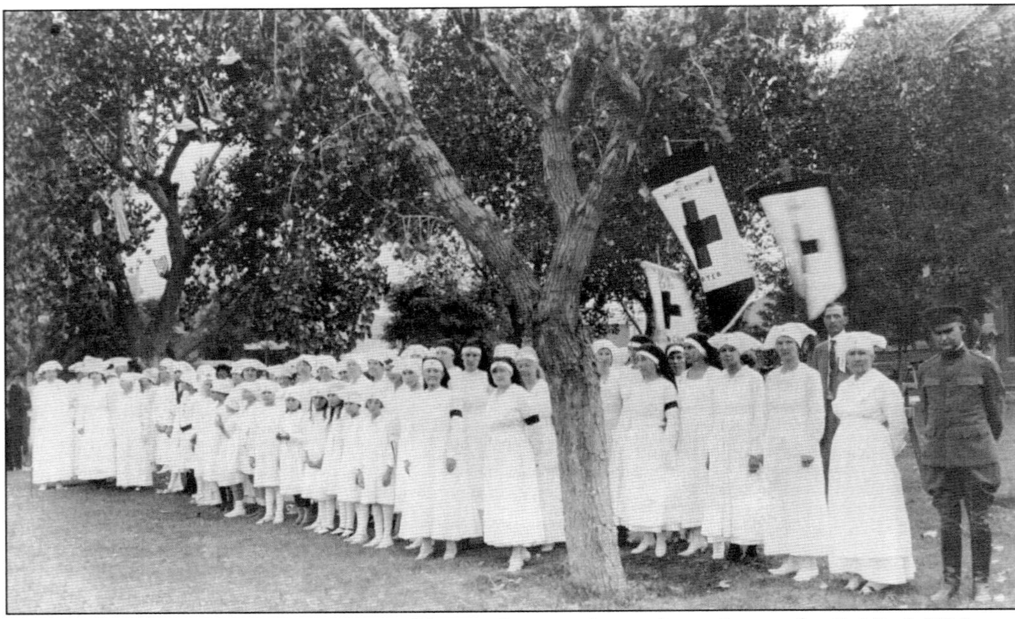

The Brewster County Red Cross assembles on the courthouse lawn during the Soldier's Welcome Home Day celebration. The uniformed man is Dr. J. R. Middlebrook, who served in the Medical Corps during World War I and was an Alpine physician from 1909 until 1922. (Courtesy of the Archives of the Big Bend.)

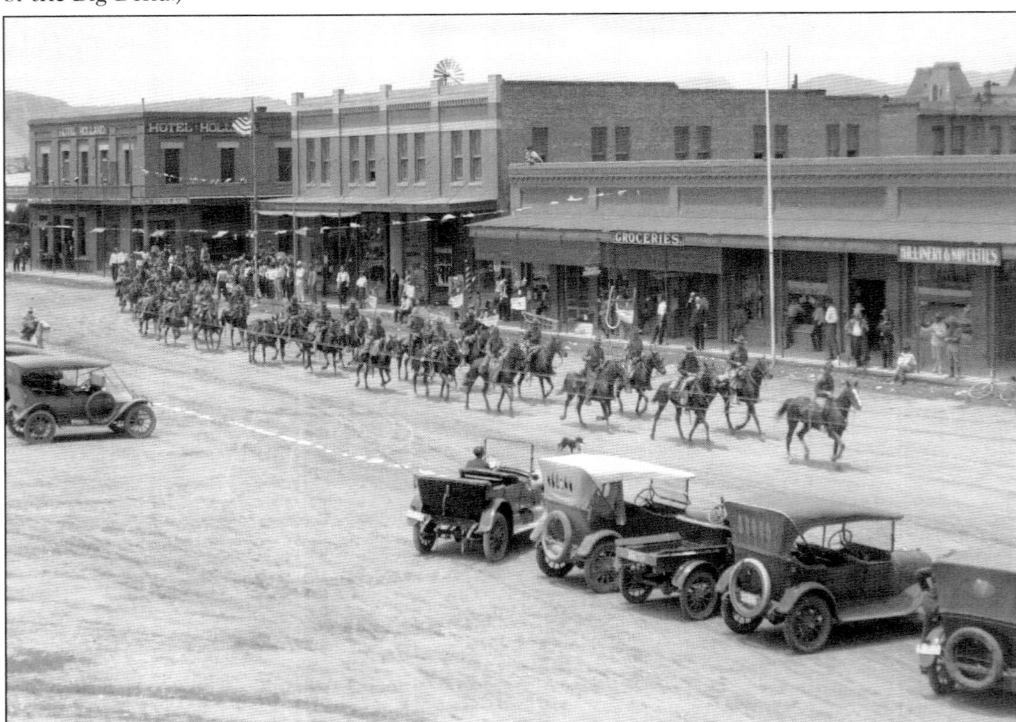

The 8th Cavalry band parades down Front Street as part of the Soldier's Welcome Home Day celebration. Under Col. George T. Langhorne, 700 troopers had marched from Marfa to Alpine to join the celebration. (Courtesy of the Museum of the Big Bend.)

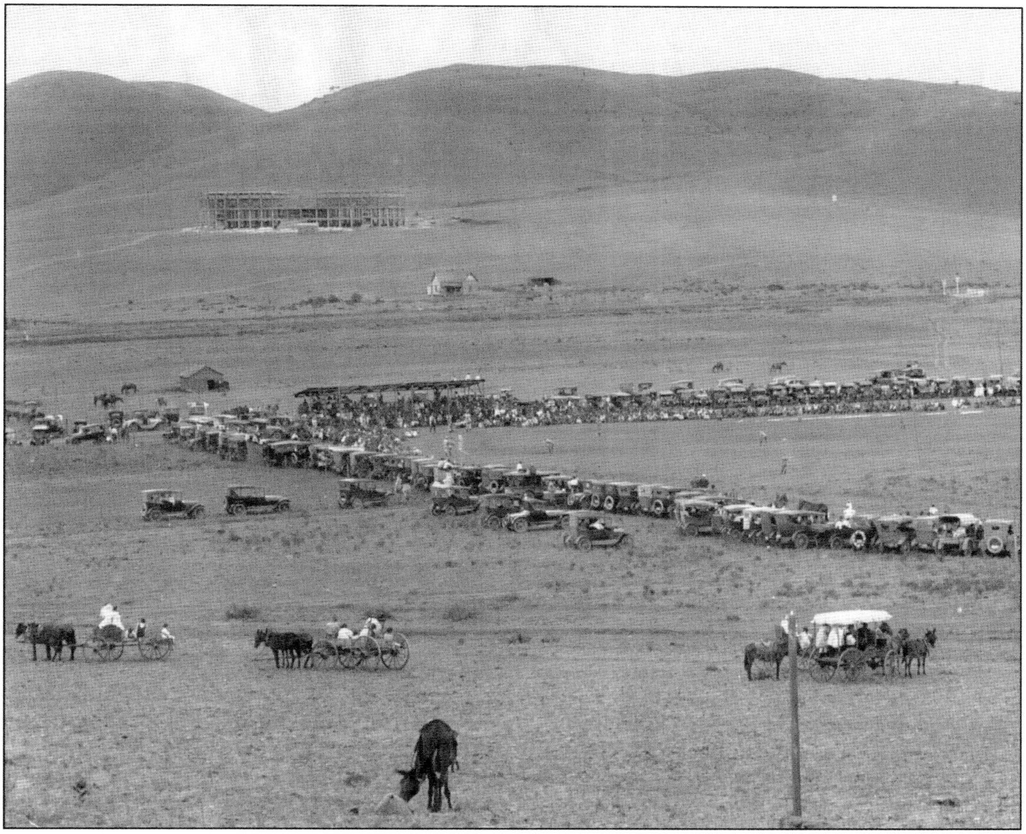

The Alpine Sluggers played against Marfa as part of the Soldier's Welcome Home Day celebration. The playing field was outlined in cars though some spectators came in wagons to watch the game. In the background, Sul Ross State Normal College is under construction. (Courtesy of the Archives of the Big Bend.)

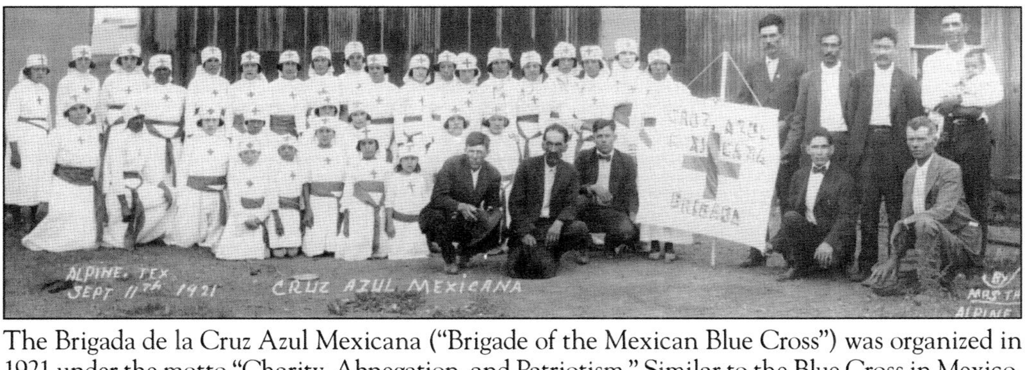

The Brigada de la Cruz Azul Mexicana ("Brigade of the Mexican Blue Cross") was organized in 1921 under the motto "Charity, Abnegation, and Patriotism." Similar to the Blue Cross in Mexico, this charitable organization was established by local Hispanic women to aid families in need. Among its several male supporters was onetime sheriff of Brewster County Everett Townsend, lower right. (Courtesy of the Archives of the Big Bend.)

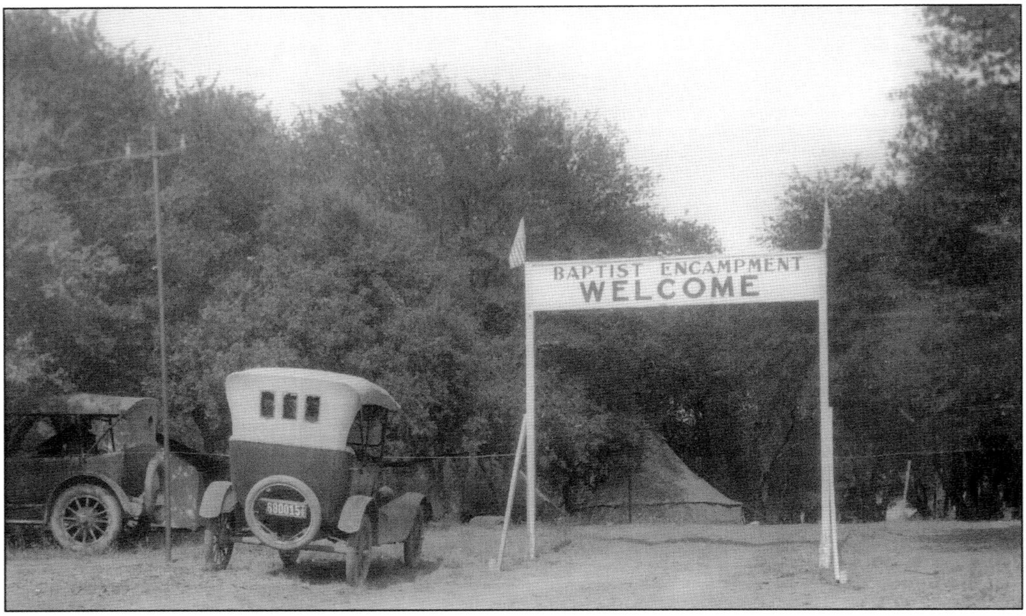

The first Paisano Baptist Encampment was held in 1921. After many years of planning and numerous delays, 1,000 acres were purchased at Paisano Pass between Marfa and Alpine. Within six years, the camp had added a tabernacle, a dining shed, and an office. (Courtesy of the Museum of the Big Bend.)

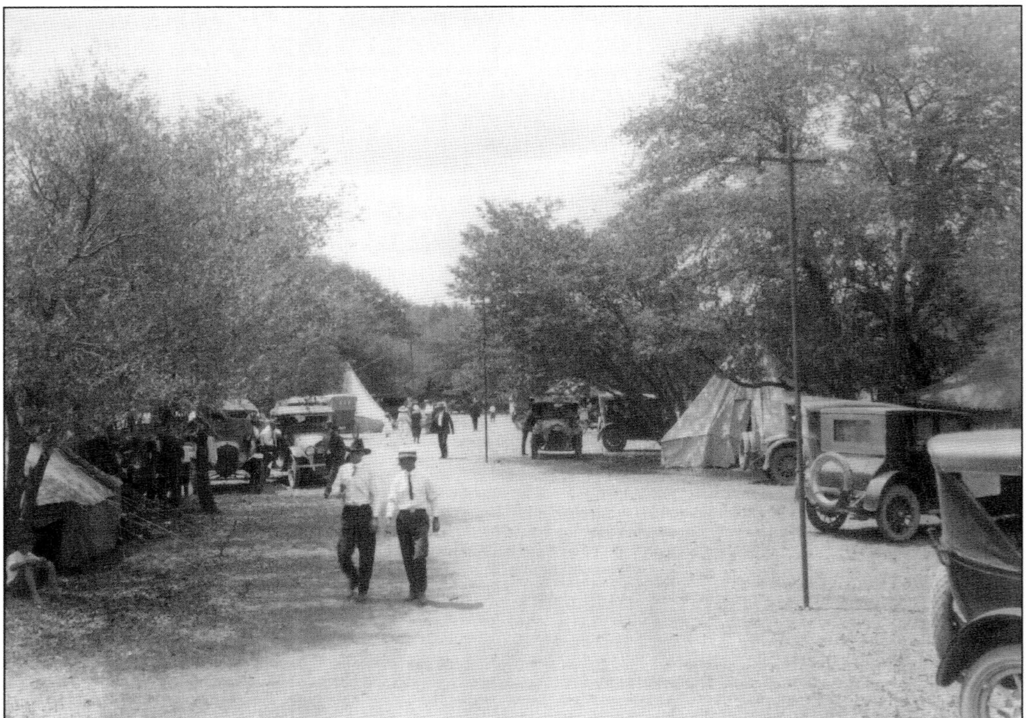

The Paisano Baptist Encampment was largely due to the work of L. R. Millican, a Baptist minister who was also a founder of the Bloys Cowboy Camp Meeting near Fort Davis. According to his wishes, he was buried on the campgrounds in 1938. (Courtesy of the Museum of the Big Bend.)

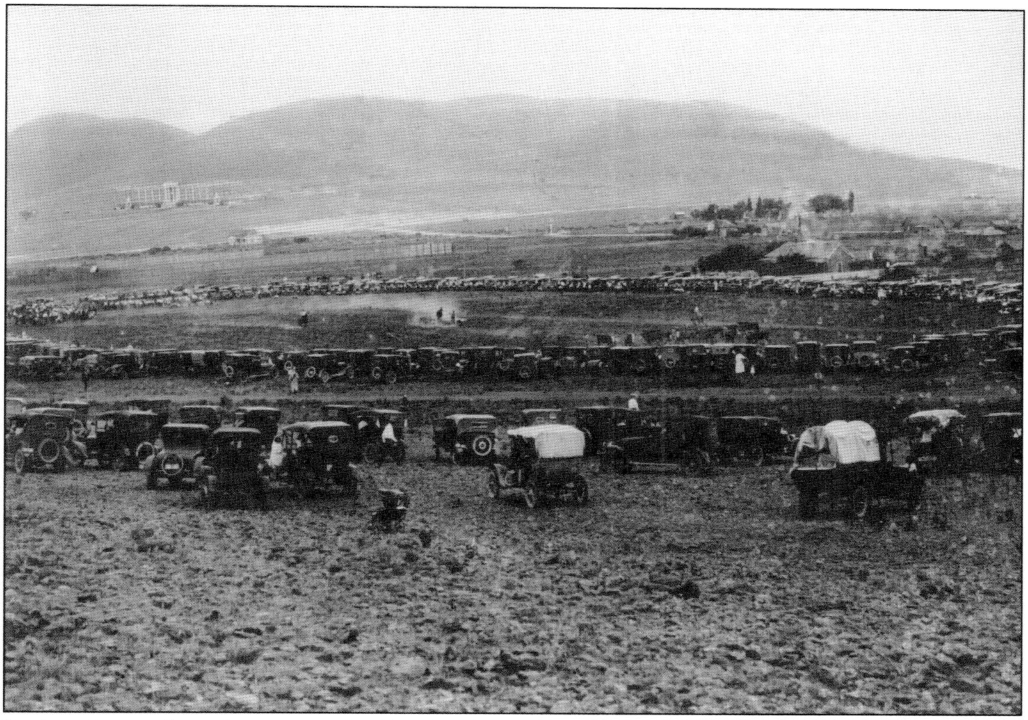

Rodeos have a long history in the Big Bend region as a way for cowboys to compete using the skills of their trade. Located where Jackson Field is today, the makeshift arena at this 1923 rodeo was created simply by the arrangement of the spectators' cars. (Courtesy of the Archives of the Big Bend.)

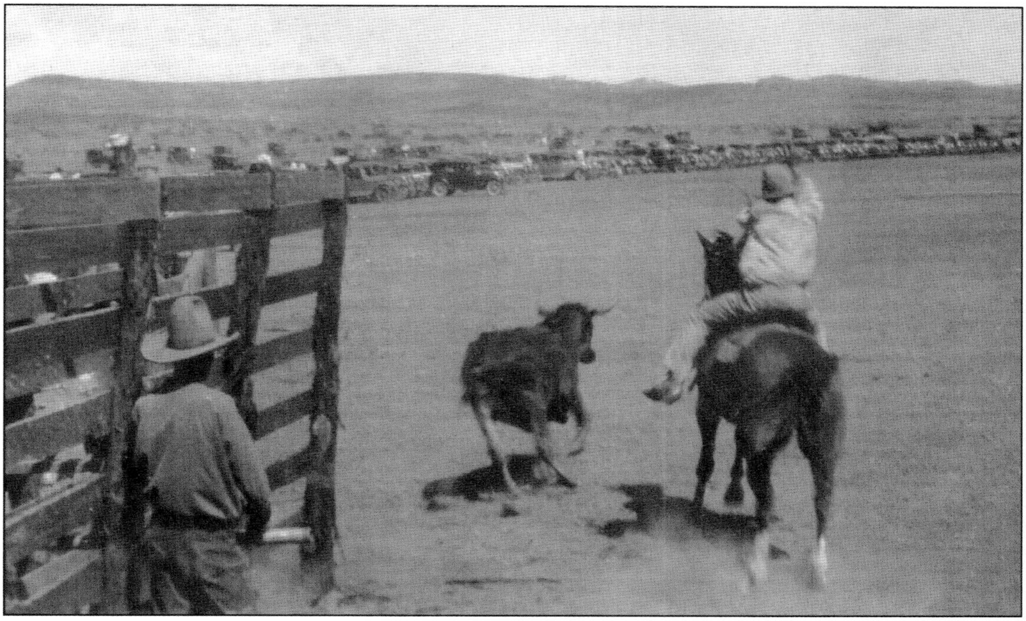

A cowboy and his horse burst out of the chute in the steer roping event at an Alpine rodeo around 1930. Another cowboy, using a pipe brace as a makeshift gate, looks on. Spectators watch from inside, or on top of, their cars. (Courtesy of the Museum of the Big Bend.)

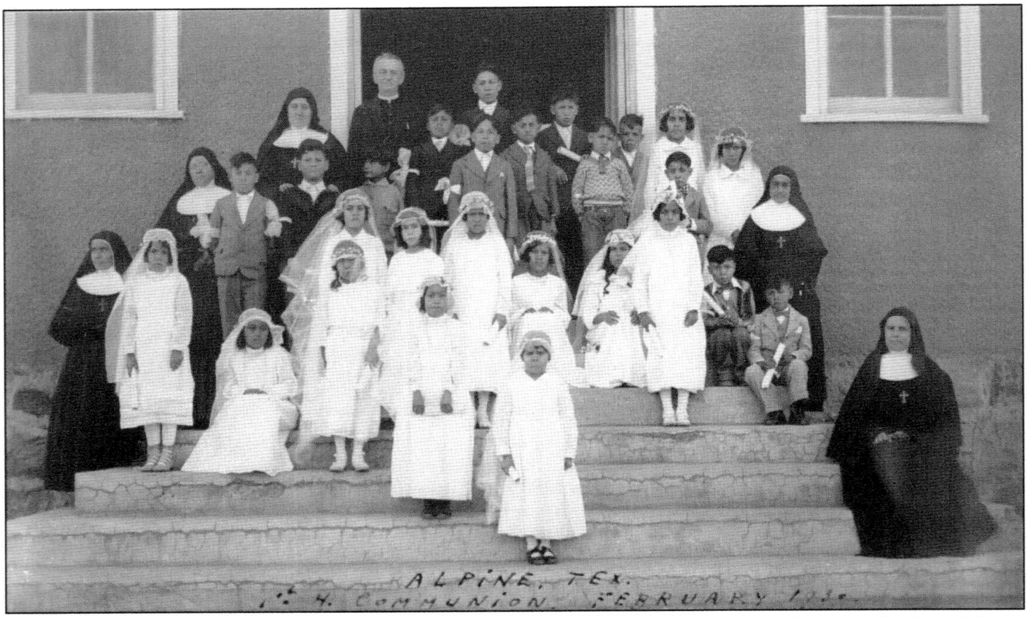

A group gathers to commemorate a First Holy Communion at Nuestra Senora de Guadalupe Catholic Church in 1930. Considered an important rite of passage in the Roman Catholic church, First Communion typically takes place at age seven or eight. The traditional white dresses and veils worn by the girls symbolize purity. (Courtesy of the Archives of the Big Bend.)

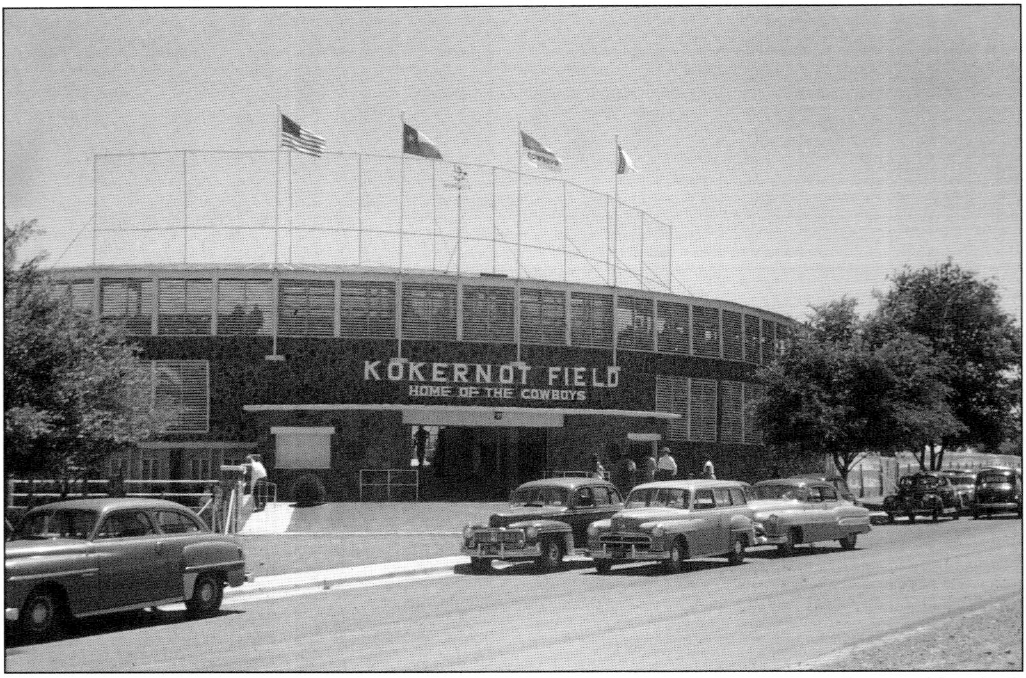

Kokernot Field was built by rancher Herbert Kokernot Jr. in 1947 for his semiprofessional baseball team. Sparing no expenses, he had red clay hauled in by boxcar from Georgia for the infield and used native stone to construct the outfield wall and grandstand, built to seat 1,400 people. Once completed, the stadium was considered to be one of the finest in the country. (Courtesy of the Hunter collection.)

Six

The Intellectual Frontier
Sul Ross State University

In 1923, Horace W. Morelock arrived in Alpine to assume the presidency of Sul Ross State Teacher's College. Over the next 22 years, he worked tirelessly to maintain the school's vitality and rose to become the most influential president in the college's history. Surrounded by the Davis Mountains, Alpine's idyllic setting became a major promotional selling point. Photographs in the Sul Ross publication, the *Rossonian*, showed students swimming in Ranger Canyon, picnicking at Mitre Peak, climbing the Twin Sisters. Beside them Morelock wrote, "No other place in Texas offers so rare a combination of work and play . . . Health, happiness, and a new lease on life result."

The West Texas Historical and Scientific Society, founded in 1926 by Sul Ross faculty and area citizens, was an unprecedented interdisciplinary endeavor that celebrated the region's vast array of natural and cultural resources. The Big Bend Memorial Museum that was started by the society gained a museum building during the 1930s so impressive it was hailed as one of the finest in the state.

The 1930s saw Sul Ross rise to new heights. With various educational trips, the Summer Art Colony, the Historical and Scientific Society, the new museum, and the large-scale building projects spawned by Roosevelt's New Deal, the scene on campus was in striking contrast to the hardships suffered by the town and surrounding ranches.

Ironically, as the wetter conditions of the 1940s brought renewed hope to ranchers and reinvigorated the economy, Sul Ross enrollment plummeted with the start of World War II. Had it not been for Morelock's ingenuity in developing new programs and attracting the Women's Army Corps, the college would have faced certain closure.

But Sul Ross managed to survive, and starting in the 1950s, even as ranges surrounding the college began to dry up as the worst drought of the century descended, enrollment climbed out of its wartime slump. By the 1960s, the number of students would soar higher than ever before.

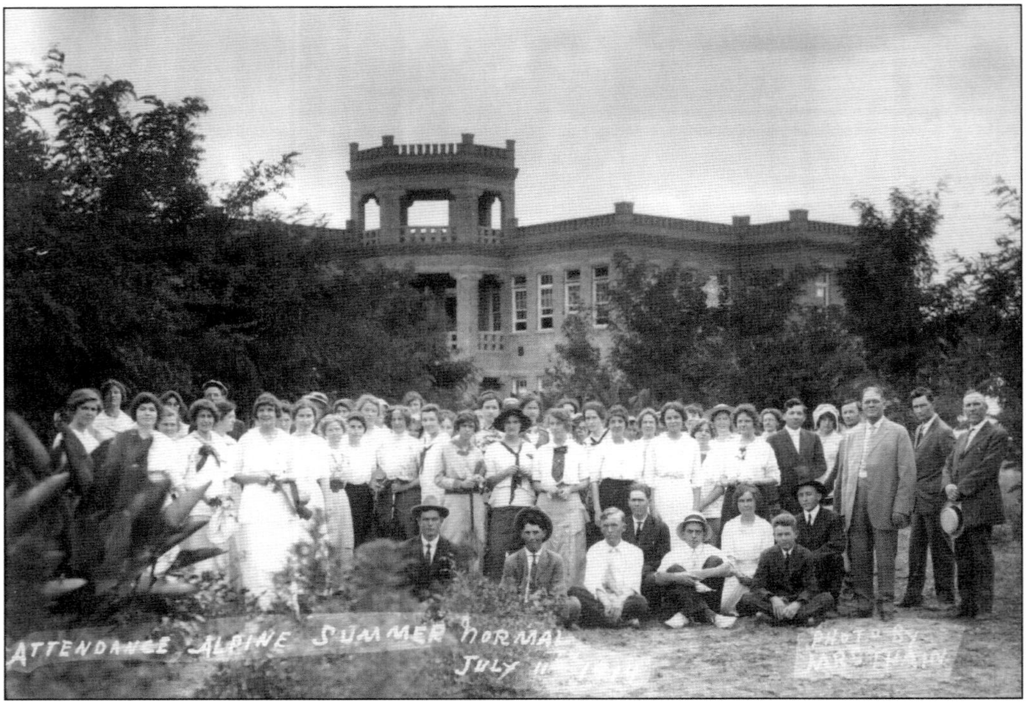

The Alpine Summer Normal, the predecessor to Sul Ross State Normal College, was partly inspired by the impressive new two-story Gothic Revival Alpine public school building. The summer normal was held in the building for a decade before the college opened in 1920. Here students and faculty pose in front of their brick schoolhouse in 1914. (Courtesy of the Smith collection.)

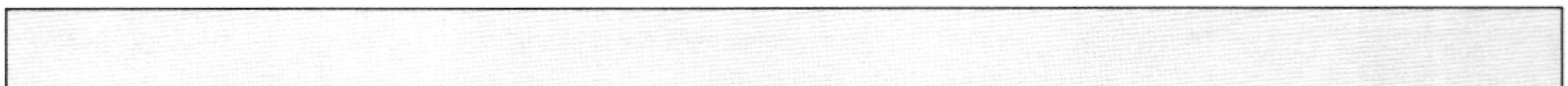

Sul Ross State Normal College, shown here shortly after it was completed in 1920, was built in the classic Greek Revival style and featured massive two-story columns supporting a portico, pilasters (recessed columns), and pediments. It is an architectural model evocative of Greek democracy and education and, if not resonant with the vernacular, was appropriate enough for an institute of higher learning. (Courtesy of the Archives of the Big Bend.)

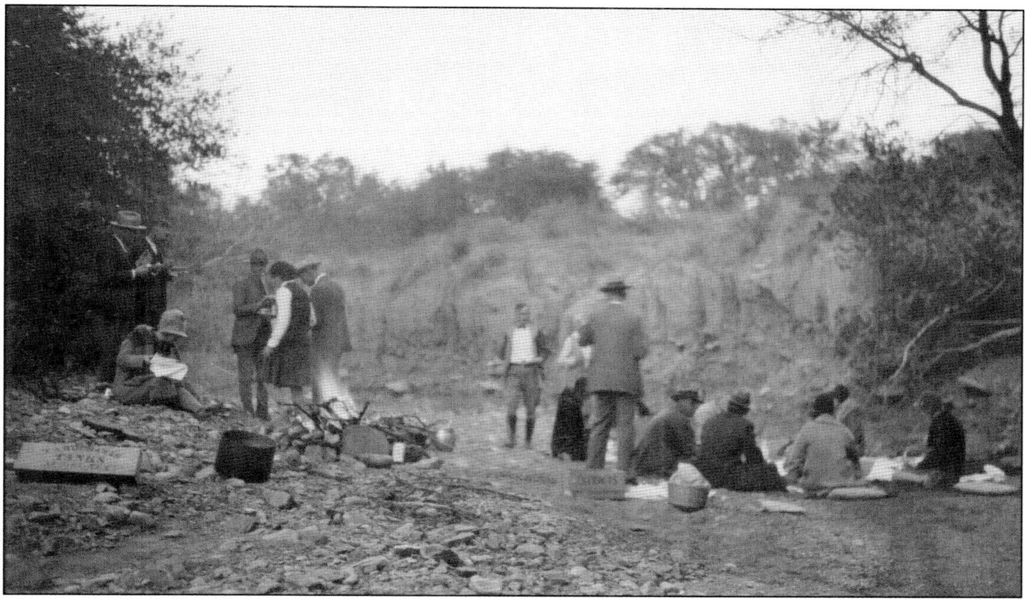

Picnics for Sul Ross faculty, such as this one in Sunny Glen Canyon, were common in the early days. Ranchers were eager to accommodate the new college and frequently extended invitations to their ranches for such school functions. (Courtesy of the Archives of the Big Bend.)

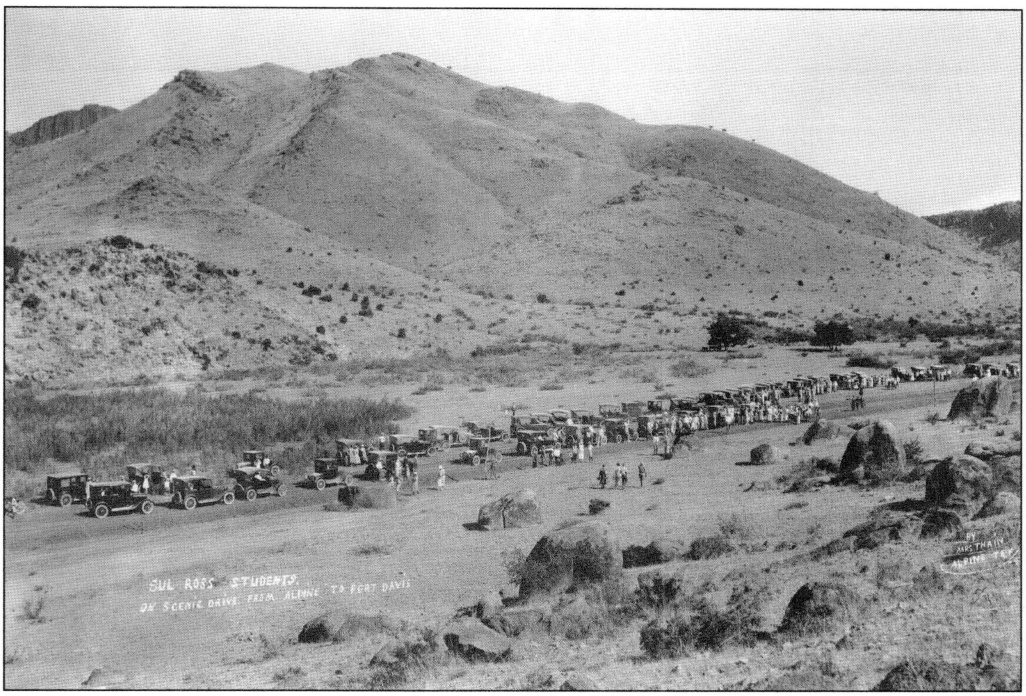

Sul Ross students pause at one of several stops along a scenic drive through the Davis Mountains around 1925. Such excursions were highlights of the summer session, culminating in a big barbeque at the end of the day. The beauty of the surrounding countryside was a major selling point in attracting students, and outings were regular events during the school year. (Courtesy of the Archives of the Big Bend.)

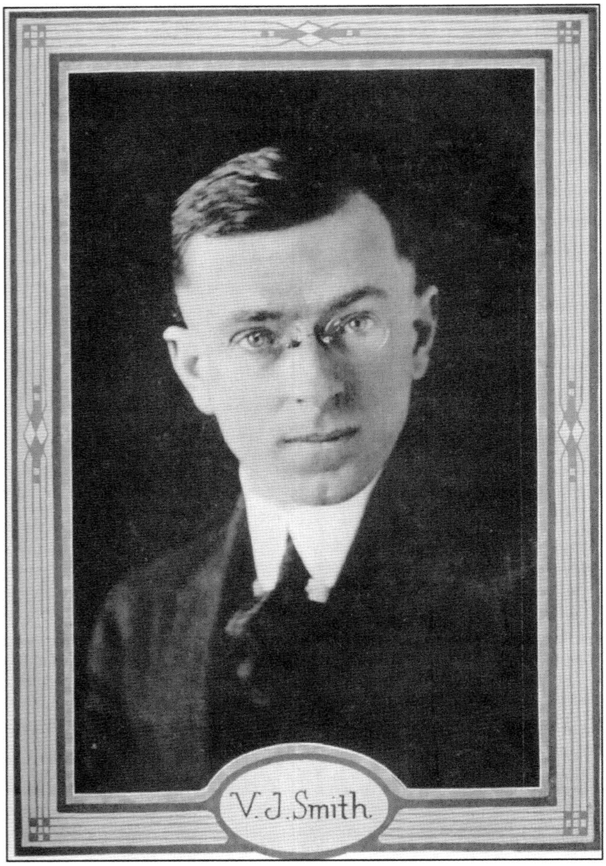

Victor Smith was the first faculty member at Sul Ross, joining shortly after his arrival in 1919 to supervise the construction of the college. During his 30-year career, he would play a key role in the construction of almost every new building on campus, organize the West Texas Historical and Scientific Society, and publish articles on subjects ranging from adobe construction to archaeology. (Courtesy of *The Brand*, Sul Ross State University.)

Sul Ross students pose with the college's first school bus in 1928. Teacher Anne Aynesworth (in white dress) stands in center. Although many more women than men enrolled in the early days, the gender gap decreased as the college began to offer a broader curriculum. (Courtesy of the Museum of the Big Bend.)

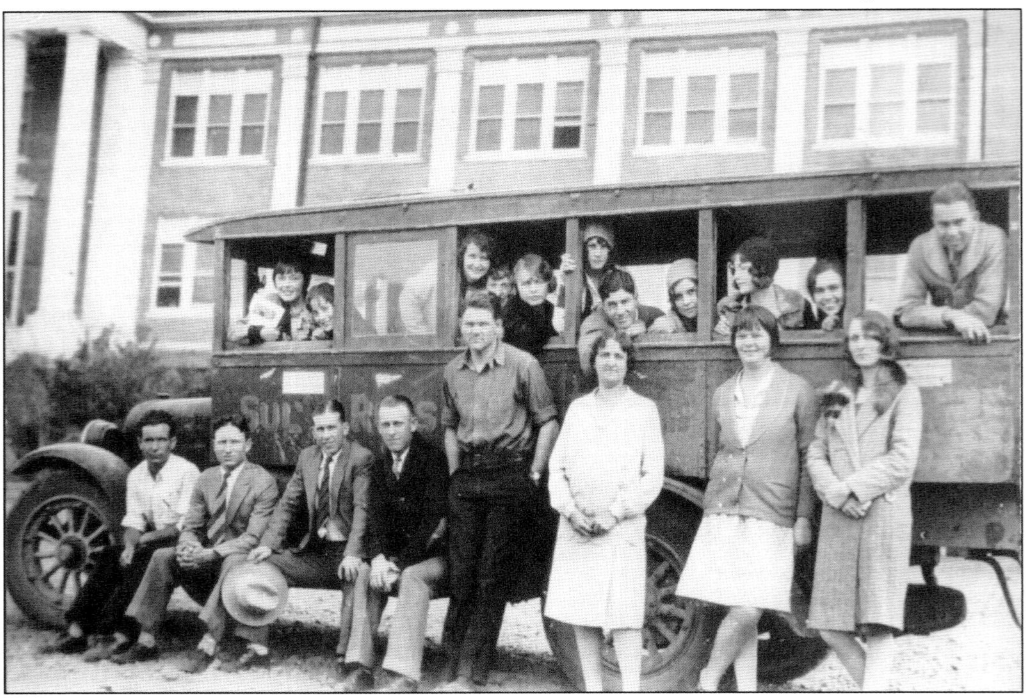

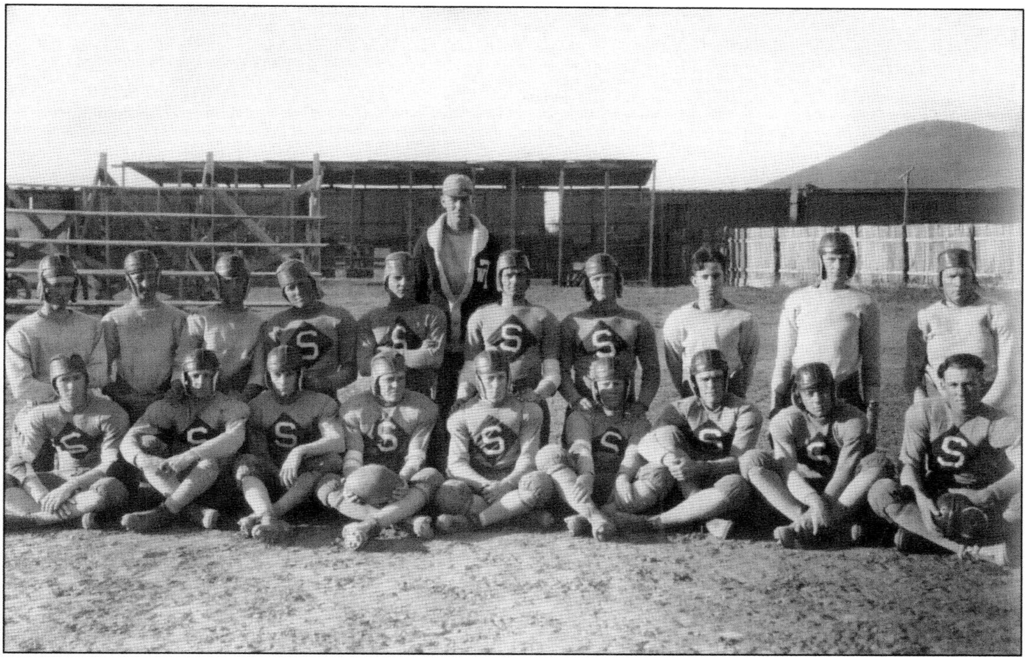

Coach B. C. Graves, who played football at West Point and West Texas State before coming to Sul Ross, stands behind the college's first football team in 1923. In the early years, the Lobos won more than 70 percent of their games. (Courtesy of the Museum of the Big Bend.)

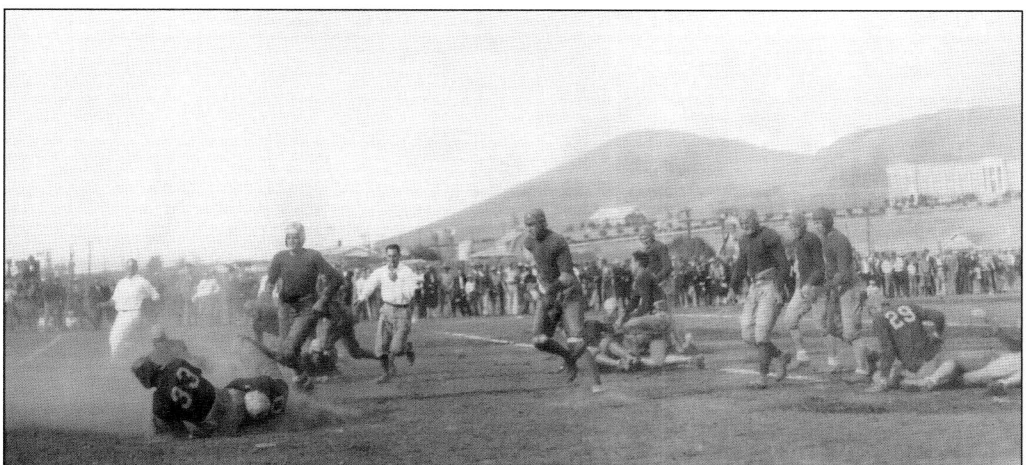

A tackle is made at a Sul Ross football game in 1928. At that time, the field, located where Jackson Field is today, was little more than a chalk outline in the dirt. Consequently, these early games were often dusty events. (Courtesy of the Museum of the Big Bend.)

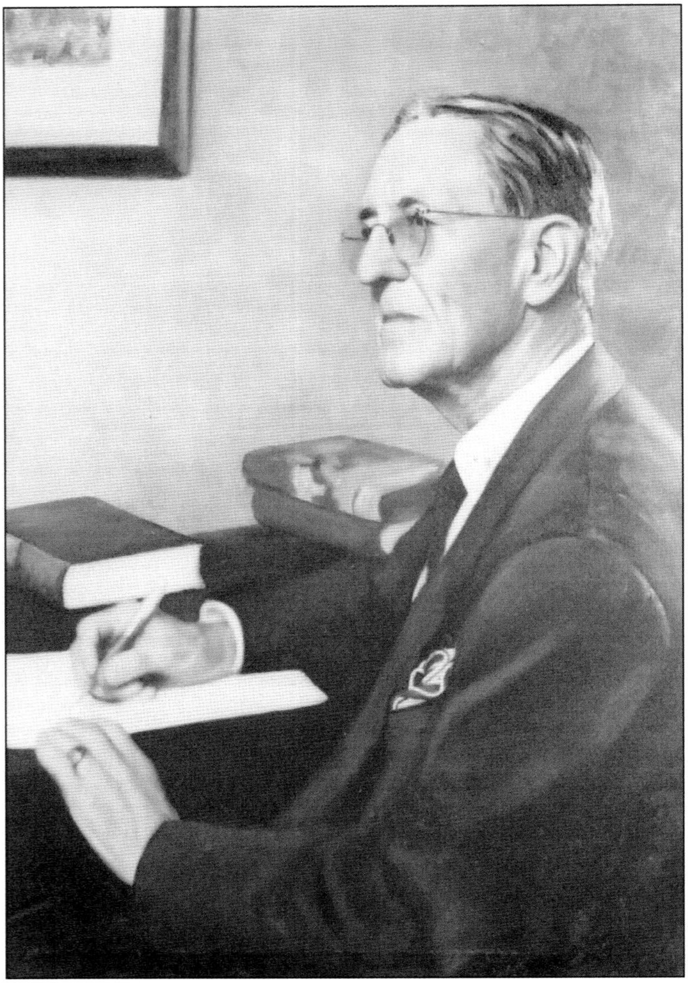

Dr. Horace Morelock, a Harvard graduate and man of letters, served as president of Sul Ross for over 20 years. He was also an early advocate of Big Bend National Park and a champion of the region's natural wonders. (Courtesy of the Archives of the Big Bend.)

During his years as president of Sul Ross, Horace Morelock was also its most enthusiastic promoter. In a series of foldout postcards, he lyrically described Alpine and Sul Ross as places that can revitalize both the mind and body. (Courtesy of the Museum of the Big Bend.)

ALPINE

"In the Heart of the Texas Rockies"

ALPINE is located on the main line of the Southern Pacific R. R. from New Orleans to San Francisco, at its junction with the Santa Fe R. R. from Topeka, Kansas, to Chihuahua, Old Mexico. It is a prosperous little town of 5000 inhabitants, and is surrounded by an imposing array of rugged mountains. This section of Texas represents the last stronghold of the primitive West, and it is noted for its fine Hereford cattle and hospitable people. Situated at the open gateway to the Davis Mountains, Alpine—with its delightful climate, its picturesque mountains, its lovely homes, paved streets, pure water, elegant hotel, and opportunities for recreation—is rapidly becoming a favorite resort for Texas people who desire rest, recreation, and spiritual uplift within easy distance of their homes. In summer the nights are uniformly cool, and the winters are mild.

SUL ROSS

"The Summer Home for Texas Teachers"

Sul Ross State Teachers College is situated on a lofty hill overlooking the town of Alpine, and from the windows of every recitation room a panorama of gorgeous mountains greets the eye. Teachers from all parts of Texas attend the Summer School of this institution for its program of "Rest, Recreation and Study". At the close of the session they return to their homes better equipped physically and mentally for service in the school room.

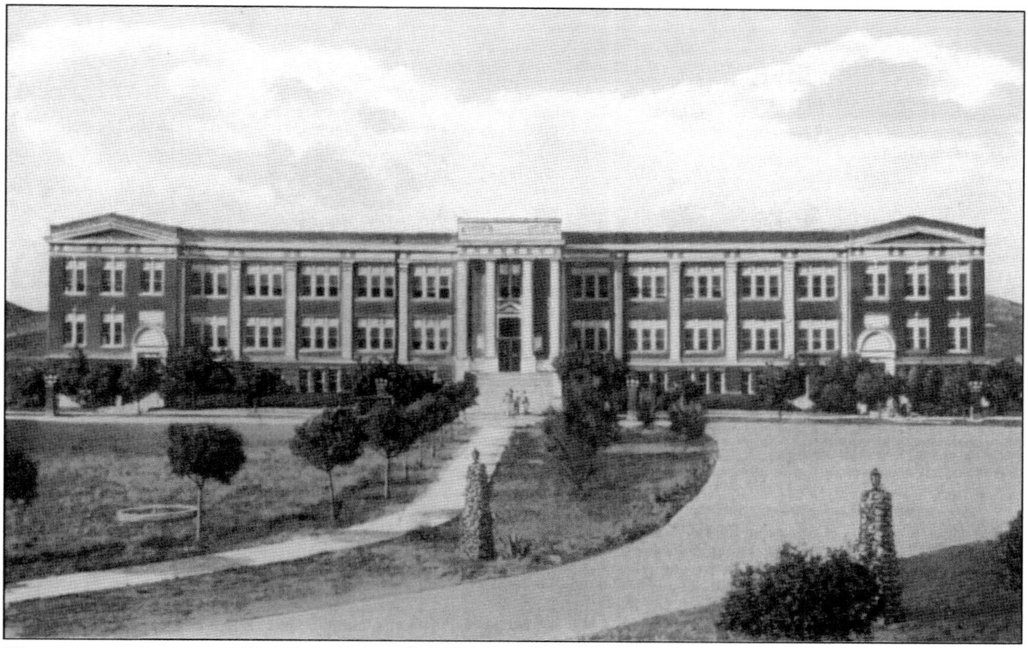

This postcard image of Sul Ross State Teacher's College in 1930 was included in a series of images dedicated to promoting the college and the town of Alpine. It was one of a number of promotional efforts that Sul Ross president Morelock employed over the years to strengthen enrollment and increase funding. (Courtesy of the Museum of the Big Bend.)

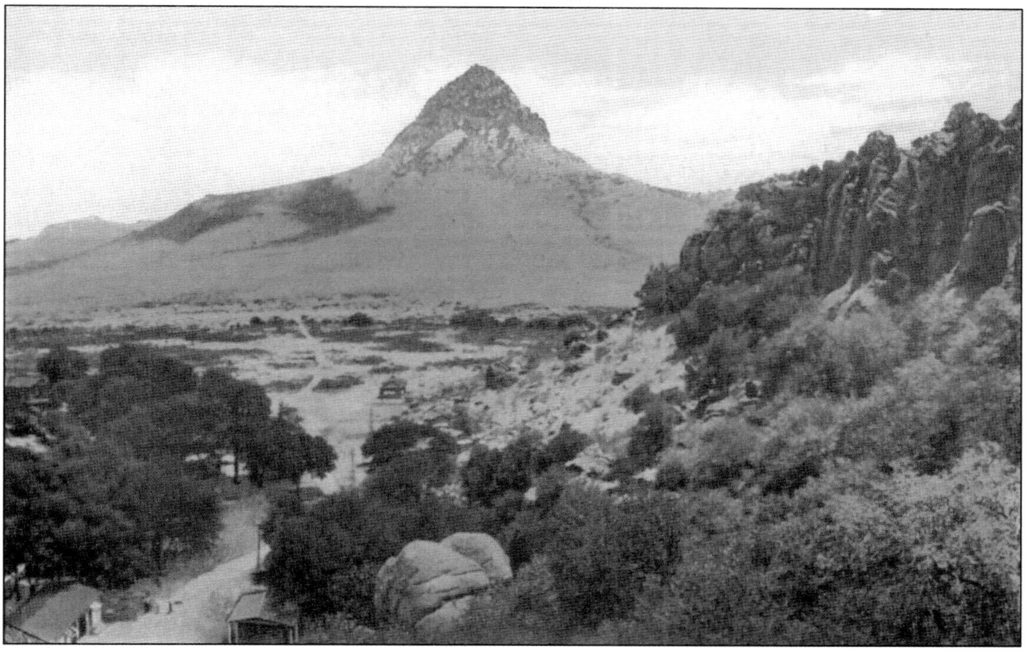

Mitre Peak on the Tippit Ranch was one of many local landmarks used to advertise the area's outdoor recreation potential. In one of the published school "Bulletins," President Morelock wrote, "Those who are brave enough to toil through the three hours necessary to scale its peak are rewarded with a magnificent view of the surrounding country." (Courtesy of the Museum of the Big Bend.)

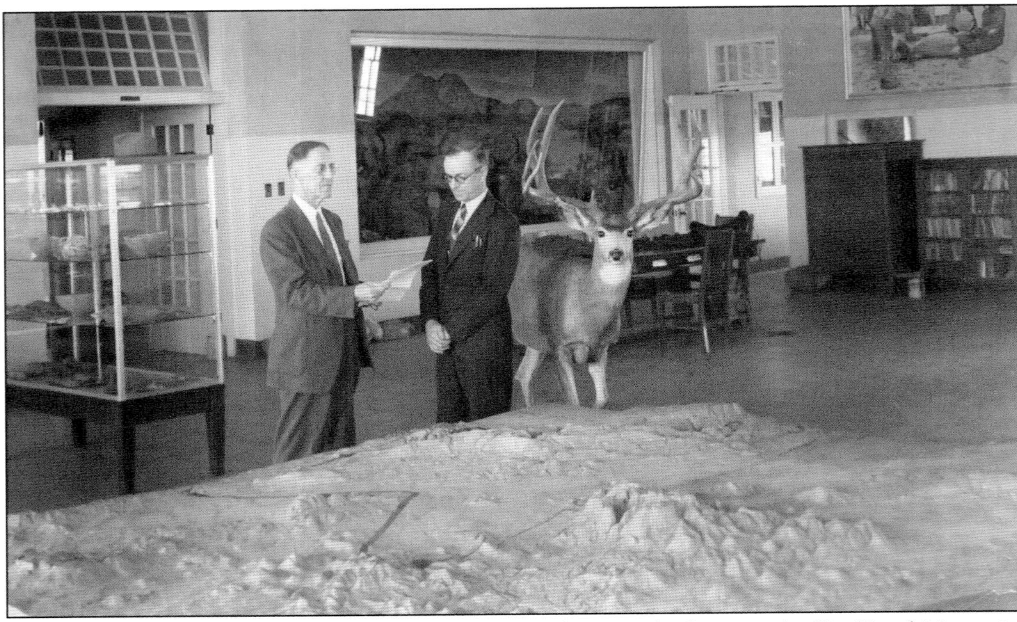

With the founding of the West Texas Historical and Scientific Society, the Big Bend Memorial Museum was established within Sul Ross State Teacher's College. Dr. Horace Morelock (left) and museum founder Victor Smith stand inside the first museum, complete with mounted wildlife specimens, a molded relief map, dioramas, murals, and an array of historic and prehistoric artifacts. (Courtesy of the Archives of the Big Bend.)

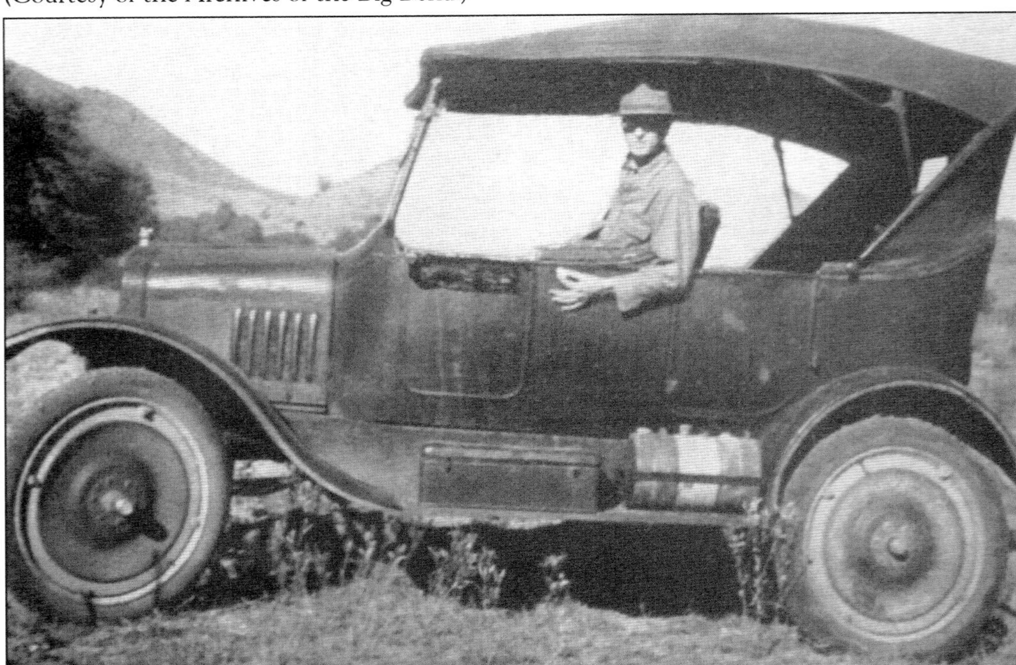

Victor Smith proudly displays an artifact collected while on one of his many archaeological excursions in his beloved Model T Ford touring car. Although not a professional archaeologist, Smith recorded more than 200 prehistoric sites in the Big Bend, with his specially outfitted car serving as the sole transportation. (Courtesy of Sul Ross State University.)

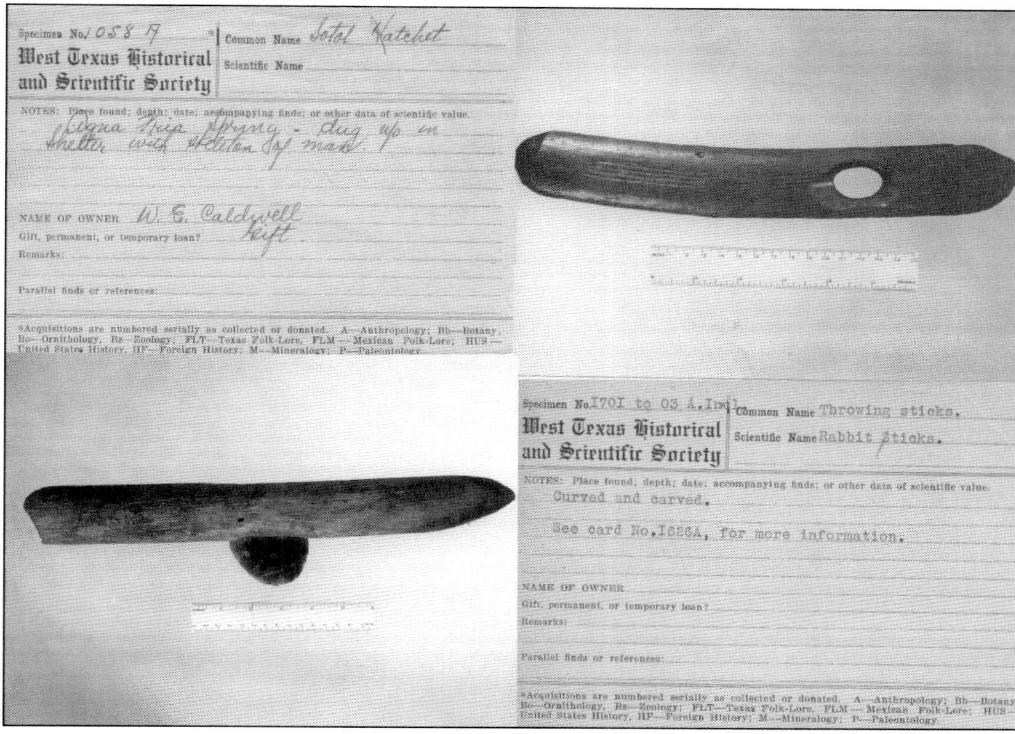

Accession cards such as these were used to document artifacts to be curated at the museum. Victor Smith filled out hundreds of these as he added prehistoric and historic artifacts to the museum collection. Here a "sotol hatchet" recovered from a human burial and a decorated (carved) "rabbit stick" are shown. (Courtesy of the Museum of the Big Bend.)

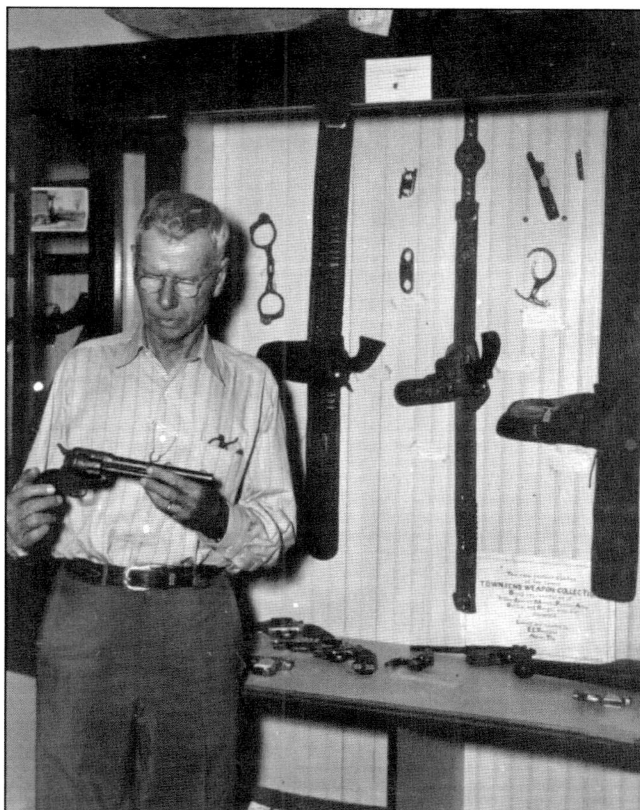

Everett Townsend examines one of the many guns in the collection he donated to the museum. Townsend, known as the Father of Big Bend National Park, was curator of the museum for several years. He made many donations to the museum, including his famous weapon collection that included—among others—examples of Indian, Spanish, Mexican, and outlaw weaponry. (Courtesy of the Museum of the Big Bend.)

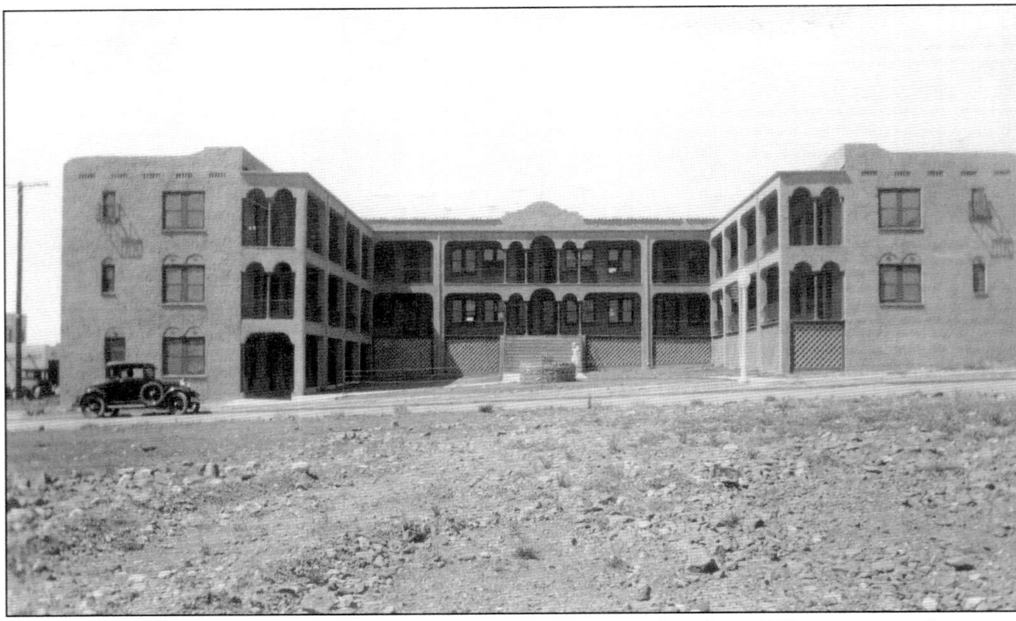

College Apartments, located just west of campus, were completed in 1929 as a privately owned student apartment complex. This Spanish mission building was acquired by Sul Ross in 1937 and was later operated as a co-op where students did household chores to pay rent. Later known as Fletcher Hall, it was renovated in 1956. (Courtesy of the Archives of the Big Bend.)

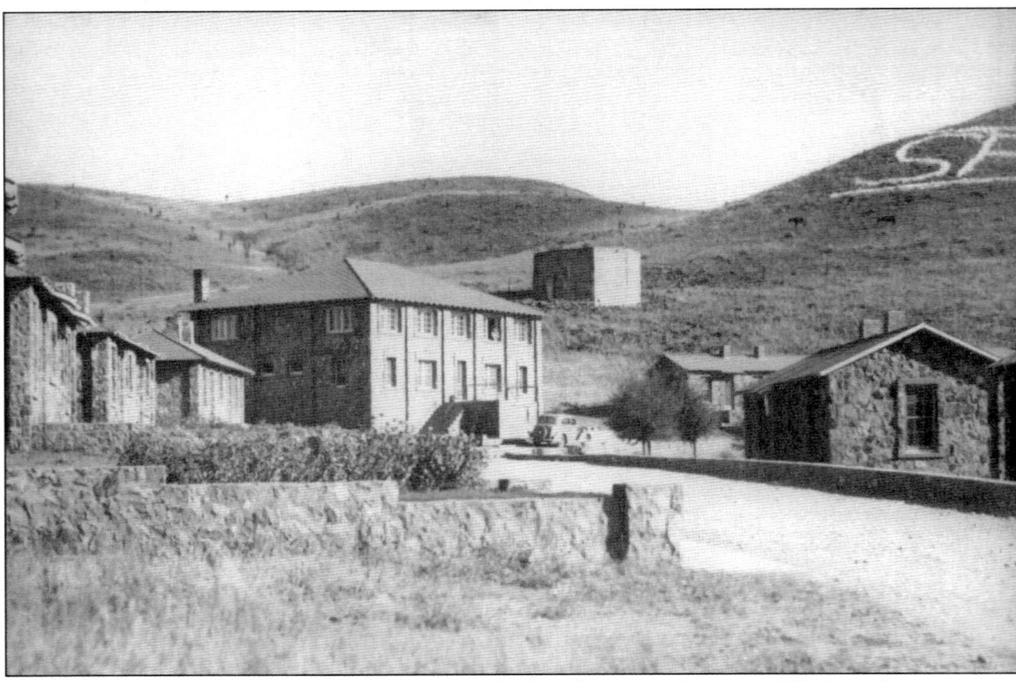

The rock cottage village was built by local relief workers and the Civil Works Administration in 1935. In appreciation, Morelock wrote, "In years to come these men will point with pride to those monuments of beauty and usefulness to which they devoted their hand and heart and which will be a blessing to the community for all time to come." (Courtesy of *The Brand*, Sul Ross State University.)

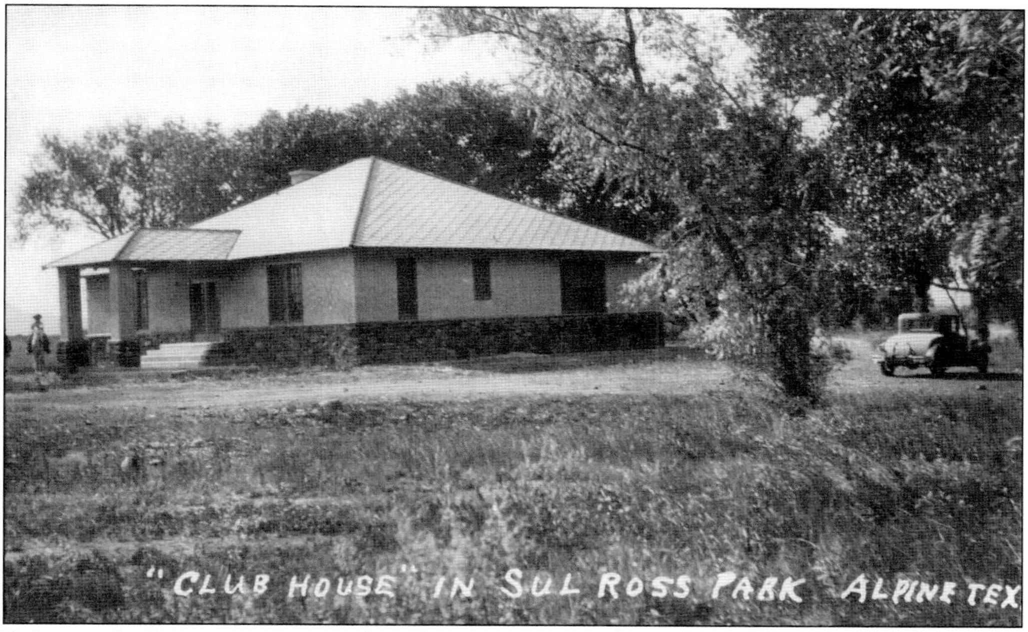

Kokernot Lodge was constructed in the 1930s using a $10,000 appropriation from the state legislature and New Deal relief labor on land donated by the Kokernot family. Initially serving as a clubhouse, it was the central feature on the 35 acres surrounding historic Kokernot Springs. The lodge, as well as the outdoor theater, was dedicated in 1934. (Courtesy of the Museum of the Big Bend.)

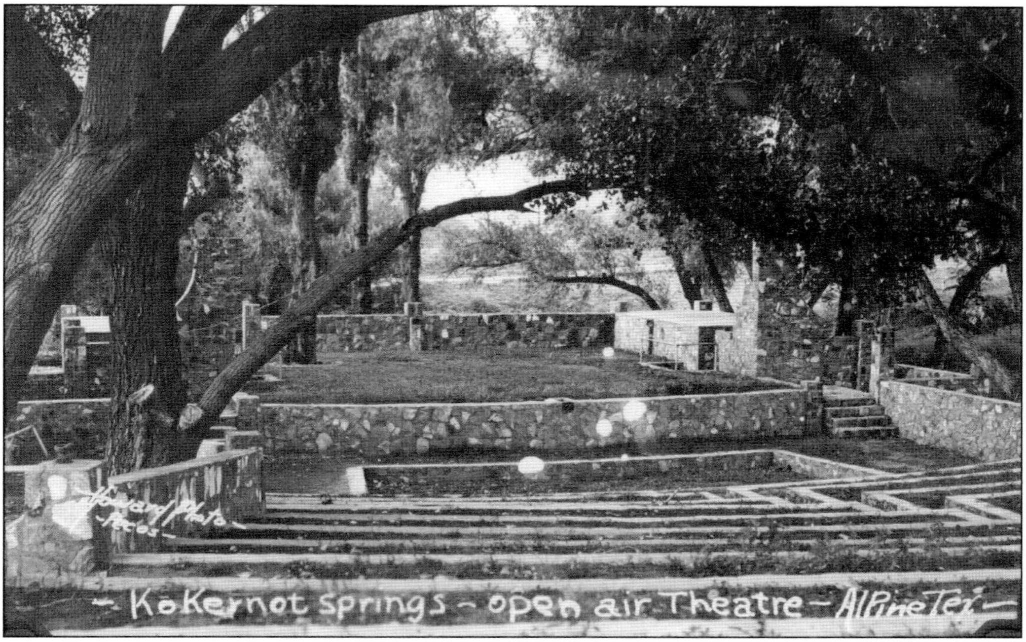

The Kokernot outdoor amphitheater was dedicated in 1934 along with the lodge. This facility, constructed of native stone beside Kokernot Springs, was used for many Sul Ross outdoor performances until 1970, when a more modern outdoor theater was built. (Courtesy of the Ivey collection.)

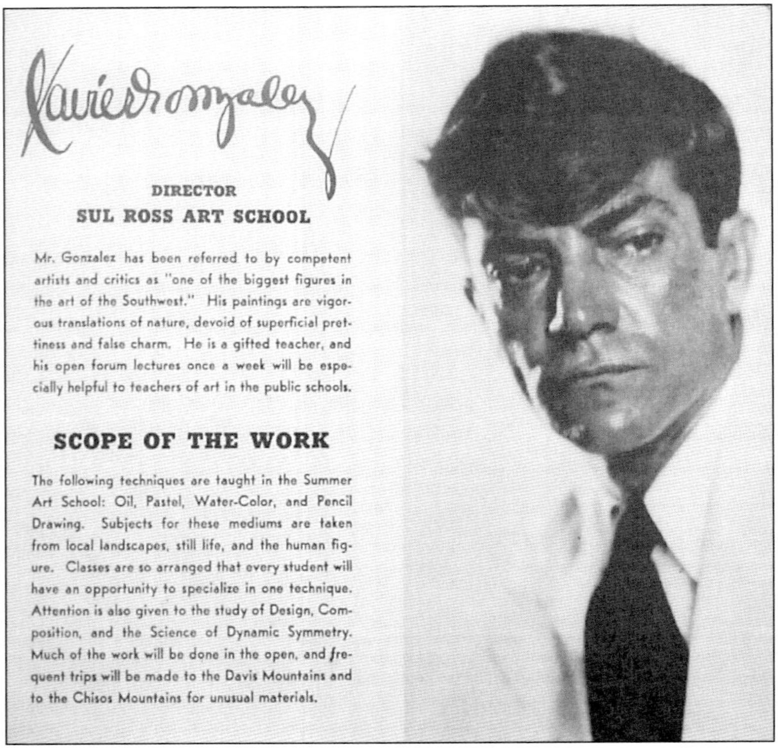

DIRECTOR

SUL ROSS ART SCHOOL

Mr. Gonzalez has been referred to by competent artists and critics as "one of the biggest figures in the art of the Southwest." His paintings are vigorous translations of nature, devoid of superficial prettiness and false charm. He is a gifted teacher, and his open forum lectures once a week will be especially helpful to teachers of art in the public schools.

SCOPE OF THE WORK

The following techniques are taught in the Summer Art School: Oil, Pastel, Water-Color, and Pencil Drawing. Subjects for these mediums are taken from local landscapes, still life, and the human figure. Classes are so arranged that every student will have an opportunity to specialize in one technique. Attention is also given to the study of Design, Composition, and the Science of Dynamic Symmetry. Much of the work will be done in the open, and frequent trips will be made to the Davis Mountains and to the Chisos Mountains for unusual materials.

Xavier Gonzales was hired in 1932 to teach the first Sul Ross summer Art Colony. Born in Spain, Gonzales possessed great artistic versatility, although he was best known as a muralist, a style developed during years spent in Mexico. The Art Colony featured the natural landscape of the region as a primary subject, and many classes were conducted outdoors. (Courtesy of the Museum of the Big Bend.)

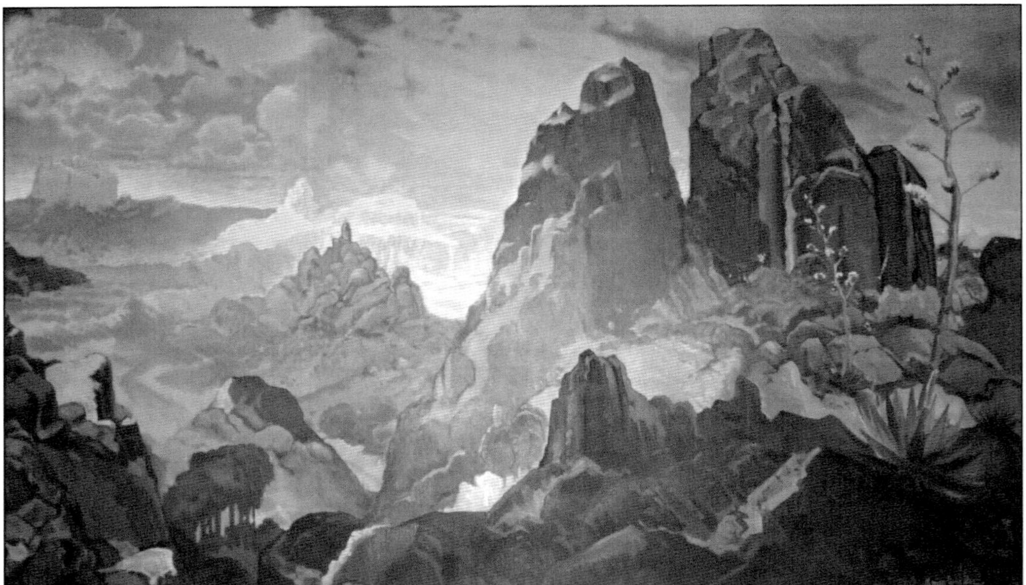

Moonlight over the Chisos was painted by Xavier Gonzales during the 1934 summer Art Colony. This large (4-foot-by-12-foot) oil on canvas mural depicts the Chisos Mountains in Big Bend National Park bathed in a surreal light. Gonzales claimed, "Art is the link between ourselves and nature." (Courtesy of the Museum of the Big Bend.)

Julius Woeltz became director of the art department in 1932. During his relatively brief time at Sul Ross, he produced a number of large paintings, primarily of landscapes and ranching activities in the Big Bend. For several years, Woeltz taught beside Xavier Gonzales at the Sul Ross Summer Art Colony. (Courtesy of the Museum of the Big Bend)

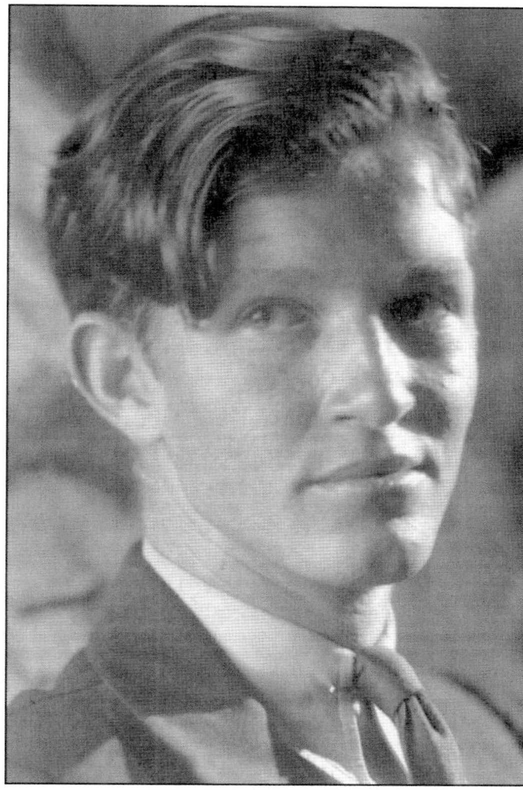

The Branding Crew was painted by Julius Woeltz sometime between 1932 and 1936. Typical of his work, the subjects are stylized, the colors often muted. Based on a photograph by W. D. Smithers, the painting depicts cowboys at work on the Cathedral Mountain Ranch. (Courtesy of the Museum of the Big Bend.)

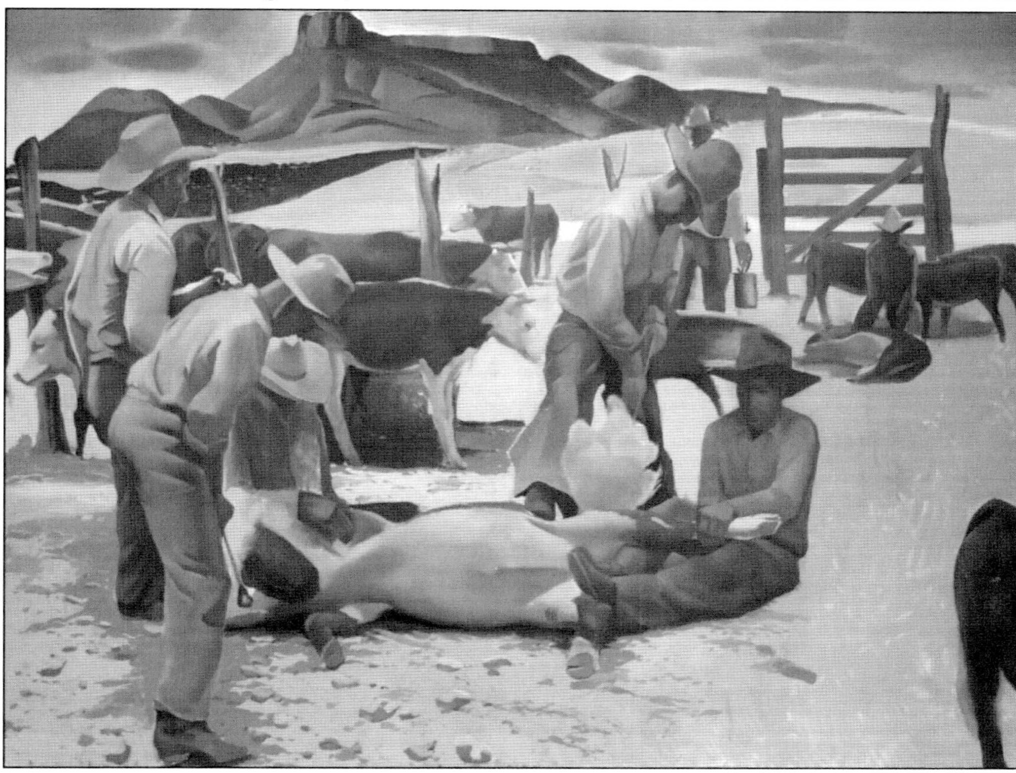

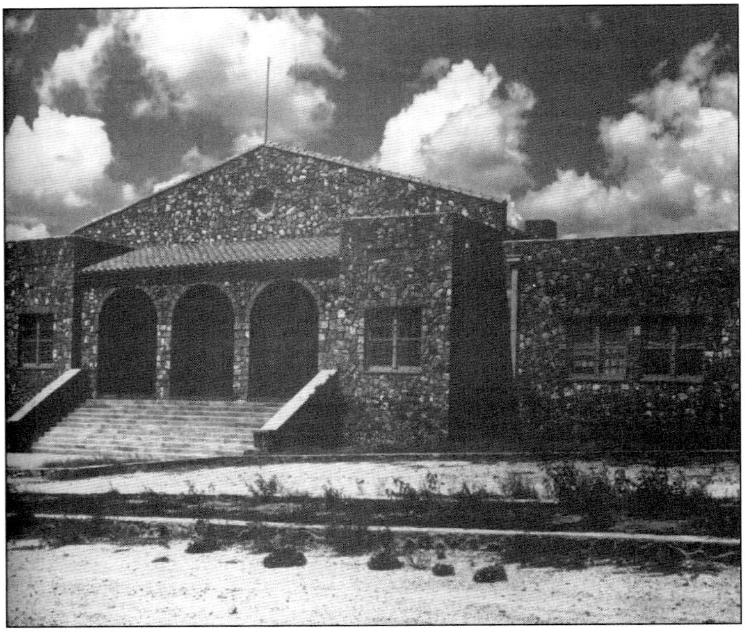

The Big Bend Memorial Museum, originally housed in the administration building, was later moved to this native stone structure designed by Victor Smith and built by relief workers using funding from the Texas Centennial fund and the Works Progress Administration. For many years, it was celebrated as the best museum between San Antonio and El Paso. (Courtesy of *The Brand*, Sul Ross State University.)

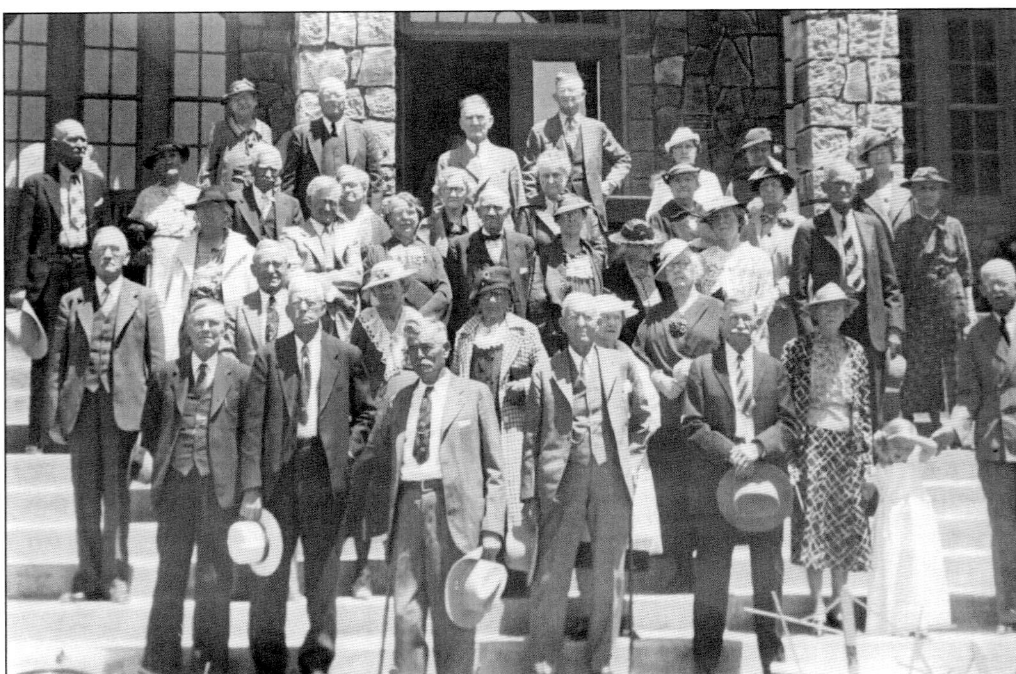

The Big Bend Memorial Museum was dedicated on May 1, 1937, in a ceremony that honored the region's pioneers and leading citizens, shown here on the steps of the new building. More than 40 pioneers who had arrived in the region before 1890 participated. (Courtesy of the Archives of the Big Bend.)

Clifford Casey joined the faculty at Sul Ross in 1929 and served as the head of the history department until his retirement in 1962. For 30 years, he also served as director of research for the West Texas Historical and Scientific Society. His encyclopedic histories of Alpine, Brewster County, and Sul Ross remain the definitive sources on the subjects. (Courtesy of *The Brand*, Sul Ross State University.)

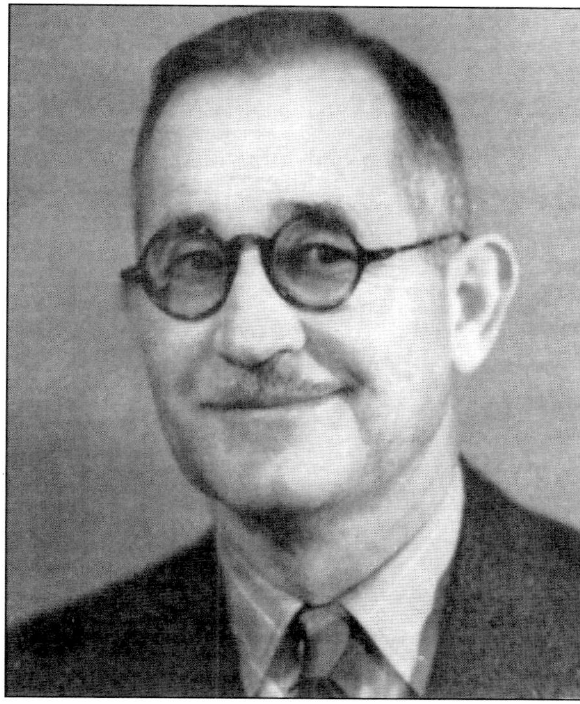

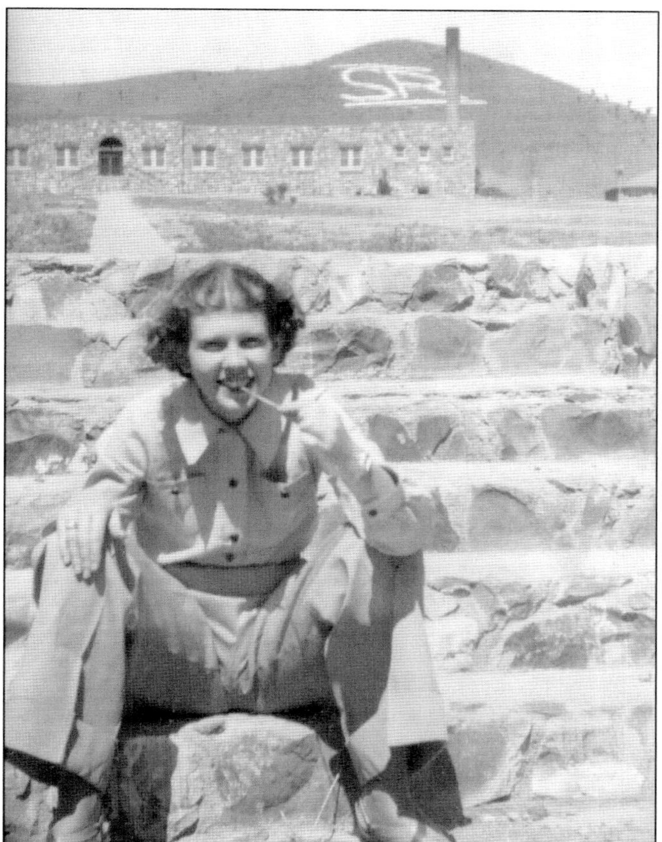

Katherine Carr sits on the rock steps below the men's dormitory around 1936 while she was attending Sul Ross. Born in Olney, Texas, in 1918, she taught school in Shafter, Valentine, and Marfa after graduating from Sul Ross. In 1942, she married rancher Rex Ivey Jr. and raised two sons. (Courtesy of the Ivey collection.)

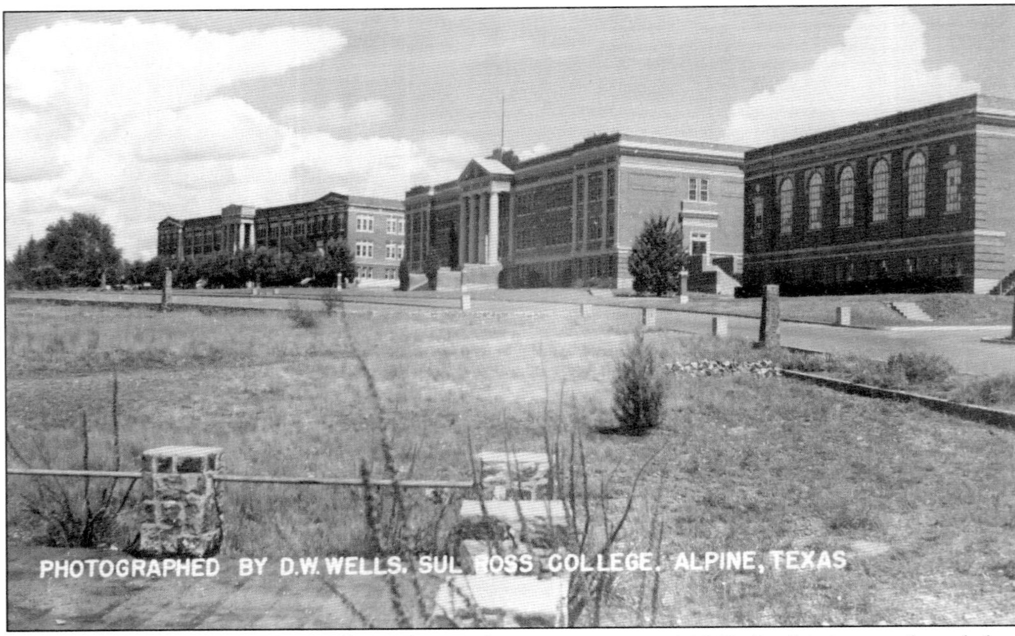

The Sul Ross campus is shown from the south entrance around 1940. In this image, from left to right, are the administration building constructed in 1919, the library and classroom building constructed in 1930, and the gym constructed in 1928. Between 1928 and 1940, the campus grew dramatically, most of which was made possible with New Deal funding. (Courtesy of the Museum of the Big Bend.)

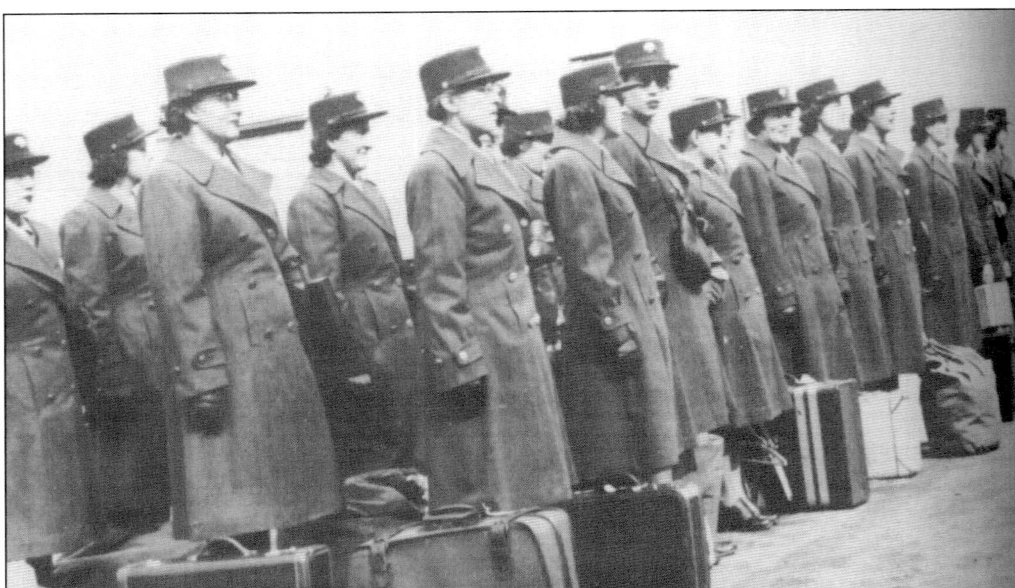

For a brief period from 1943 to 1944, Sul Ross hosted the Women's Auxiliary Army Corps (WAAC). World War II had caused a precipitous decline in male enrollment, and the WAAC training and a United States Navy pilot-training program served as the college's lifelines during the war. (Courtesy of *The Brand*, Sul Ross State University.)

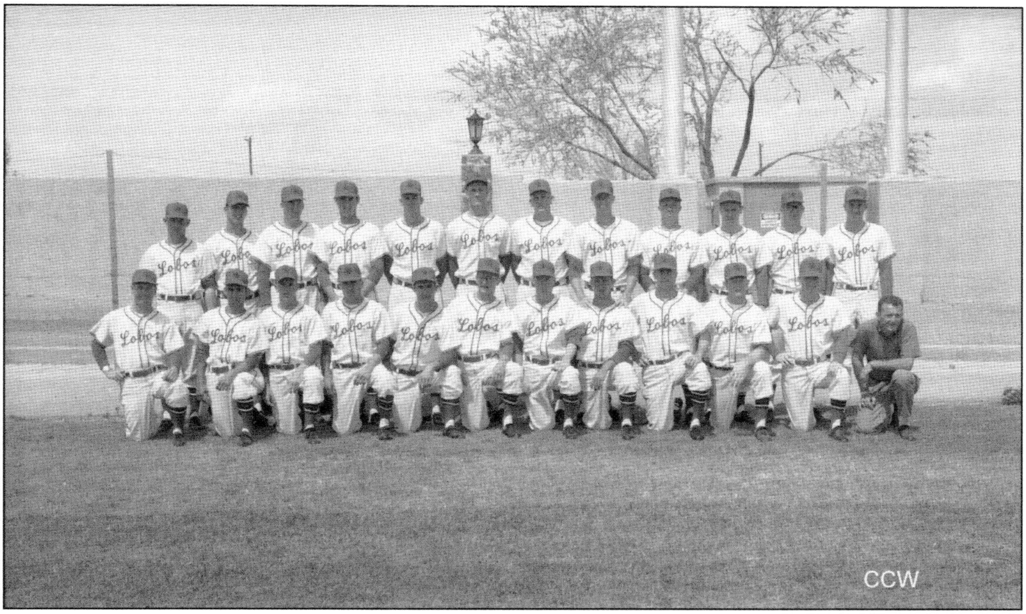

The Sul Ross Lobos baseball team poses for a photograph at Kokernot Field around 1952. The intercollegiate sports program had been reinstated in 1945 following a 5-year hiatus. Throughout the 1950s, Sul Ross maintained a strong team, largely due to the scholarship support of Herbert Kokernot Jr. In 1957, the Lobos baseball team would win the national championship at their home field. (Courtesy of the Williams collection.)

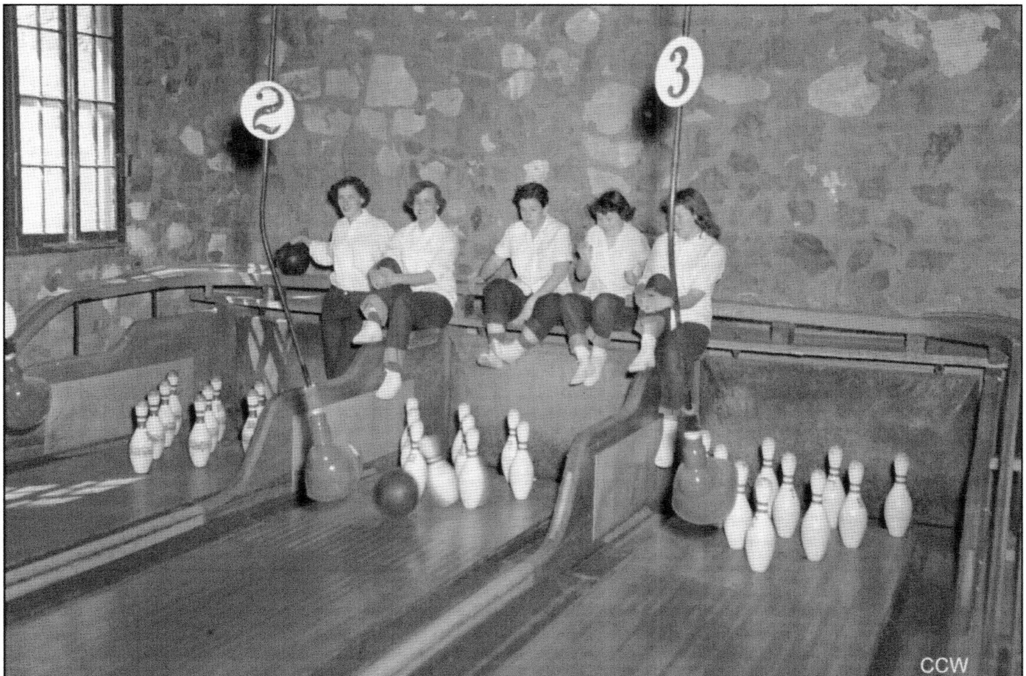

The Sul Ross bowling alley was another of the New Deal construction projects built in the 1930s. Here several Sul Ross students enjoy a close view of the action at the far end of the lanes. (Courtesy of the Williams collection.)

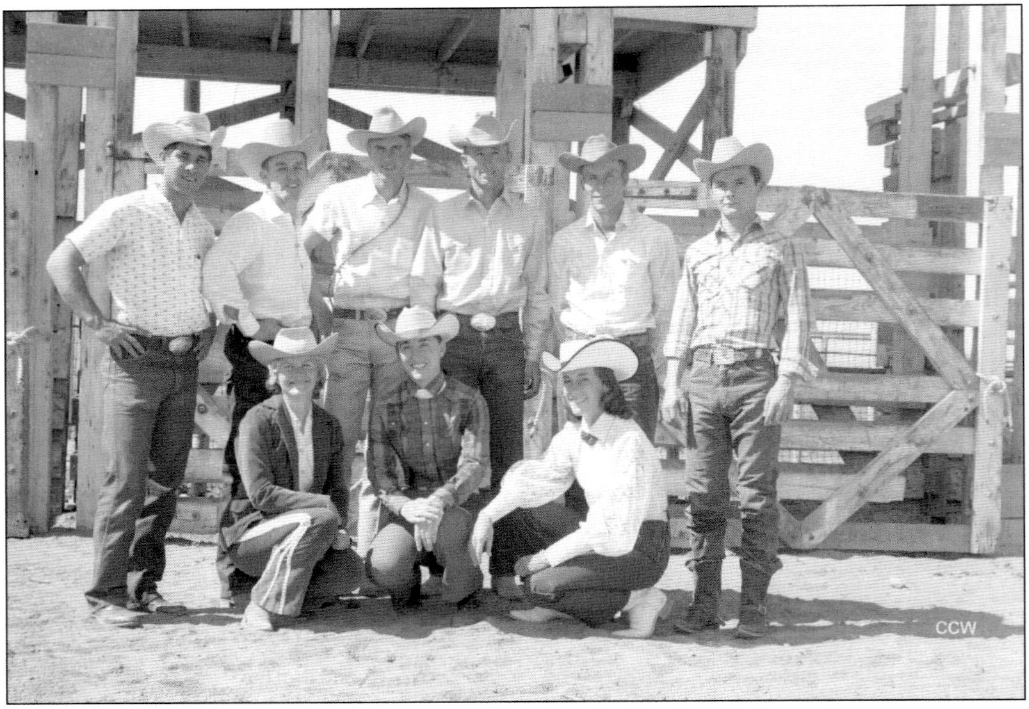

The Sul Ross rodeo team poses in their arena around 1952. The Bar SR Bar rodeo association was organized in 1947, and the first intercollegiate rodeo sponsored by Sul Ross was held in November 1948. In 1949, rodeo team president Hank Finger helped organize the National Intercollegiate Rodeo Association; the same year, Sul Ross won the national championship. (Courtesy of the Williams collection.)

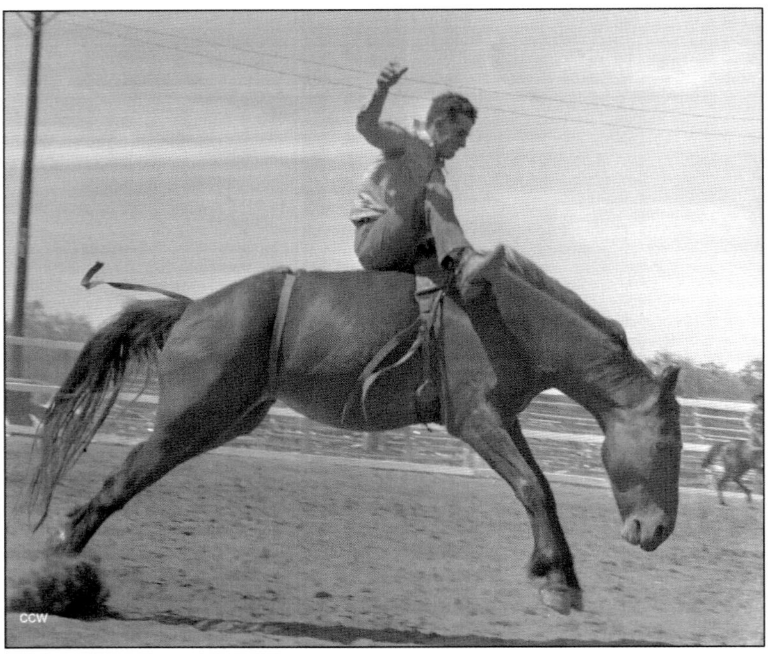

A Sul Ross bareback bronc rider holds tight to his rigging as he tries to make the eight-second buzzer at an intercollegiate rodeo around 1952. Rodeos have a long history in Alpine, and the Sul Ross rodeo team was instrumental in putting college rodeo on a par with other intercollegiate sports. (Courtesy of the Williams collection.)

Seven

The Years Between
Decades after World War II

The years following World War II were promising for Alpine. With the establishment of Big Bend National Park, the founding of Alpine's own semiprofessional baseball team, and the start of its first radio station, the troubles of the previous decade seemed far behind. Sul Ross was able to regain the student enrollment it had lost during the war. And Alpine's population climbed by 36 percent during the decade, at least some of which was the result of an influx of workers from the Terlingua mines as they quit operations.

By the 1950s, Alpine's economy had grown less dependent on ranching, so the effects of the drought on the town were not as pronounced. Still, population declined during the decade, and the pace of growth slackened. But there were modest gains. In 1954, Highway 118 was completed to Big Bend National Park, and in 1957 Alpine finally gained its first hospital. The following decade would see population gains and significant strides in civil rights. Although segregation had been declared unconstitutional in 1954, it persisted in Alpine until 1969, when schools finally integrated following a desegregation battle led by Pete A. Gallego, the first Hispanic elected to the school board.

But it was also during the 1960s and 1970s that Alpine slid into something of a cultural recession. It had been a subtle, gradual change that was expressed primarily by the loss of historic buildings, most poignantly the demolition of the old Central School. Then, in 1969, the Holland Hotel—a business that had served as a barometer of Alpine's economic and cultural health—saw its last guest depart. Chain stores and fast food restaurants started to move in, and uninspired construction began to mar the town's historic charm. But Alpine's centennial celebration in 1982 signaled the beginning of a new era that would once again recognize the value of the past, a sentiment that for decades had fallen by the wayside.

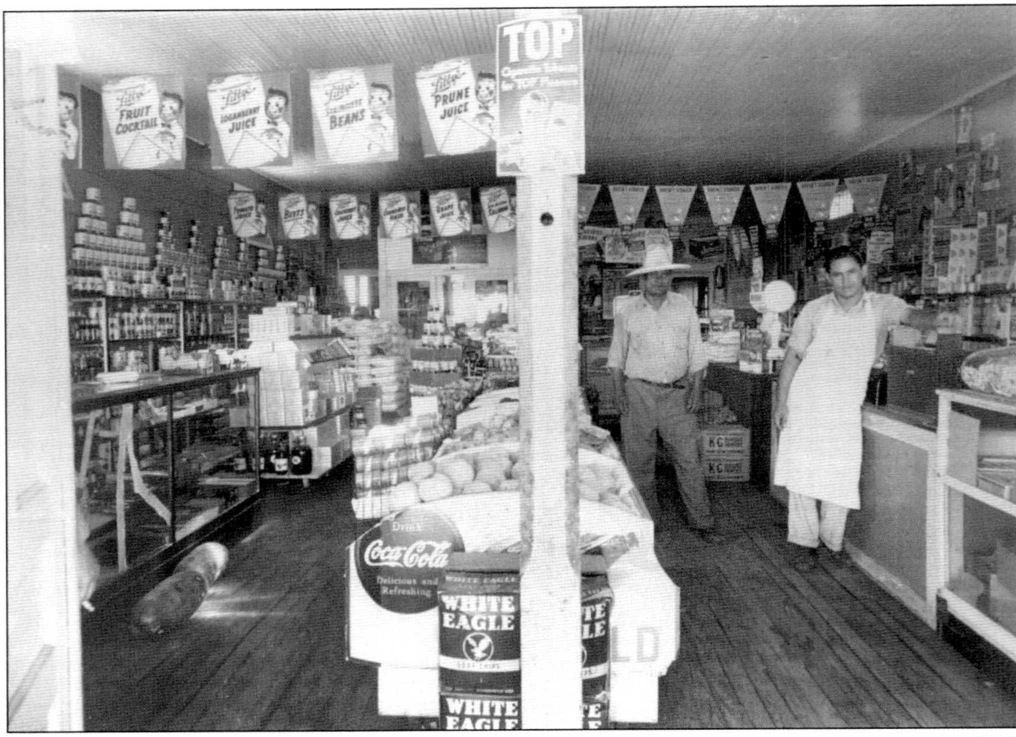

Tomás Valadez (left) and his son Manuel stand inside Valadez Grocery, located on South Fifth and Murphy Streets in 1940. One of the more successful merchants in town, Valadez was known for his generous extension of credit to his customers. The store, one of several south of the tracks, operated until 1972. (Courtesy of the Archives of the Big Bend.)

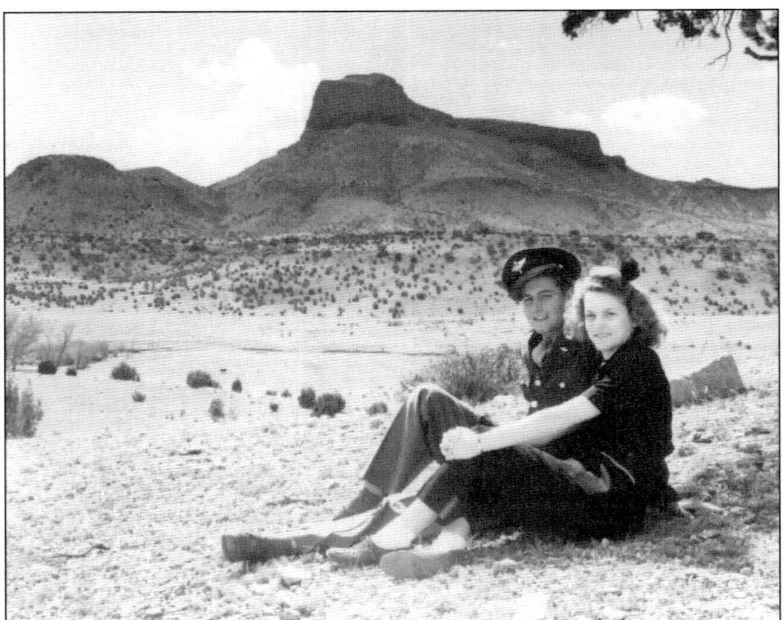

Willeen Smith and an unidentified pilot from the Marfa Army Airfield pose below Cathedral Mountain in 1942. Although the airfield and Fort D. A. Russell had much less affect on Alpine than on neighboring Marfa, they nevertheless provided a ready supply of eligible bachelors for area women during World War II. (Courtesy of the Smith collection.)

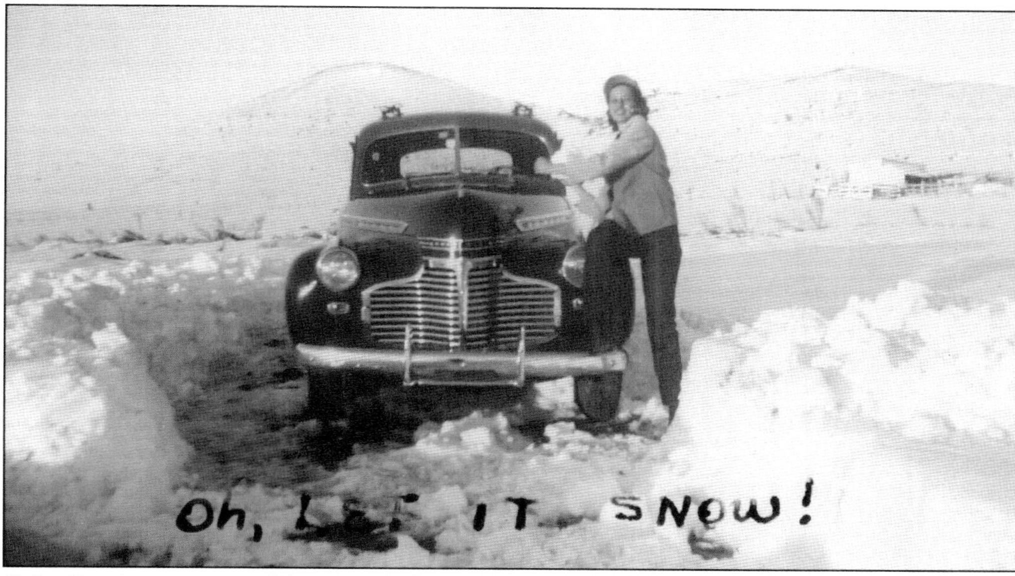

Celia Smith prepares to lob a snowball at the camera in 1946 following a record snowfall that dropped over 26 inches in Alpine. Because water lines were frozen, a fire that started in the second Southern Pacific depot could not be extinguished. A porter on a passing train remarked, "The folks in Alpine burned the depot to warm the town." (Courtesy of the Smith collection.)

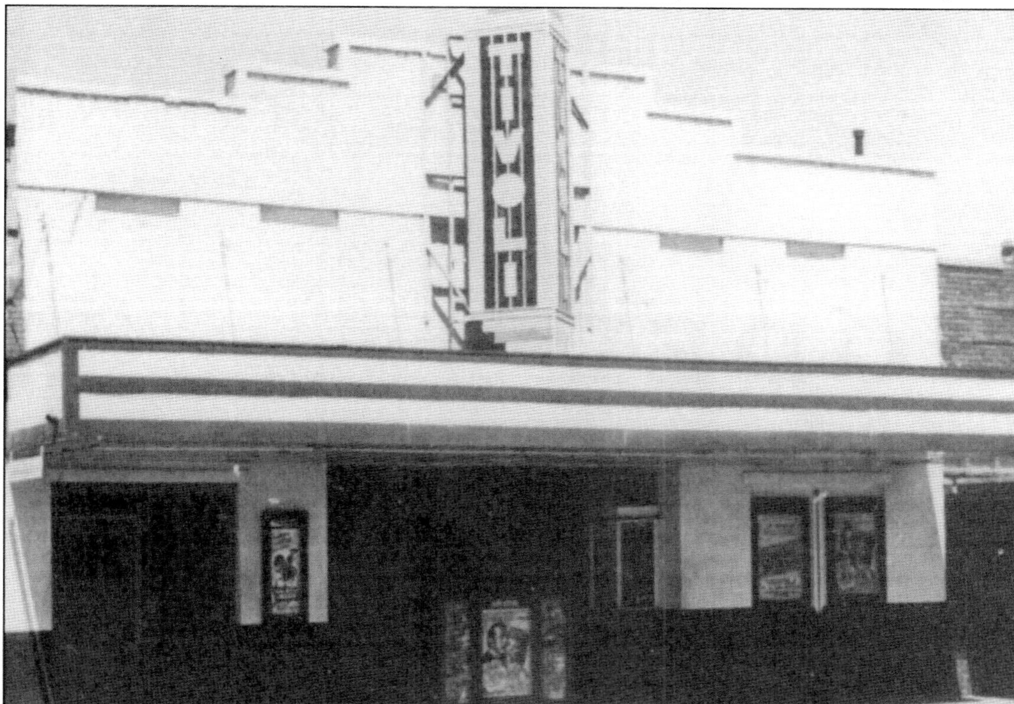

By the late 1940s, the old Mojave Theatre had been remodeled and devoted to showing Spanish-language motion pictures. Originally built by Benjamin Berkeley in 1921 to host traveling shows and vaudeville acts, in 1929 owner E. C. Moseley upgraded it to include "moving picture talkies," and it became Alpine's second movie theater, in addition to the Granada. (Courtesy of *The Brand*, Sul Ross State University.)

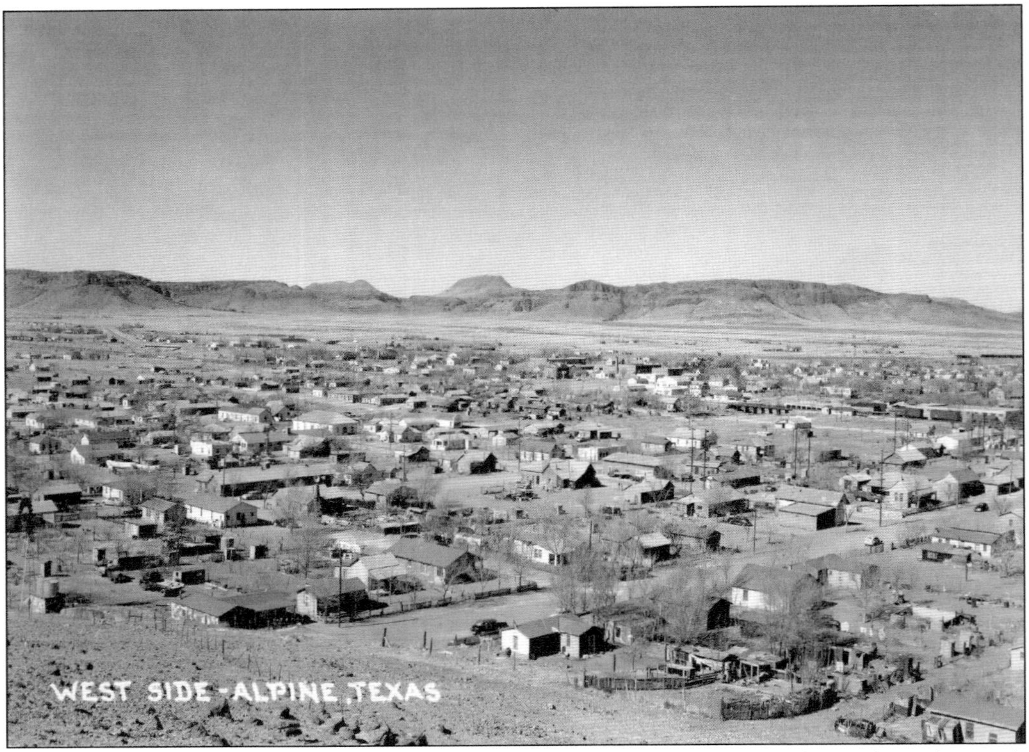

This and a companion postcard photograph to the right show Alpine around 1952 from the north slope of A Mountain. The expansive Sunny Glen area (upper left of photograph) was still open ranchland. A collection of outhouses sits in the lower left of the photograph; most of the homes on the south side of Alpine would not have indoor plumbing for another decade. (Courtesy of the Archives of the Big Bend.)

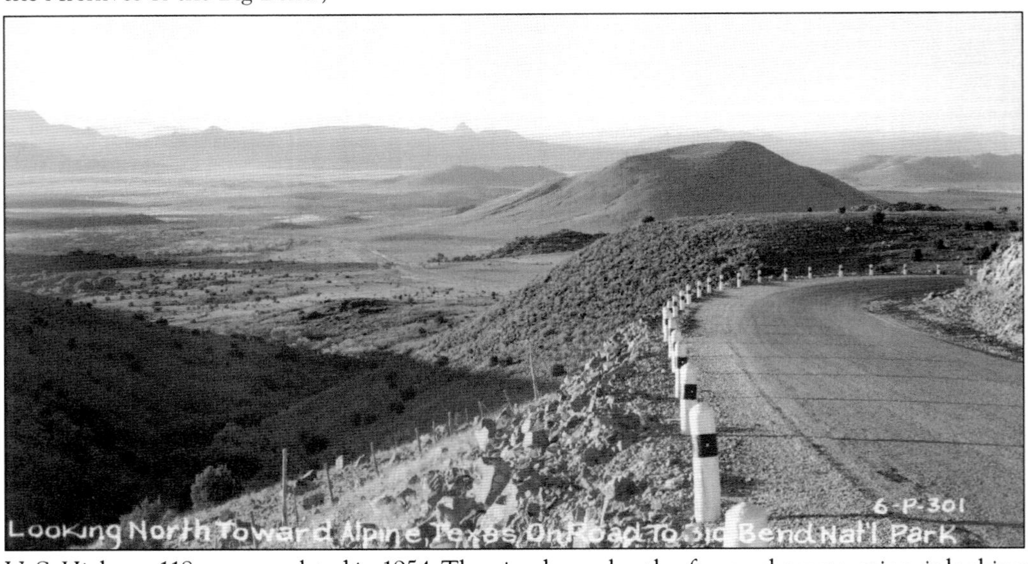

U. S. Highway 118 was completed in 1954. The view here, shortly after road construction, is looking north from the top of Big Hill south of Alpine. Paved highways came slowly to Alpine, and 118 was the last, but it assured Alpine's place as a gateway to Big Bend National Park. (Courtesy of the Archives of the Big Bend.)

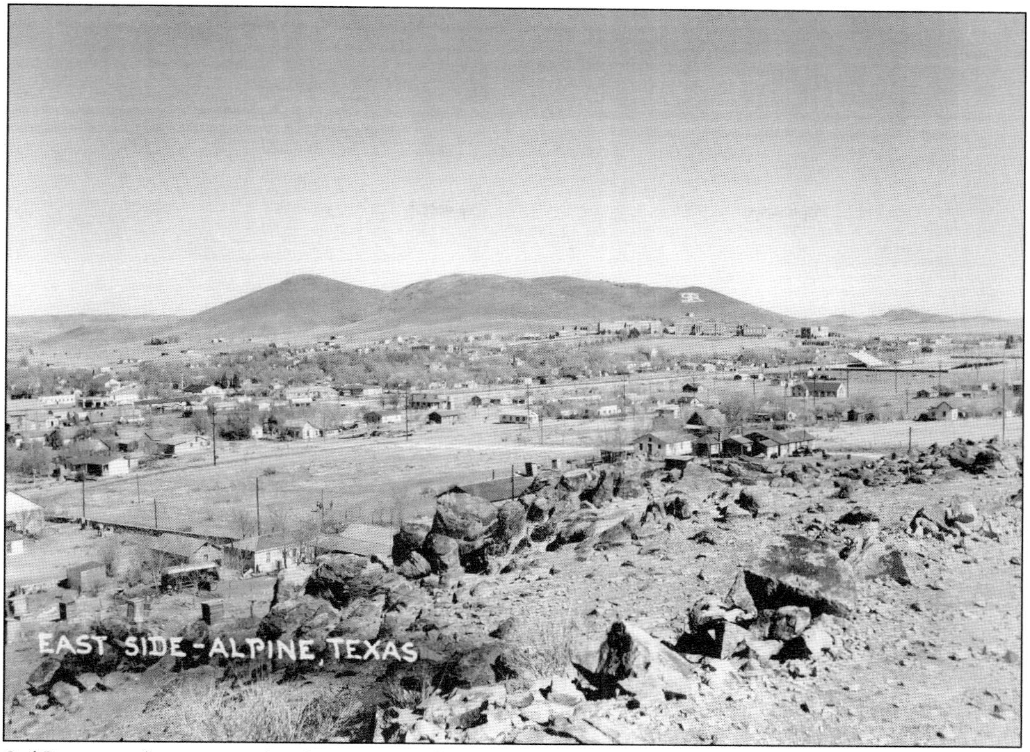

Sul Ross can be seen in the distance on the flanks of Hancock Hill in this east view over Alpine from A Mountain around 1952. The large open lot in the lower portion of the photograph had been the location of the ornate three-story Garnett Hotel which burned down in 1943. The lot became Baines Park in the 1970s. (Courtesy of the Archives of the Big Bend.)

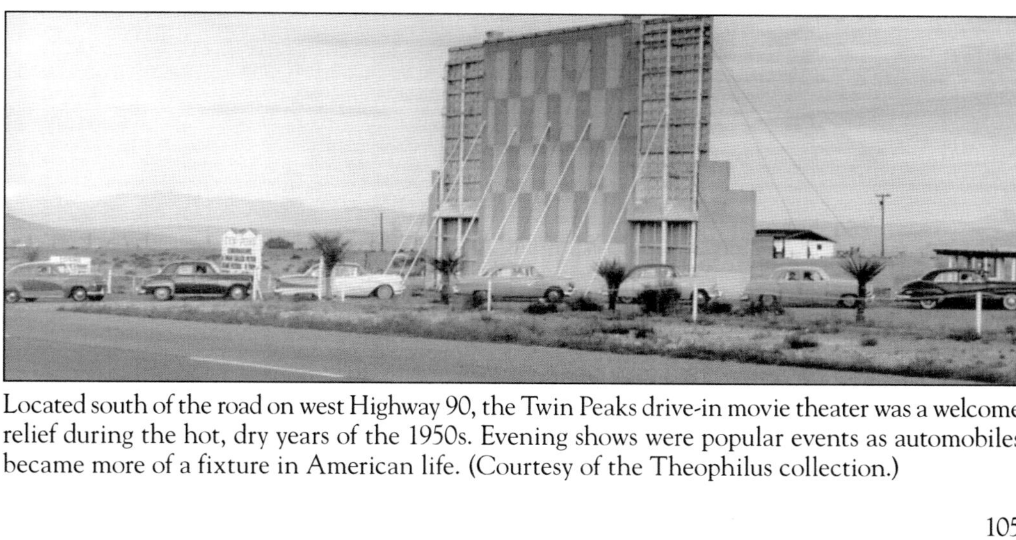

Located south of the road on west Highway 90, the Twin Peaks drive-in movie theater was a welcome relief during the hot, dry years of the 1950s. Evening shows were popular events as automobiles became more of a fixture in American life. (Courtesy of the Theophilus collection.)

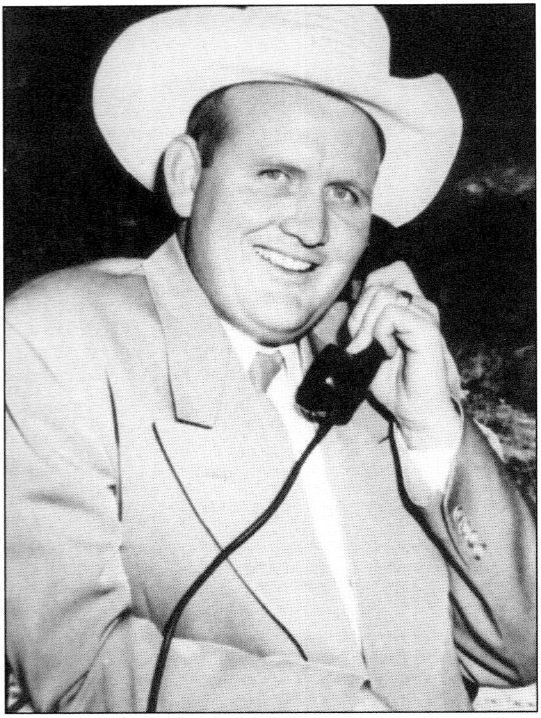

Gene Hendryx talks to Sen. Lyndon B. Johnson on the first long-distance telephone call from Big Bend National Park in 1955. Hendryx was active in Alpine civic affairs and in the mid-1950s became owner and operator of Alpine radio station KVLF. (Courtesy of the Museum of the Big Bend.)

A bird's-eye view shows the Alpine Cowboys playing at Kokernot Field around 1955. The team was established by Herbert Kokernot Jr. in 1946 when he retooled the Alpine Cats into the Cowboys. From then until 1958, the team won a dozen regional titles and was runner-up in the national championship in their final year. (Courtesy of the Archives of the Big Bend.)

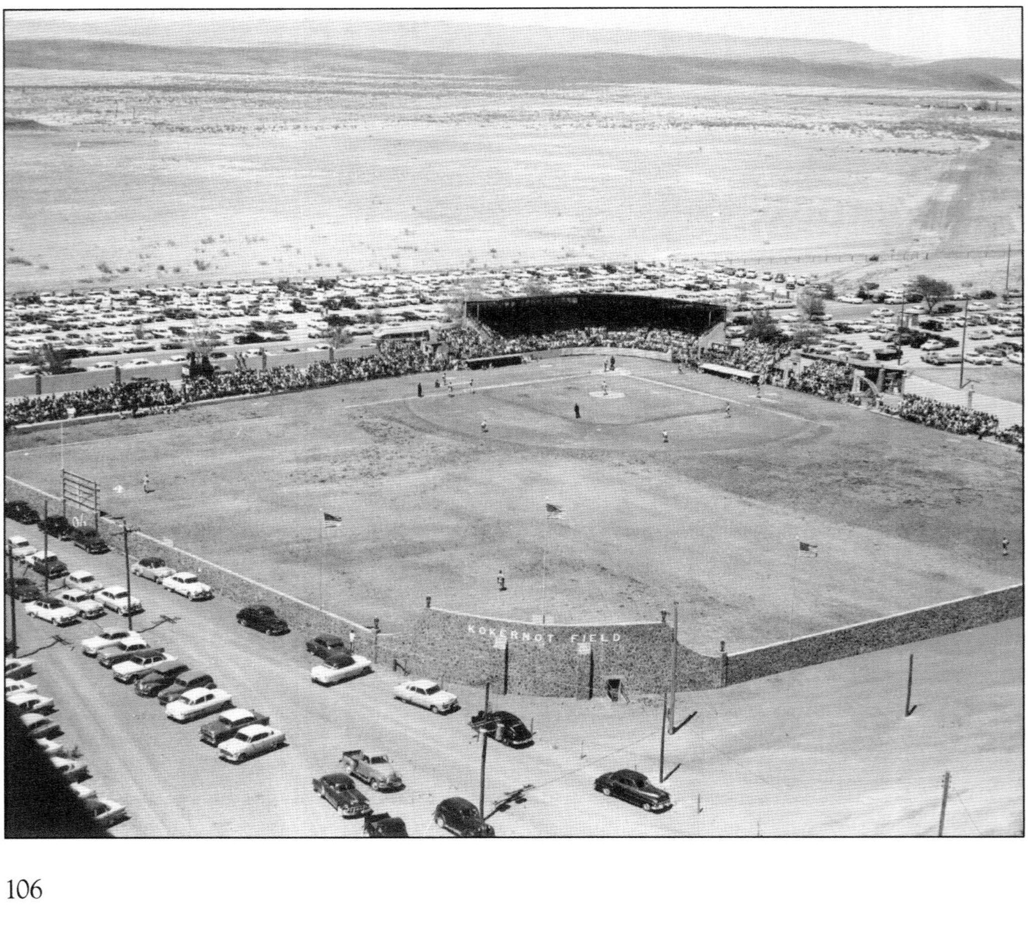

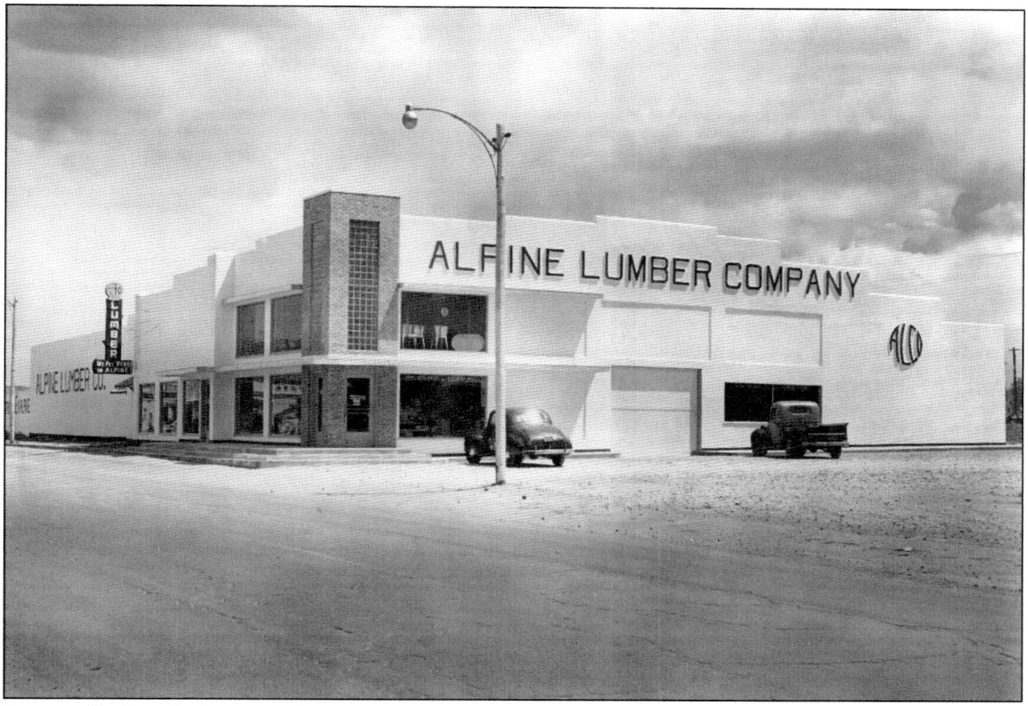

Originally founded in 1904 by W. B. Mitchell and Frank E. Gillett, the Alpine Lumber Company grew from humble beginnings in a small frame building along the railroad to this large, modern facility in the 1960s. (Courtesy of the Archives of the Big Bend.)

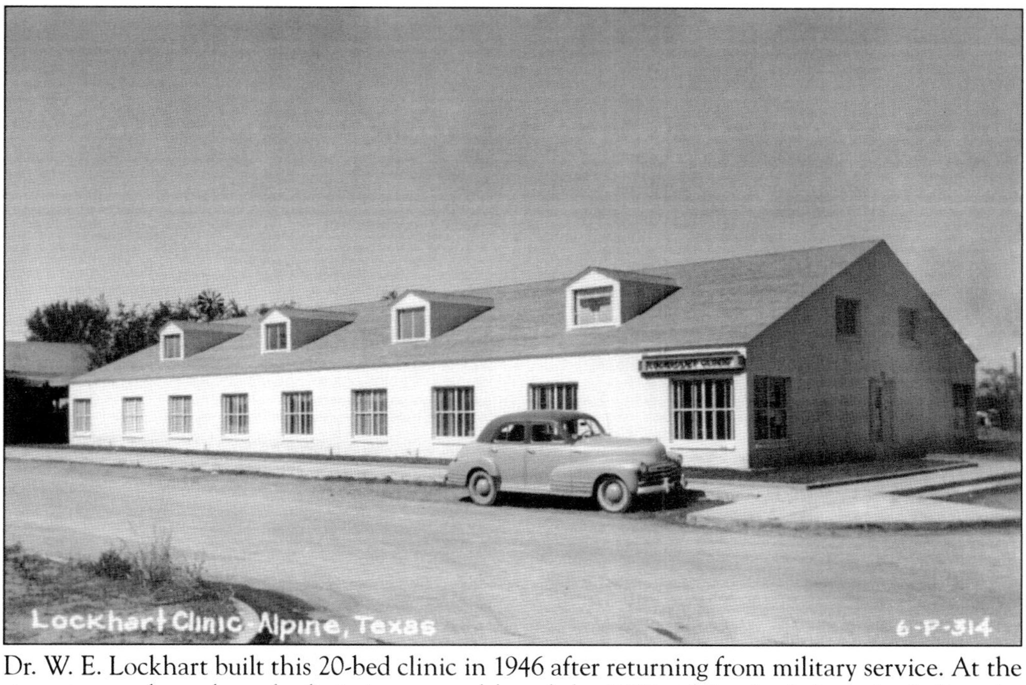

Dr. W. E. Lockhart built this 20-bed clinic in 1946 after returning from military service. At the time, it was the only such clinic in town, although by 1950, Alpine had three, including the Wright Clinic and the Jeter-Hill Clinic. In 1957, Alpine would gain the Brewster County Memorial Hospital. (Courtesy of the Archives of the Big Bend.)

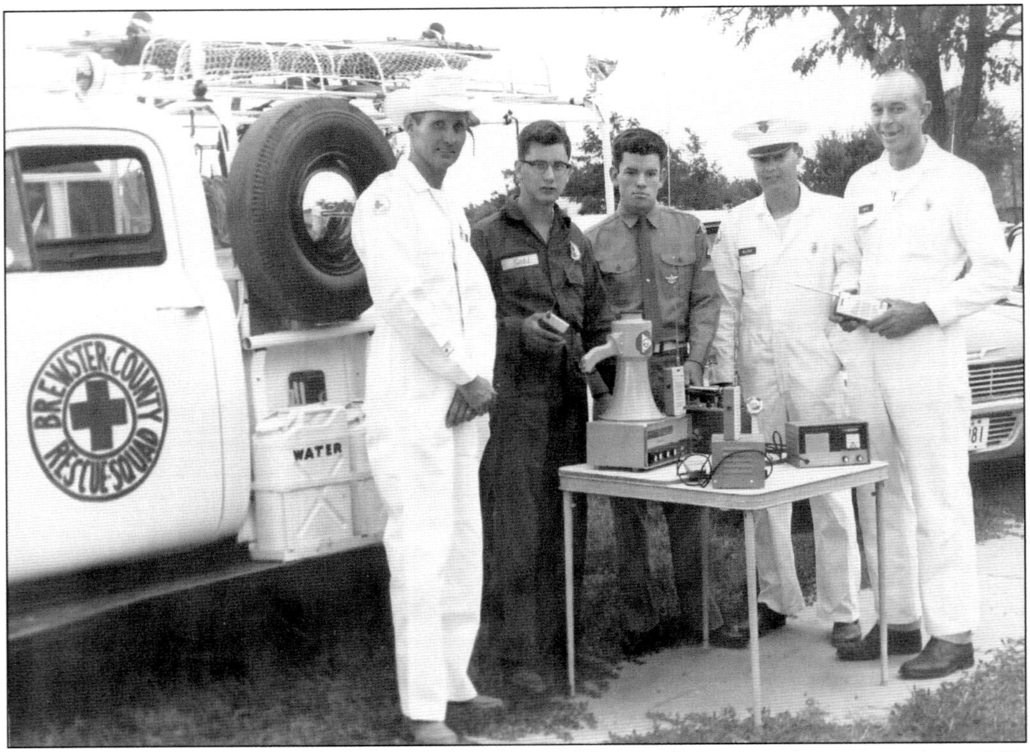

The Brewster County Rescue Squad stands in front of their well-appointed rescue truck in 1962. They are, from left to right, Bud Powers, Rick Sohl, Martin Theophilus, Carl Williams (who would later become Brewster County sheriff), and Ray Baker. The all-volunteer squad was the first on the scene of the tragic Sanderson Flood of 1965 that claimed the lives of 26 residents. (Courtesy of the Theophilus collection.)

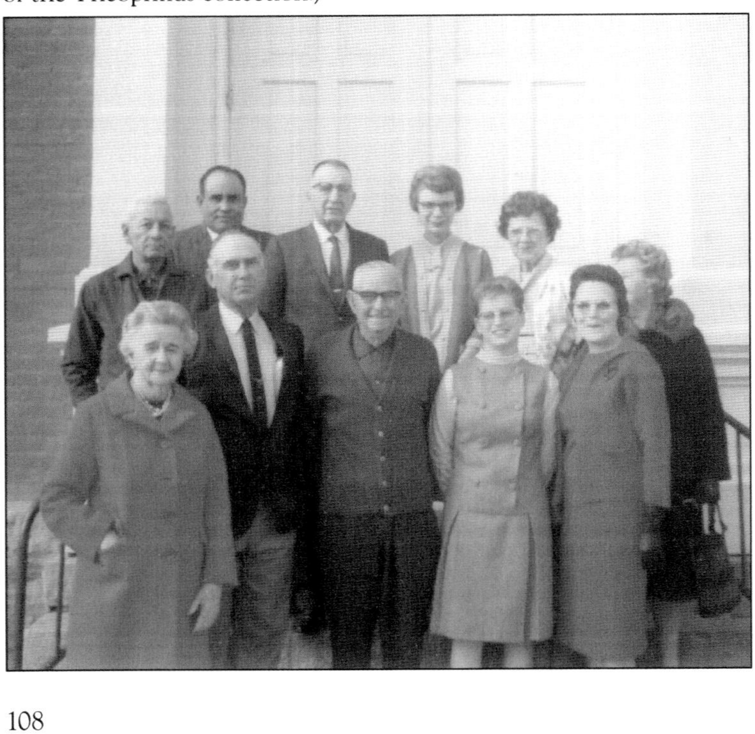

Newly sworn-in Brewster County officers stand on the courthouse steps in 1963. They are, from left to right, (first row) Hallie Stillwell, Rex Ivey Jr., Levi Bell, Joyce Combs, Avora Owens; (second row) Tom Carney, Robert Valadez, Felix McGaughy, Helen Crane, Sara Pugh, and ? Hill. (Courtesy of the Ivey collection.)

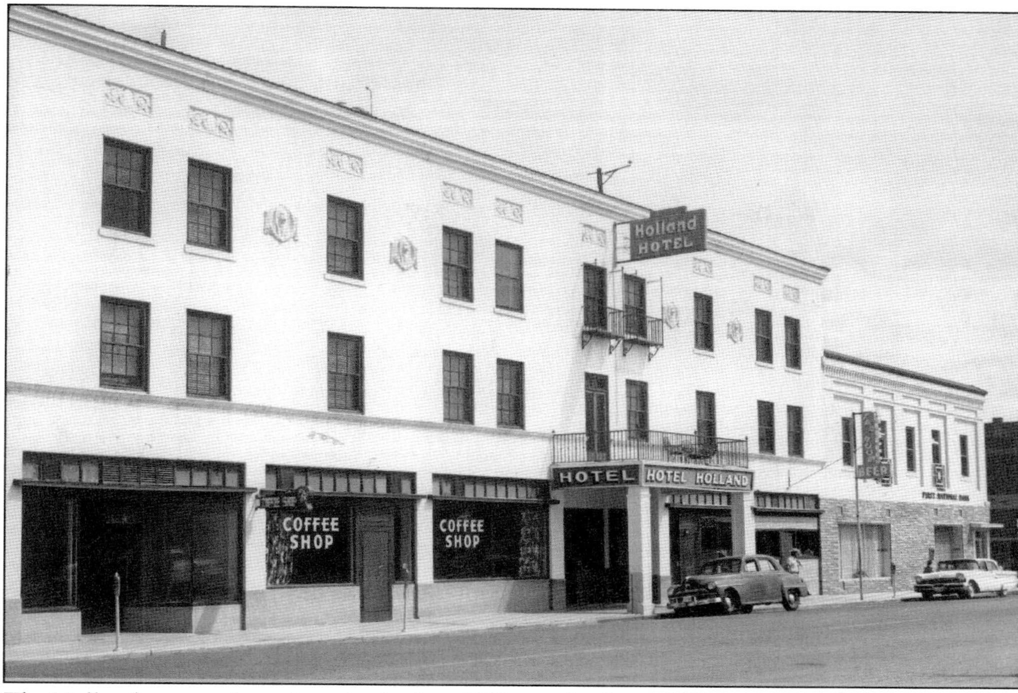

The Holland annex, shown here in the late 1950s, was built in 1927 in a freehanded interpretation of the Spanish Colonial style. The ground floor included the Holland Coffee Shop, where local ranchers and businessmen gathered and where a lot of important business deals occurred over the years. (Courtesy of the Archives of the Big Bend.)

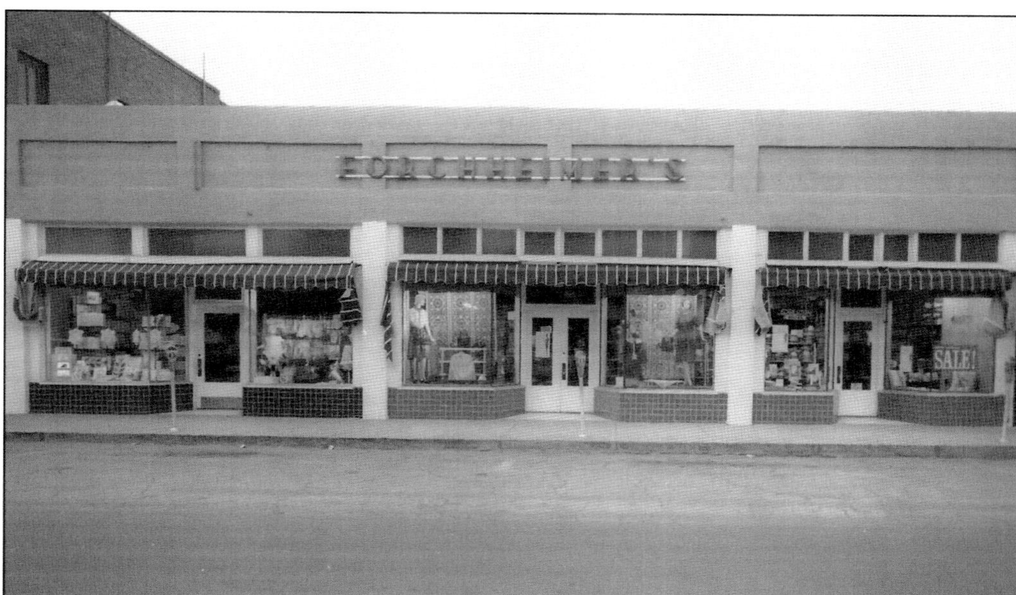

German immigrant Louis Forchheimer operated a wholesale dry goods business in New York City before moving to Alpine in 1921. The retail store he started on Holland Avenue grew from one front door to three as it gradually expanded. A town fixture, Forchheimer's served Alpine for over 75 years. (Courtesy of the Halpern-Forchheimer collection.)

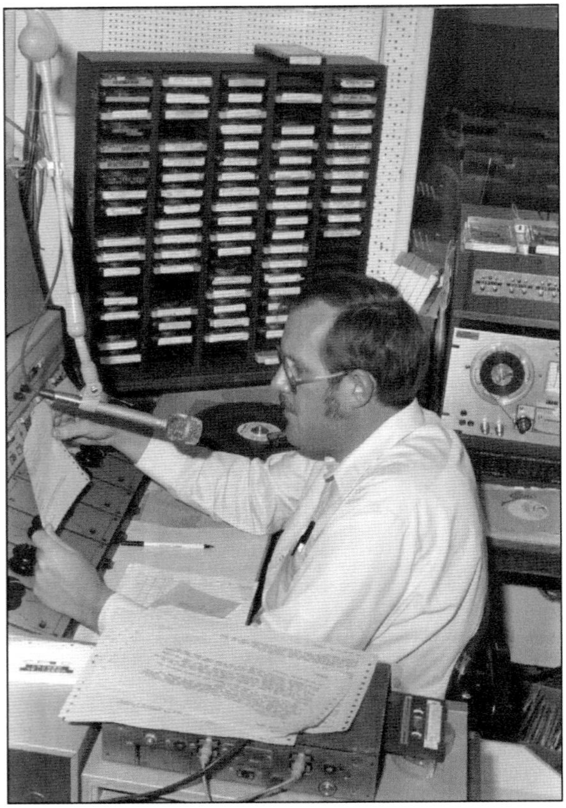

The "Voice of the Last Frontier," Ray Hendryx is shown at the console of the KVLF studio around 1986. Ray's father, Gene Hendryx, had been with the station since 1947, eventually becoming its sole owner and manager. Originally located in the front of the Holland Hotel, the station moved in 1950 to the transmitter site beside Kokernot Field. (Courtesy of the Museum of the Big Bend.)

A parade during Alpine's Centennial Celebration in April 1982 featured the O6 Ranch chuckwagon and a flag-bearing cavalcade. The three-day celebration included two dances, three parades, four rodeo performances, stagecoach rides, a beard-growing contest, a theatrical gunfight, a fireworks display, two barbeques, and a chuckwagon breakfast. (Courtesy of the Museum of the Big Bend.)

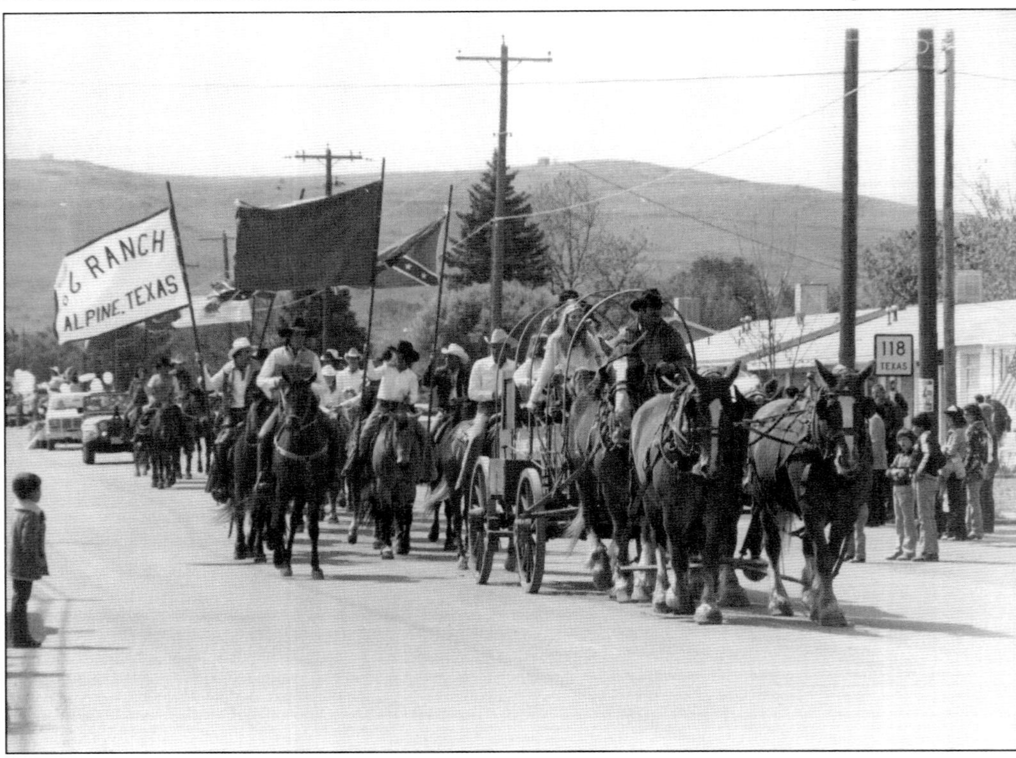

Eight

Modern Alpine
The Last Frontier

Since the mid 1990s, Alpine has seen a resurgence in cultural sophistication and artistic refinement. The first Gallery Night in 1994 signaled the beginning of the Alpine Renaissance at about the same time that a variety of new businesses took hold. Kiowa Gallery, Front Street Books, Quetzal, the Railroad Blues, and the Reata Restaurant were all established during the decade, ushering in a trend of downtown revitalization.

Since the beginning of the 21st century, the pace of change has quickened with a host of new events like Fiesta del Sol, new literary publications like the *Cenizo*, and the addition of Marfa Public Radio. Most recently, the Holland Hotel, the Granada Theatre, and a whole block along Murphy Street have been restored and reopened. In 2009, the Big Bend Cowboys drew impressive crowds once again to Kokernot Field. And today Alpine boasts over a dozen art galleries, the beginnings of a creekside trail system, and a state-of-the-art museum—the kinds of amenities that encourage tourism even as they heighten the quality of life for citizens.

With a long history of pride in its panoramic setting, its clean air, and quaint rural town life, Alpine is recapturing a sense of itself that for a time seemed lost. Today Alpine is regaining its rightful identity as a distinguished town with a rich past and—once again—a promising future.

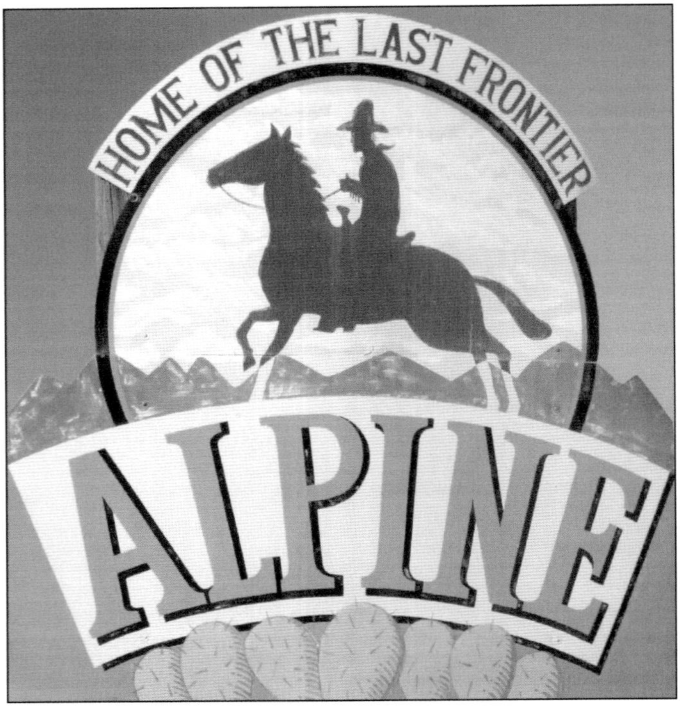

A roadside sign greets visitors driving into Alpine from the east on Highway 90. "Home of the last frontier," is one of many advertising slogans attached to the town over the years. Starting with the "Roof garden of Texas" in a 1911 edition of *Texas Magazine*, many such phrases have been coined reflecting the town's identity as a place apart. (Photograph by author.)

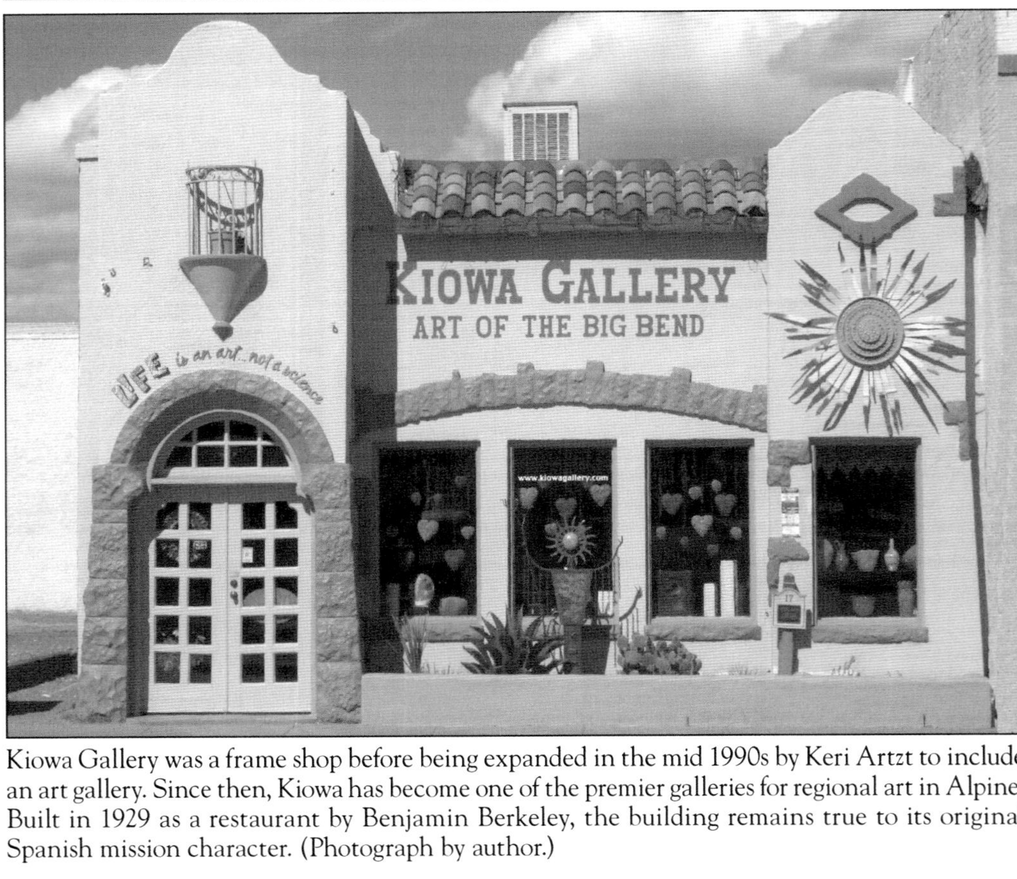

Kiowa Gallery was a frame shop before being expanded in the mid 1990s by Keri Artzt to include an art gallery. Since then, Kiowa has become one of the premier galleries for regional art in Alpine. Built in 1929 as a restaurant by Benjamin Berkeley, the building remains true to its original Spanish mission character. (Photograph by author.)

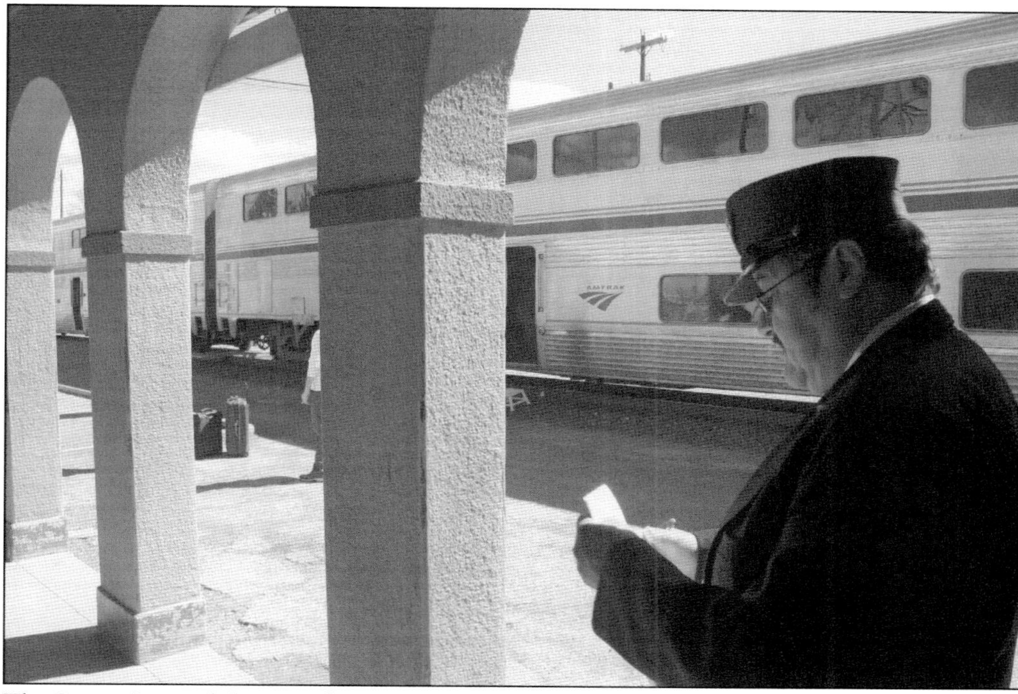

The Sunset Limited that runs between New Orleans and Los Angeles still stops in Alpine three times weekly. A trip to San Antonio costs $60 and takes about 8 hours. For another $90 (and 13 additional hours), a person can ride all the way to Los Angeles's Union Station. (Photograph by author.)

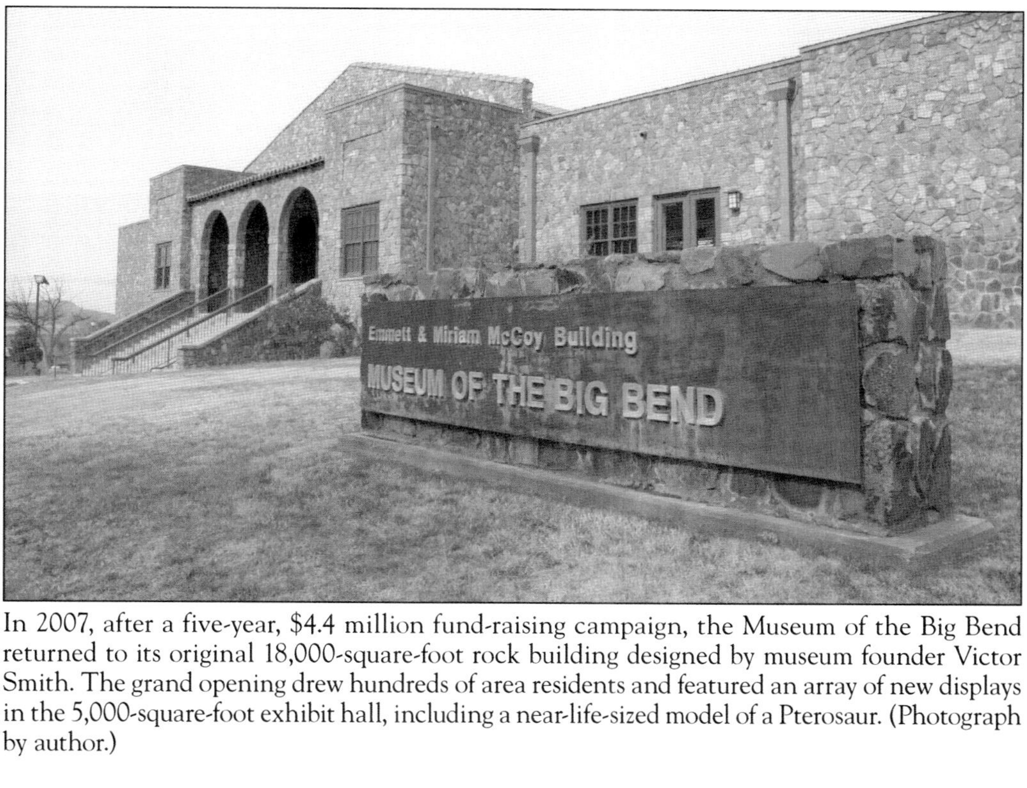

In 2007, after a five-year, $4.4 million fund-raising campaign, the Museum of the Big Bend returned to its original 18,000-square-foot rock building designed by museum founder Victor Smith. The grand opening drew hundreds of area residents and featured an array of new displays in the 5,000-square-foot exhibit hall, including a near-life-sized model of a Pterosaur. (Photograph by author.)

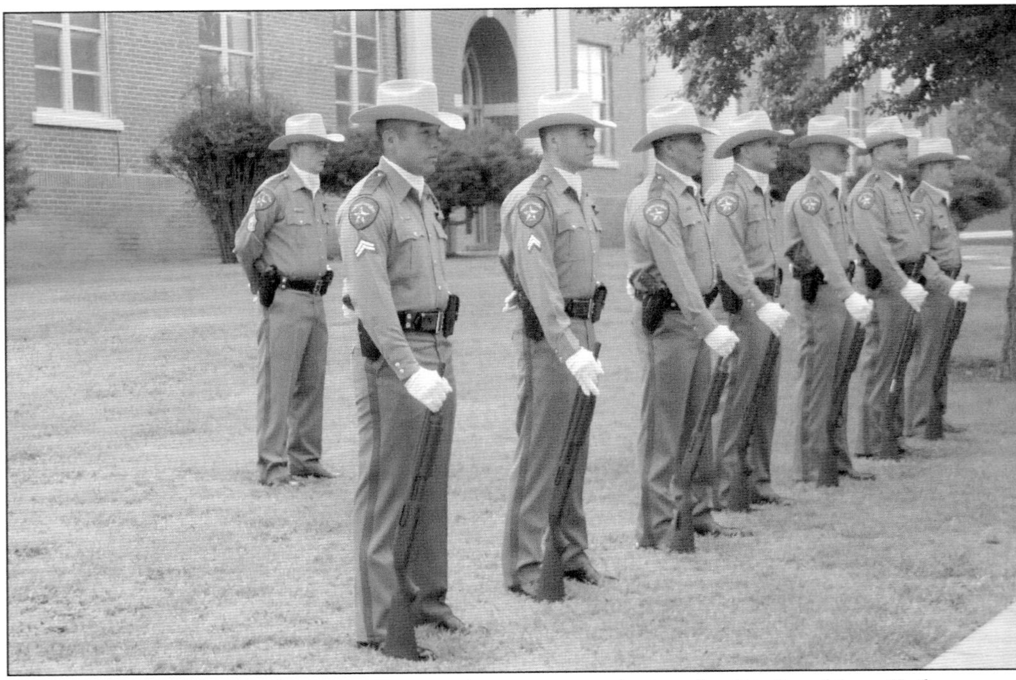

Department of Public Safety troopers stand at attention during the Big Bend Law Enforcement Officer's Memorial Ceremony. This annual event at Sul Ross, sponsored by the Big Bend Law Enforcement Officer's Association, pays tribute to officers who have lost their lives in the line of duty. (Courtesy of Sul Ross News and Publications.)

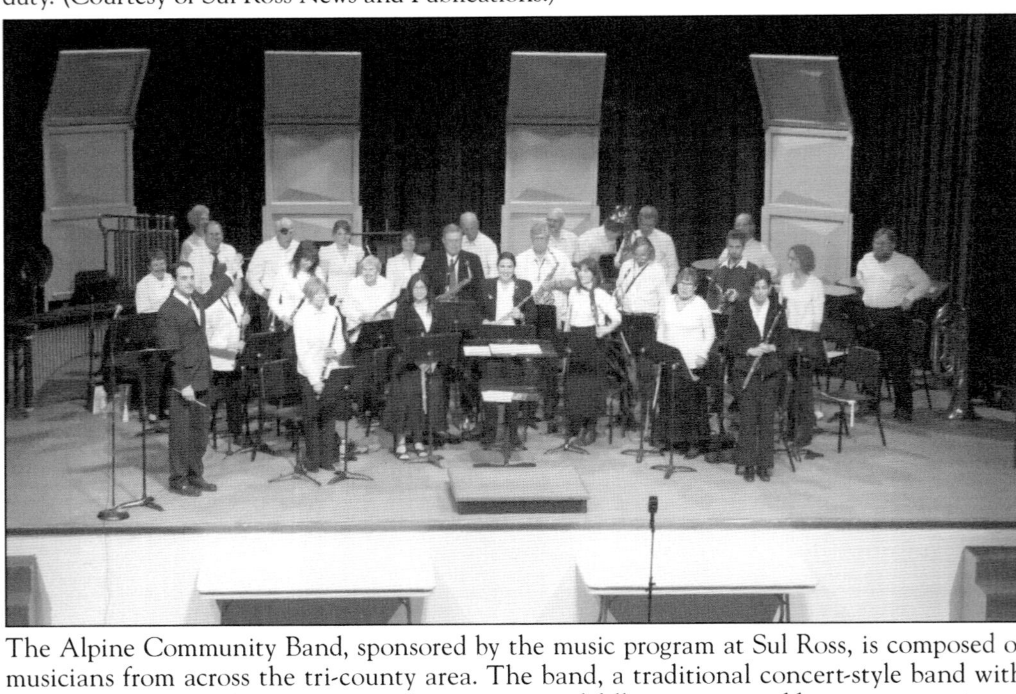

The Alpine Community Band, sponsored by the music program at Sul Ross, is composed of musicians from across the tri-county area. The band, a traditional concert-style band with woodwind, brass, and percussion, performs spring and fall concerts in addition to appearing at the Fourth of July celebration and other special events throughout the year. (Courtesy of Sul Ross News and Publications.)

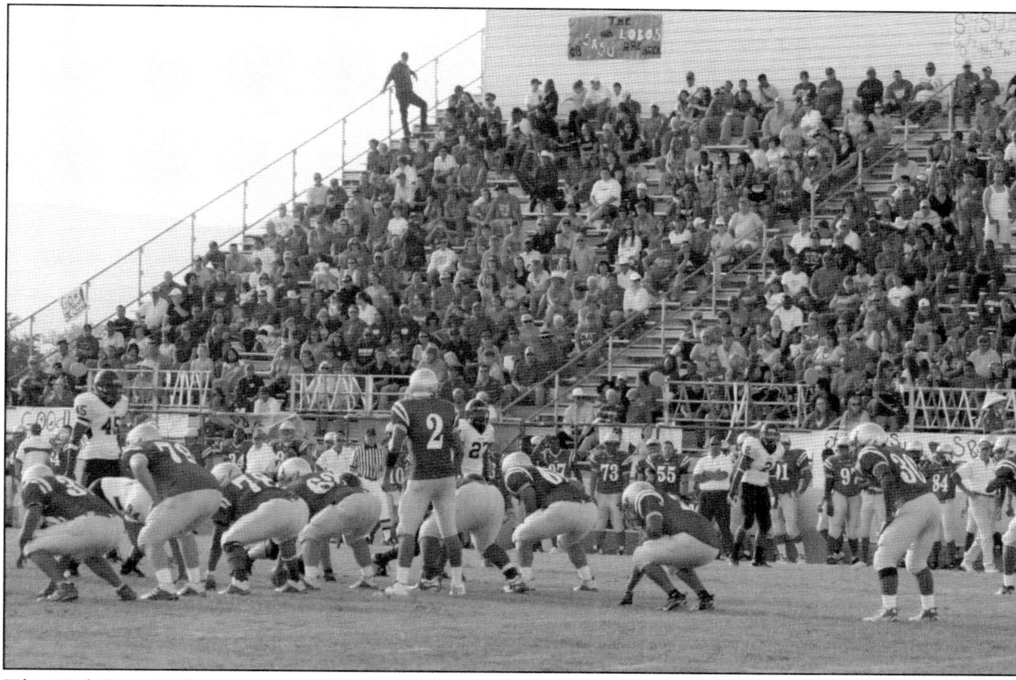

The Sul Ross Lobos square off against Texas Lutheran University's Bulldogs at Jackson Field in 2009. Although not a strong team historically, the Lobos prevailed 35 to 7 and quarterback Dominique Carson rushed for 287 yards and four touchdowns. (Courtesy of Sul Ross News and Publications.)

Baseball, perhaps the most prominent sport in Alpine's history, slowly declined following the end of the Alpine Cowboys. Ownership of Kokernot Field was turned over to Sul Ross, and later to the Alpine Independent School District after the college dropped its baseball program in 1968. Sul Ross began using the stadium again after the baseball program was revived in 1983. (Courtesy of Sul Ross News and Publications.)

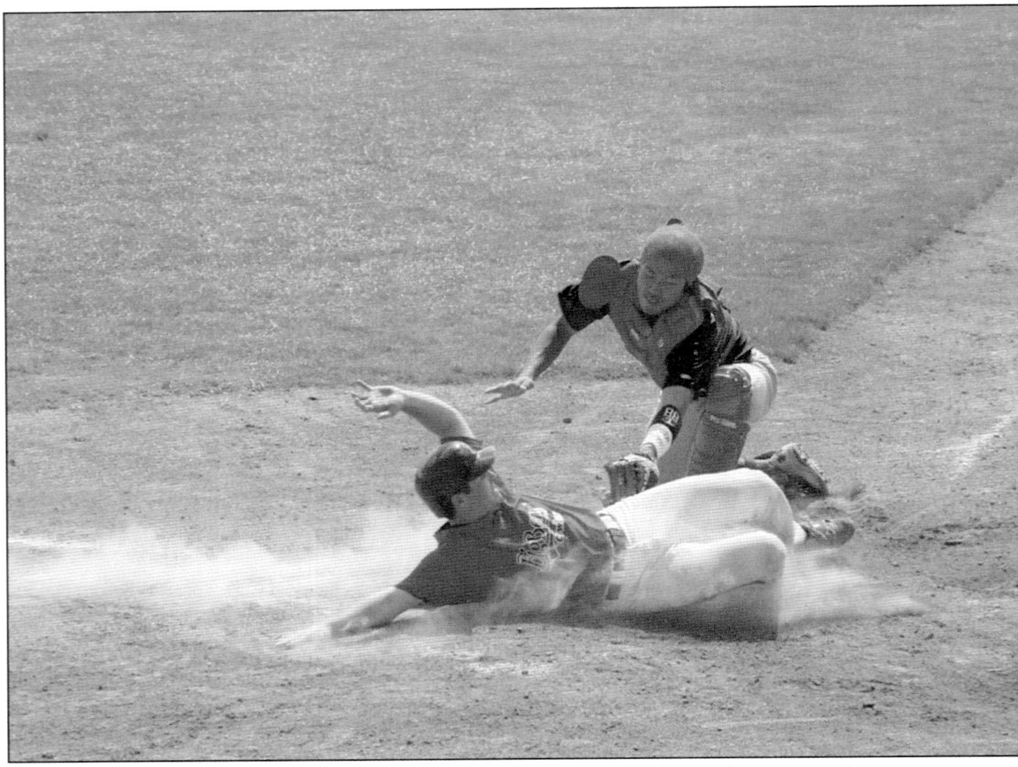

The Big Bend Cowboys formed in the spring of 2009 as an independent minor league team, part of the Continental Baseball League. A doubleheader in May 2009 marked the first professional baseball played at Kokernot Field since the final season of Herbert Kokernot's Alpine Cowboys in 1961. (Courtesy of the *Alpine Avalanche*.)

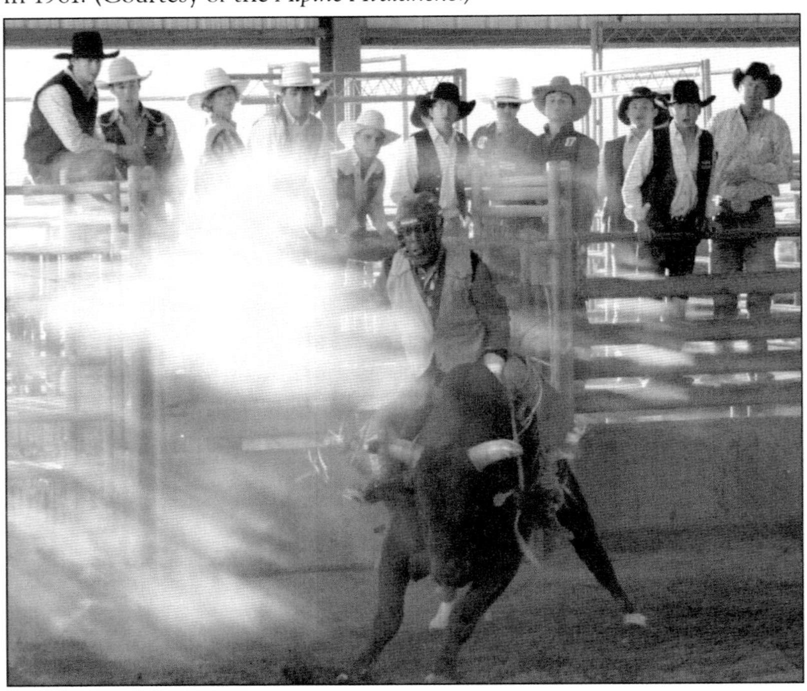

Rodeo cowboy Jamon Turner rides a bull as cowboys look on at the Sul Ross–sponsored intercollegiate rodeo in 2008. Turner went on to win the regional title in 2009. The Sul Ross rodeo team has a long history of success, including eight national titles since its origin in 1947. (Courtesy of Sul Ross News and Publications.)

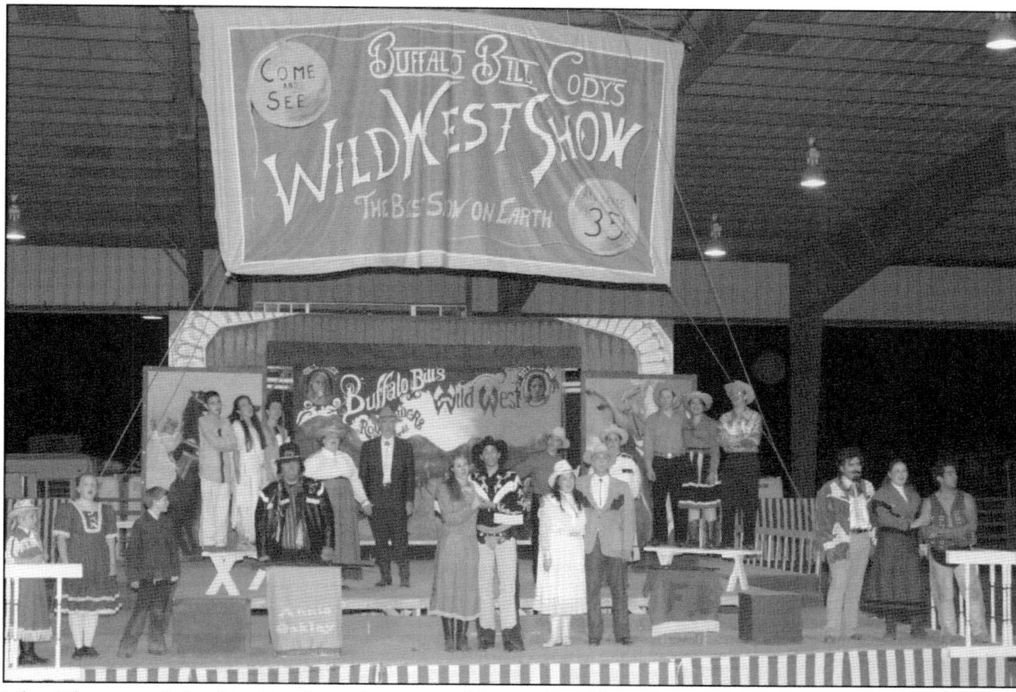

The Theatre of the Big Bend production of *Annie Get Your Gun* was performed in the Sul Ross outdoor arena allowing horses to be a part of the show to enhance the sense of an authentic Wild West show. The 1946 musical featuring music and lyrics by Irving Berlin starred local actor Terra Peters as Annie Oakley. (Courtesy of Sul Ross News and Publications.)

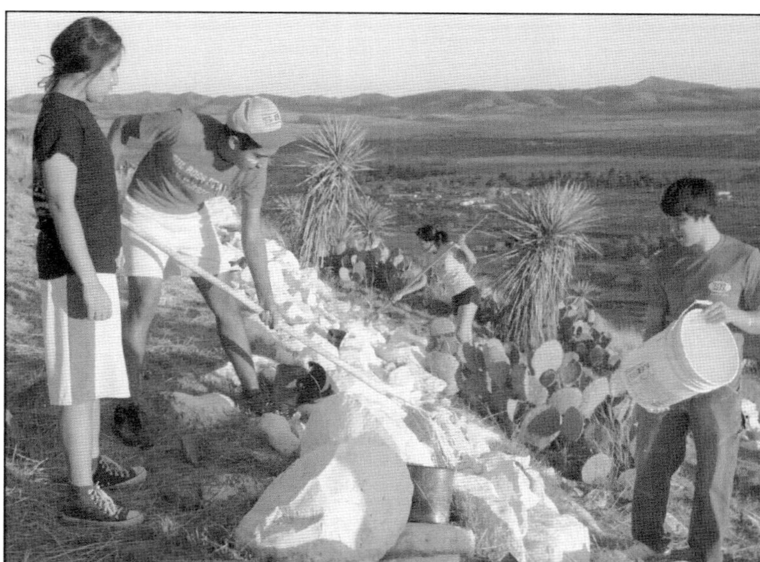
The tradition of whitewashing the Bar SR Bar on the west slope of Hancock Hill started in 1925. In April of that year, Prof. Victor Smith and his manual training students prepared the outline for the symbol and then enlisted the help of the entire student body to place and whitewash the rocks. (Courtesy of Sul Ross News and Publications.)

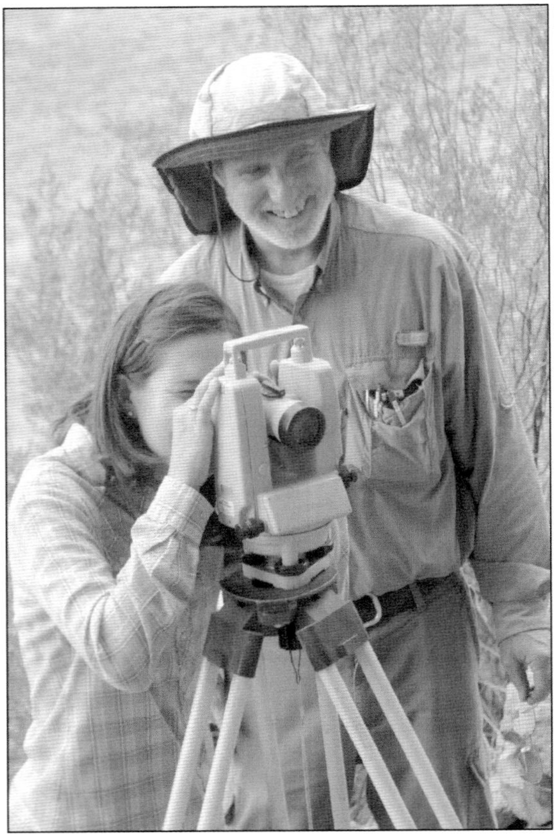

Archaeologist Andy Cloud instructs Meredith Wheelock in the use of a theodolite at a rockshelter excavation south of Alpine. The Center for Big Bend Studies at Sul Ross sponsors a field school every other year allowing students to learn archaeological methods while working on regional survey and excavation projects. (Courtesy of Sul Ross News and Publications.)

Alpine cowboy Joel Nelson performs at the annual Texas Cowboy Poetry Gathering at Sul Ross. Nelson, who has written and recited poetry for over 25 years, was the recipient of a National Heritage Fellowship by the National Endowment for the Arts. First held in Alpine in 1987, the gathering is the oldest of its kind in Texas and second oldest in the country. (Courtesy of the Texas Cowboy Poetry Gathering Committee.)

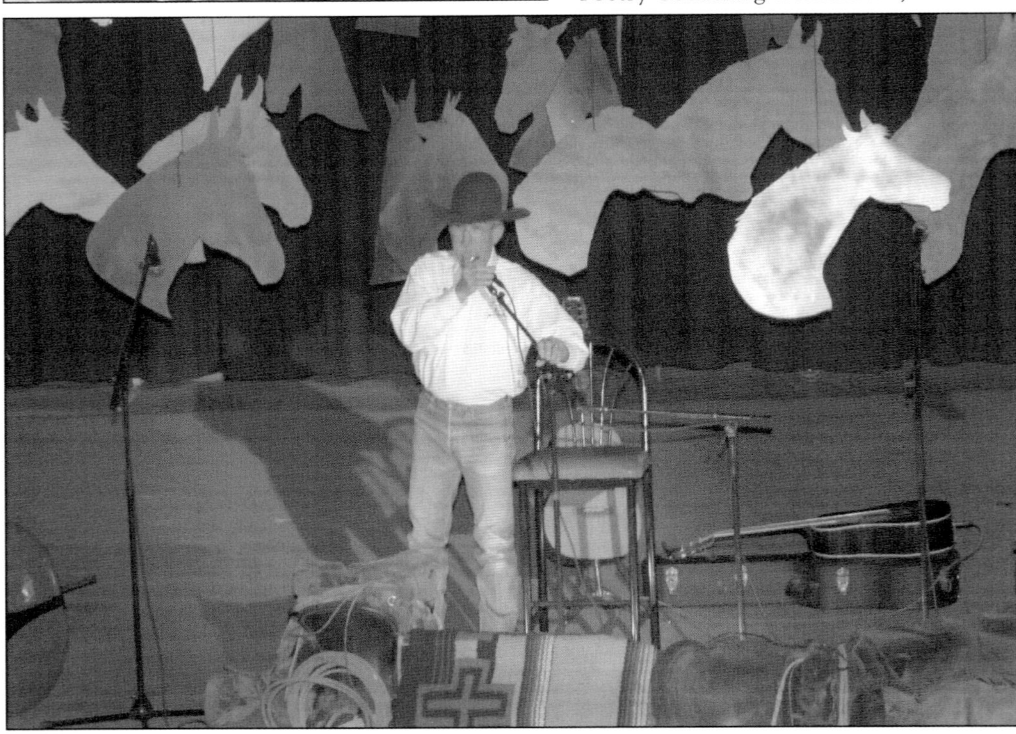

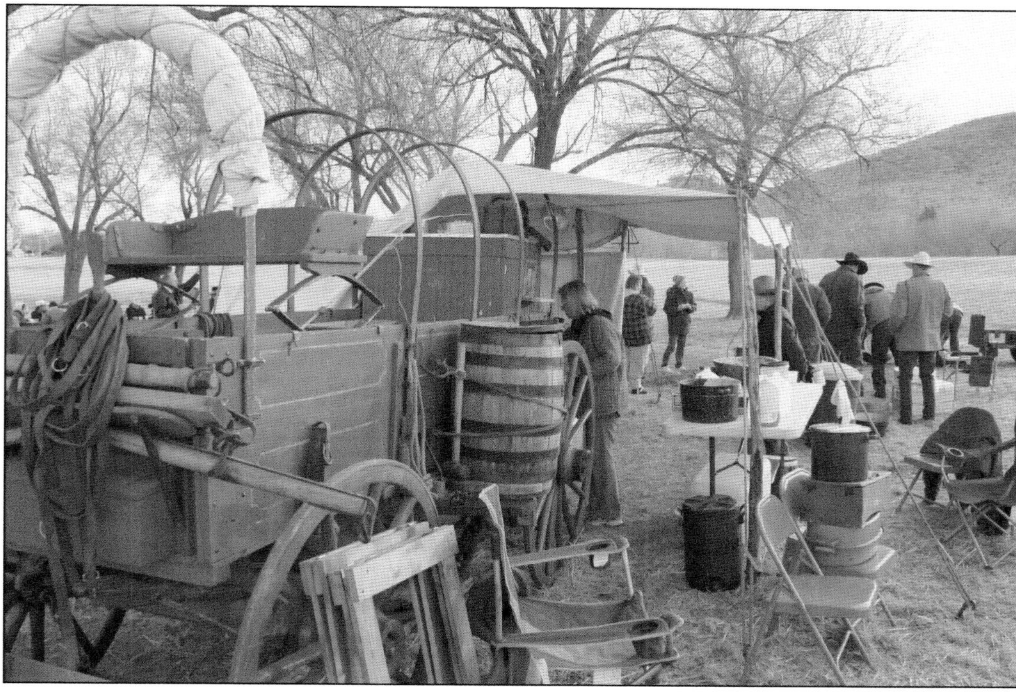

A perennial favorite chuckwagon breakfast is offered during the annual Texas Cowboy Poetry Gathering in 2010. Using Dutch ovens beside an open fire pit, the cooks prepare a standard cowboy breakfast of coffee, biscuits, gravy, and eggs at Poet's Grove in Kokernot Park. (Photograph by author.)

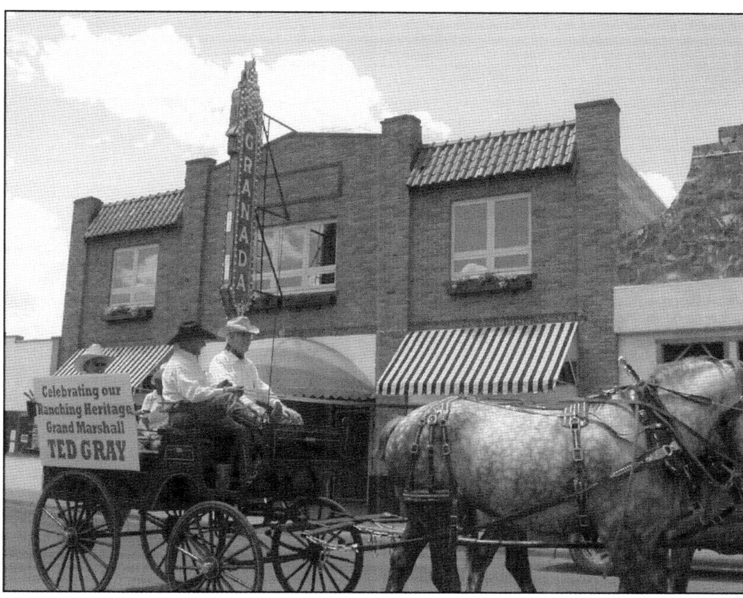

Rancher Ted Gray is honored as grand marshall at the 2009 Ranch Rodeo parade. Gray first came to the Alpine area in 1938 to work as a cowboy and would later own ranches of his own. The parade is part of the Big Bend Ranch Rodeo, a yearly event that showcases the skills of working ranch cowboys and celebrates the ranching lifestyle. (Photograph by author.)

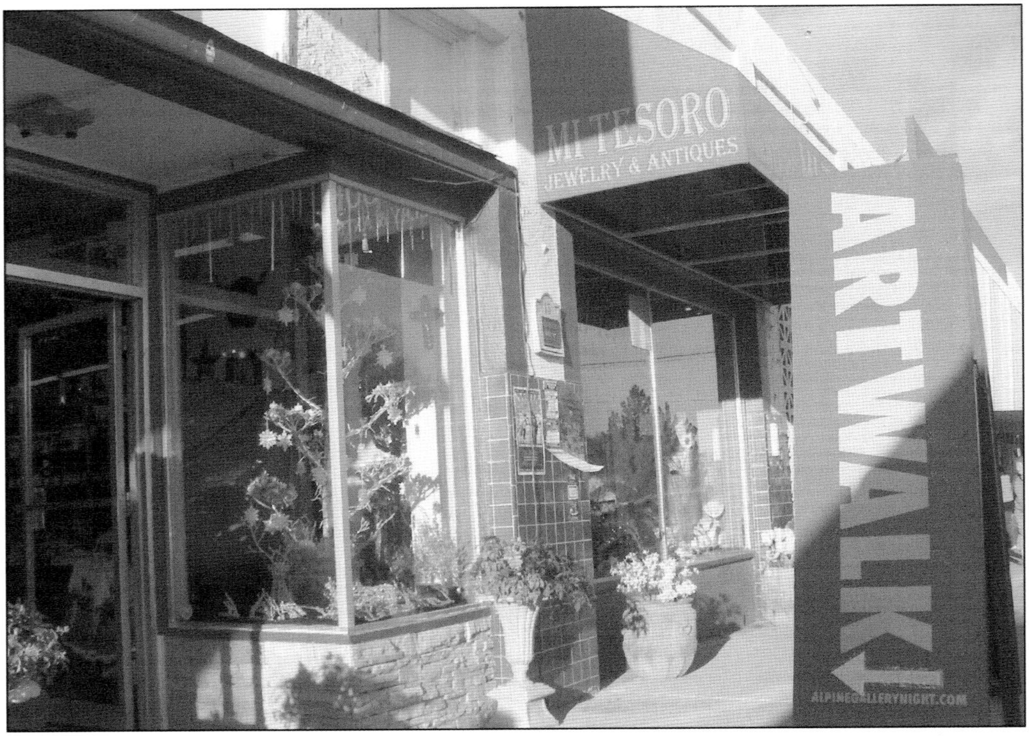

Artwalk, an annual two-day art festival held each November, draws people from across the state. Cofounded by Kiowa Gallery's Keri Artzt in 1994, the festival showcases local talent. In addition to fine art, there is free outdoor music, theater, dance performances, and a silent auction among other events. (Photograph by author.)

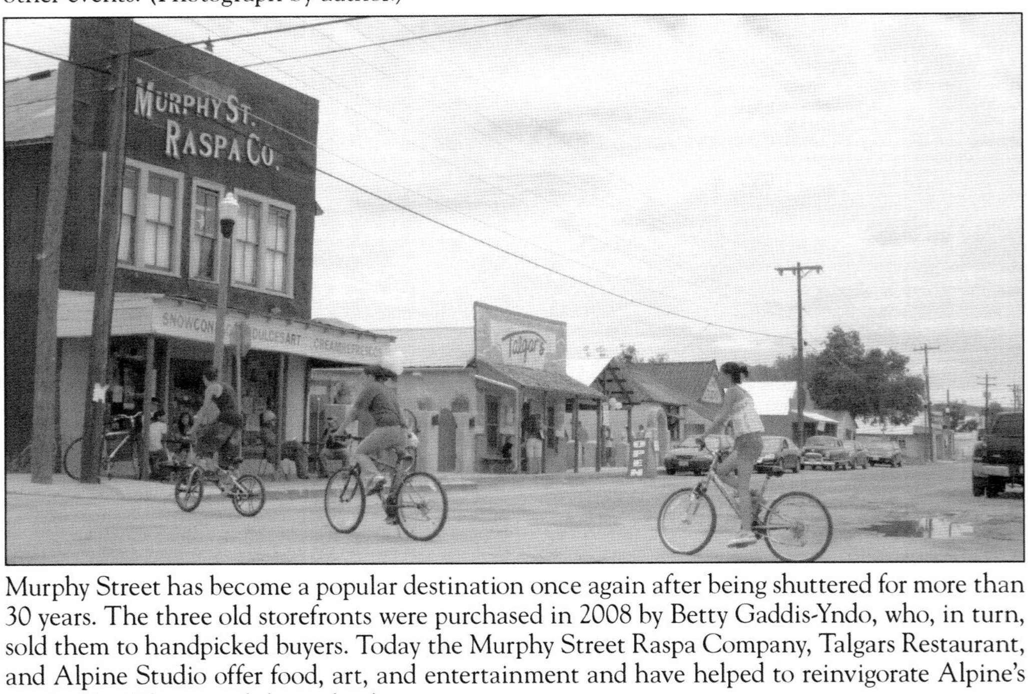

Murphy Street has become a popular destination once again after being shuttered for more than 30 years. The three old storefronts were purchased in 2008 by Betty Gaddis-Yndo, who, in turn, sold them to handpicked buyers. Today the Murphy Street Raspa Company, Talgars Restaurant, and Alpine Studio offer food, art, and entertainment and have helped to reinvigorate Alpine's south side. (Photograph by author.)

The Big Bend Balloon Bash was first organized in 1987, and has been an annual event since 1996. Held over the three-day Labor Day weekend, the event includes a variety of aerial displays by between 15 and 30 balloon pilots who come to Alpine from across Texas and New Mexico. (Photograph by author.)

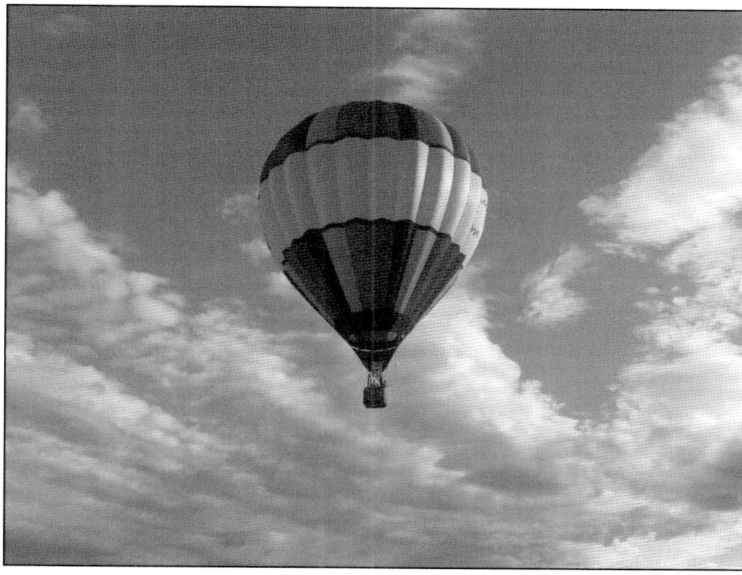

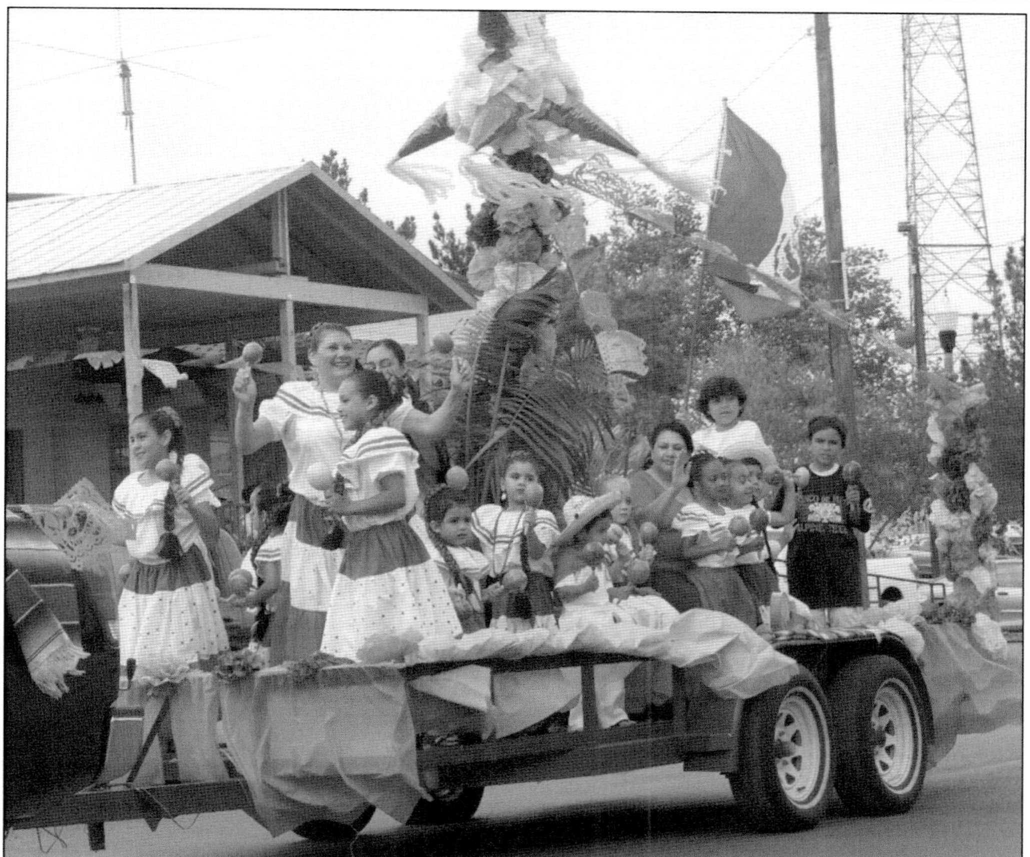

The Cinco de Mayo parade is a colorful, festive annual event that has been observed in Alpine since the early 1900s. A celebration of Mexican heritage and pride, it is a town favorite with live performances, a street dance, and plenty of food—including a cabrito and menudo cookoff. (Courtesy of the *Alpine Avalanche*.)

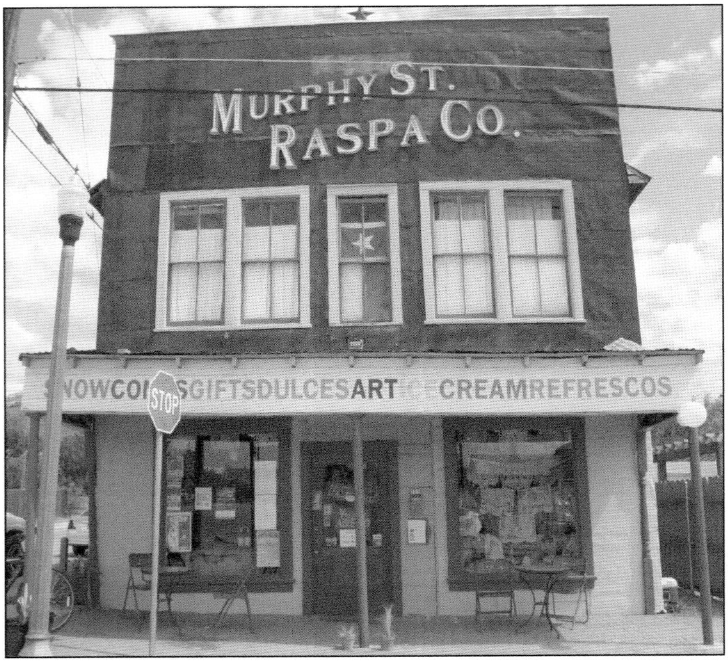

The Murphy Street Raspa Company was established in 2008 by Victor and Cristina Noriega in the old Valadez Grocery store. Promoting and celebrating Mexican culture, the store specializes in shaved ice (or *raspas* as they are called in Spanish), ice cream, coffee, and a variety of Mexican folk art and crafts. (Photograph by author.)

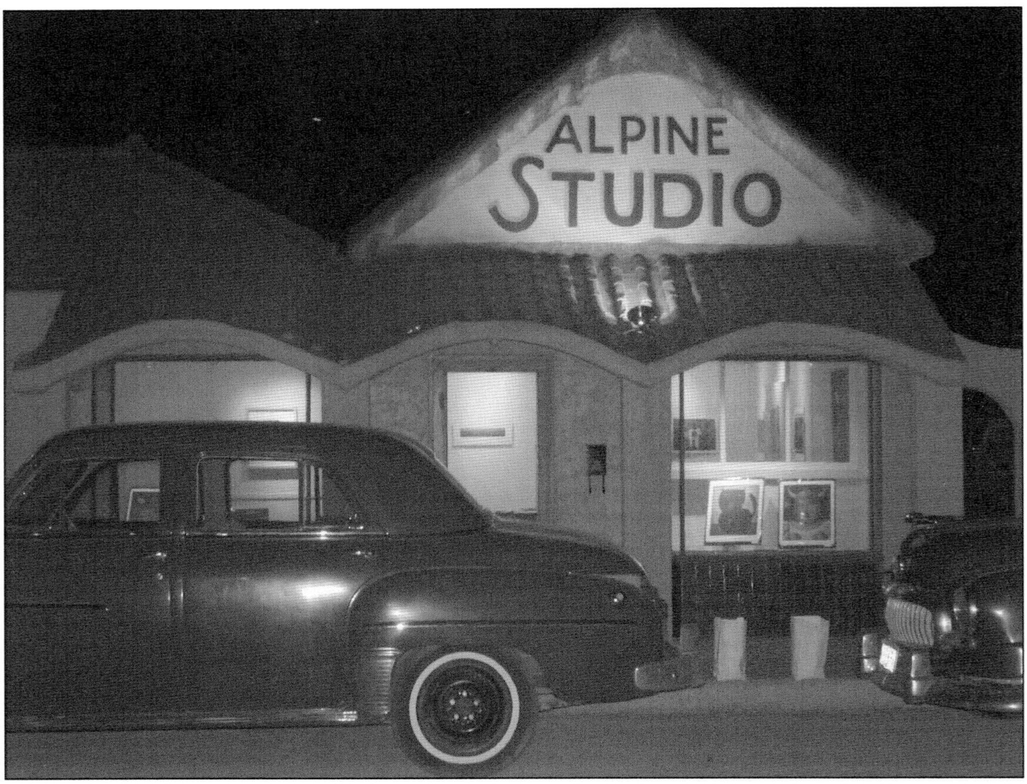

Alpine Studio, one of the restored Murphy Street businesses, was originally established as a photographic studio in 1907 by Alpine's most prolific early photographers, John and Lizzie Thain. Shown here during the annual Artwalk festival, it is now used as an art studio and gallery by local artist Tom Curry. (Photograph by author.)

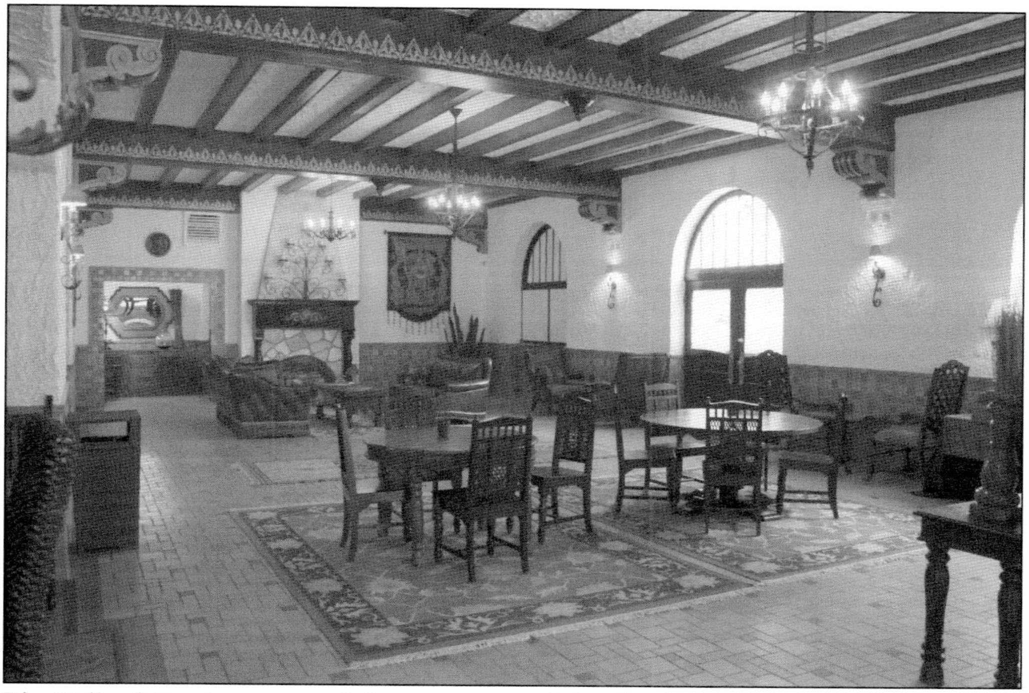

The Holland Hotel was restored close to its original detailing by South Branch Hotels in 2009. The Holland had gone through multiple reincarnations following its decline in the late 1960s, and for a while contained its own microbrewery. Its most recent facelift was also the most extensive since its original construction in 1928. (Photograph by author.)

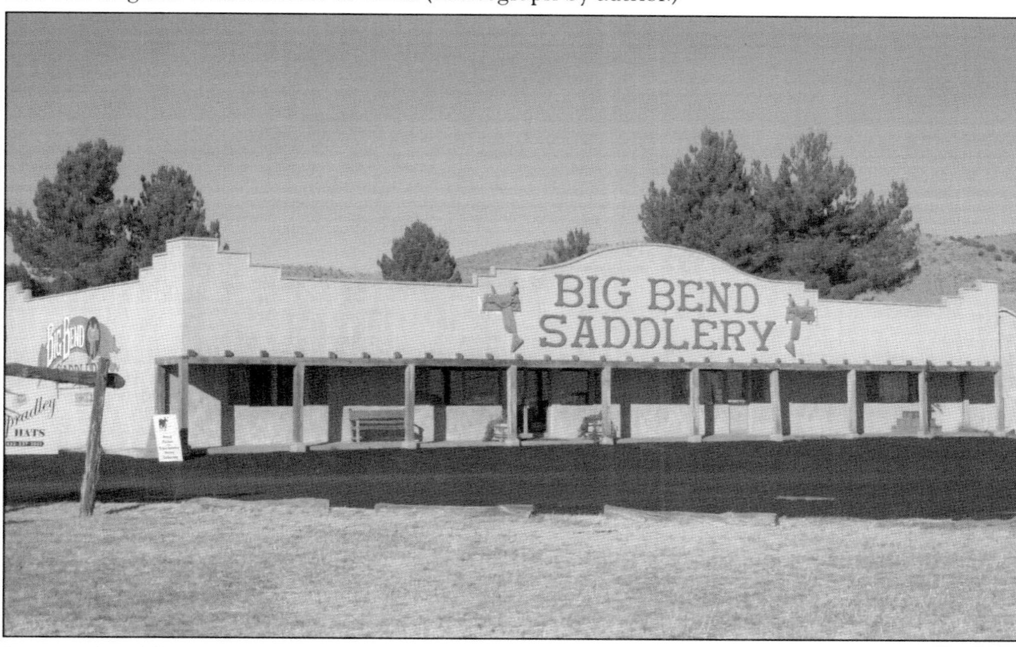

Big Bend Saddlery carries a wide variety of Western gear but specializes in custom-made saddles, bridles, chaps, and other tack. Known for many years as Alpine Saddlery, the business was first established in 1905 by J. G. Crawford and went through multiple owners before being purchased by Gary Dunshee and Bret Collier in 1983. (Photograph by author.)

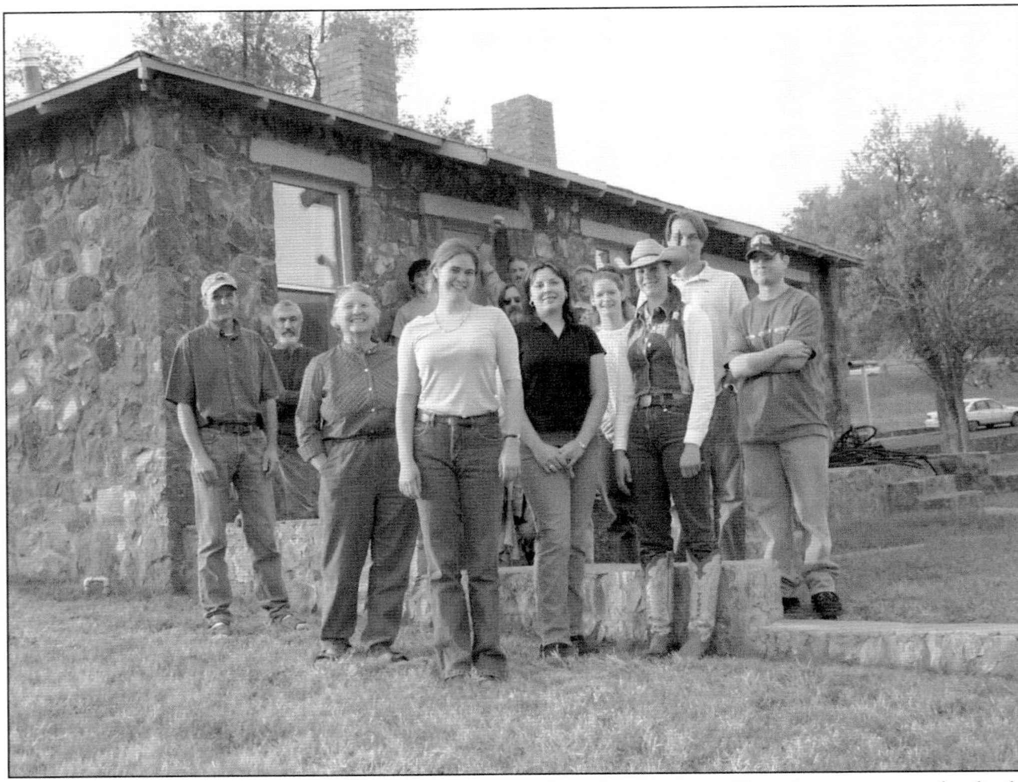

The Save the Cottages Campaign was organized by Elaine Peters (front) to prevent the little campus village from being destroyed to make way for a new student housing complex. Comprised of students, staff, faculty, and Alpine citizens, the group circulated petitions, wrote letters, and held a public forum in an effort to save the 1930s rock houses. (Photograph by author.)

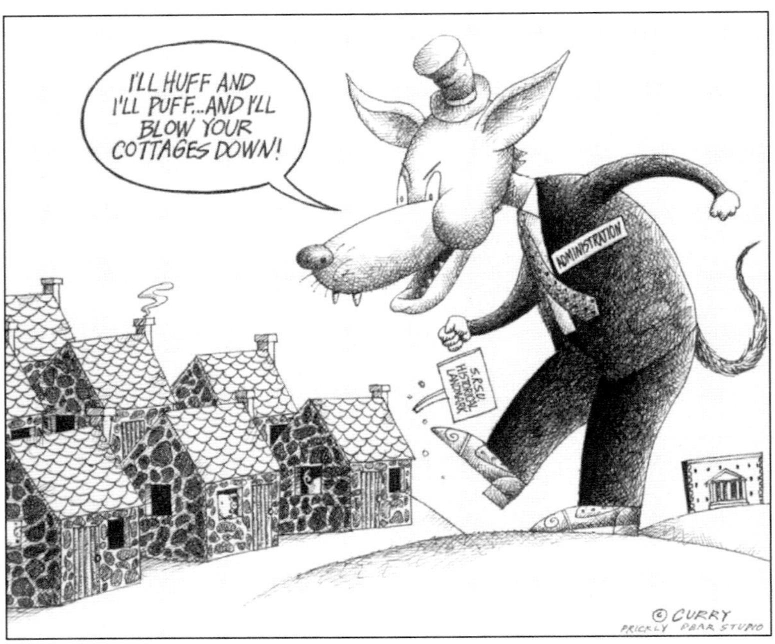

A cartoon depicting the Sul Ross administration as the big bad wolf was drawn by local artist Tom Curry to raise support for protecting the stone cottages. Despite overwhelming opposition by Alpine citizens and by preservation organizations across the state, the cottages were destroyed during the Morgan administration. (Courtesy of Tom Curry.)

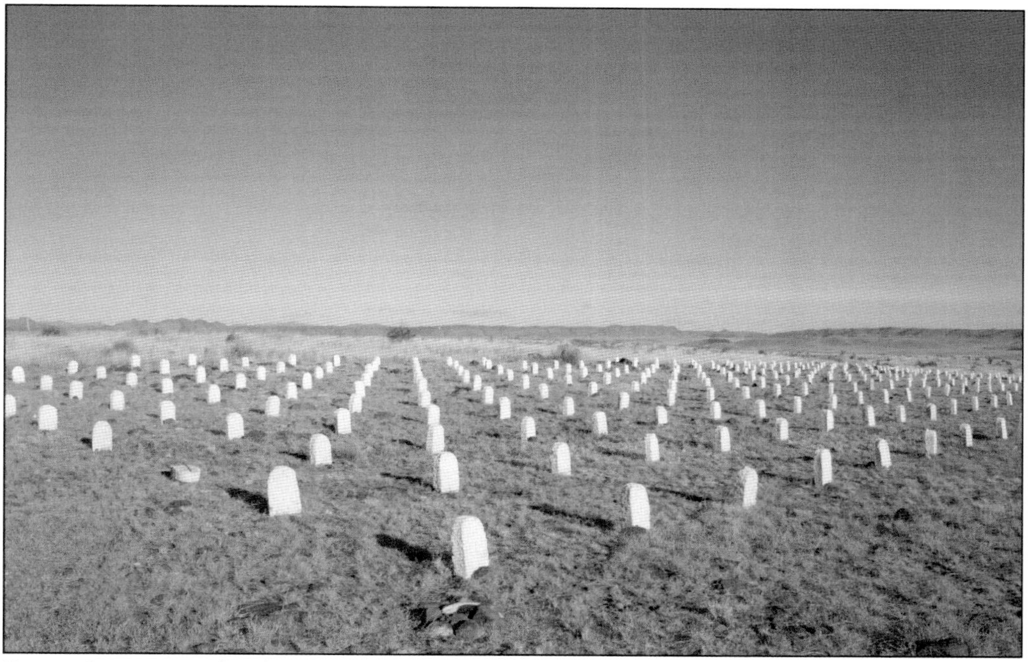

Rows of papercrete headstones stretch into the distance 4 miles east of Alpine, just north of Highway 90. Dedicated on Veterans Day in 2007 by the Big Bend chapter of Veterans for Peace, "Arlington Southwest" commemorates the hundreds of Texans who have died in the war against Iraq. (Photograph by author.)

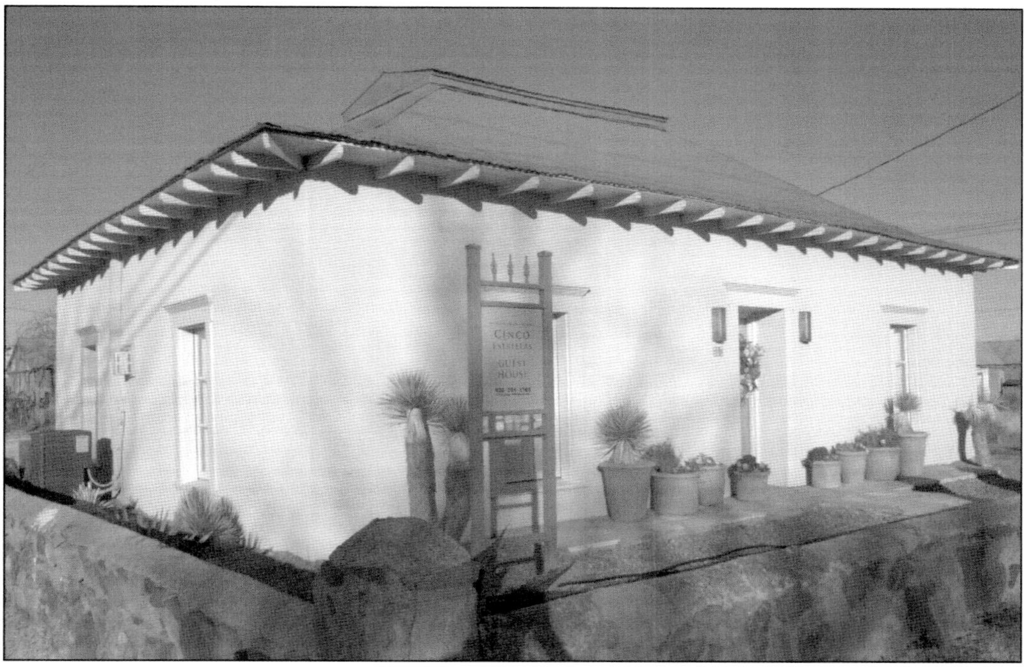

Cinco Estrellas offers home-style accommodations in Alpine's historic Pueblo Viejo. Recently remodeled into an upscale guesthouse, the historic home at one time served as the Mount Sinai Methodist Church in addition to its use as a residence. This and similar guesthouses reflect a growing interest in Alpine's historic homes. (Photograph by author.)

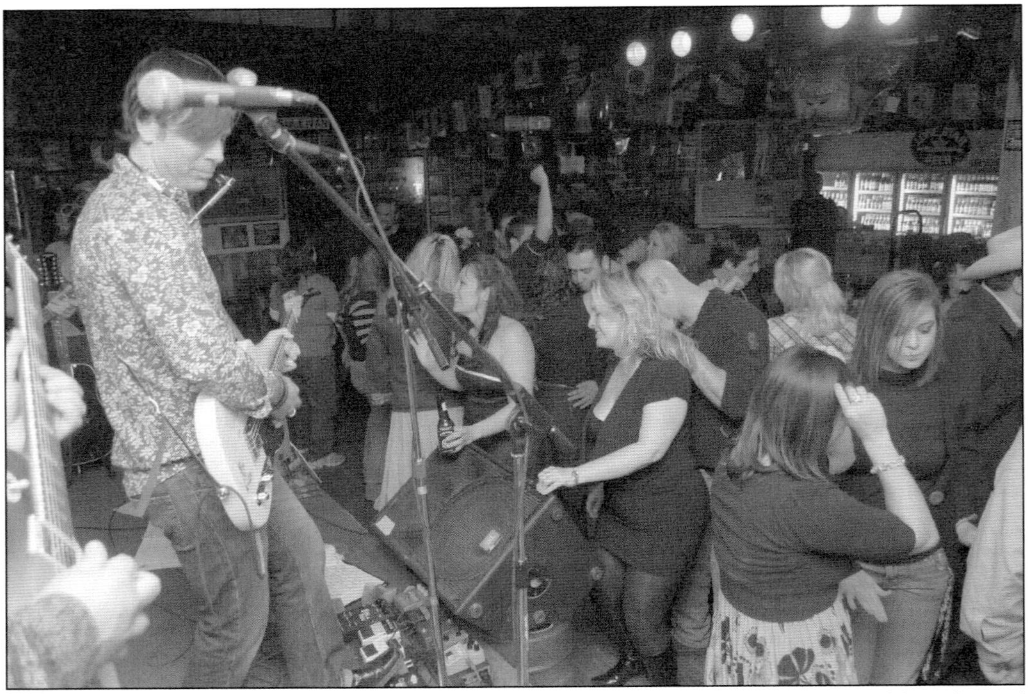

The Damn Torpedoes' Ty Hurless plays to a full dance floor at the Railroad Blues, a self-proclaimed "world famous beer and wine tourist trap." An Alpine icon since it opened in 1995, the Blues boasts the largest beer selection in the Big Bend and was voted one of the "best small town live music clubs in Texas" in *Texas Monthly* magazine. (Courtesy of Josh Ward.)

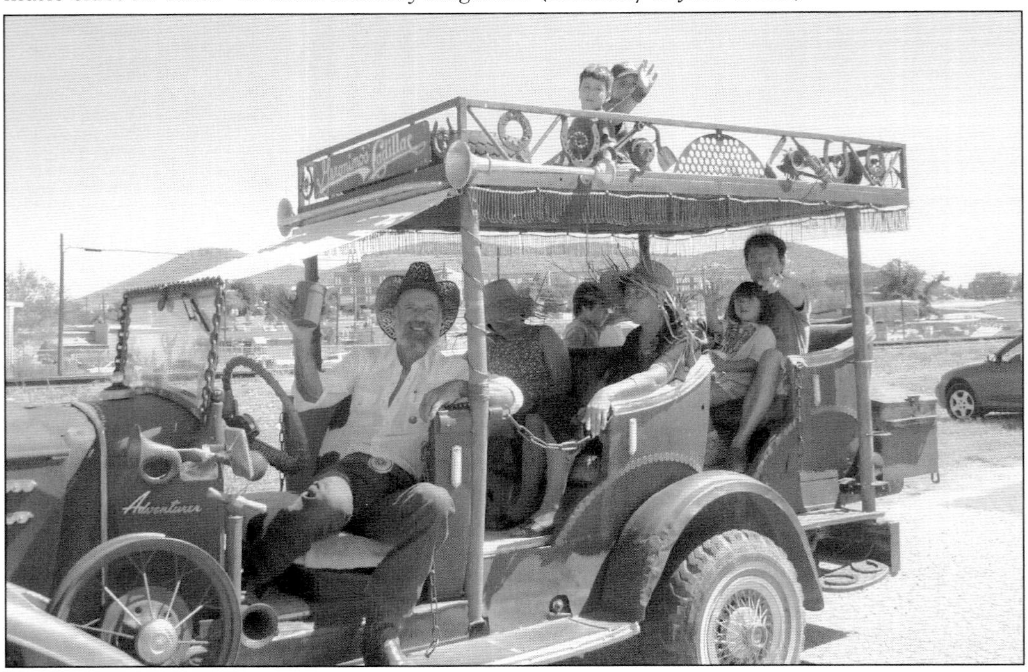

Jon Sufficool waves from Geronimo's Cadillac, one of his many artistic automobile restorations. Sufficool and his one-of-a-kind art cars are regulars in local parades, such as this one held during the dedication of the Centennial School building in 2004. (Photograph by author.)

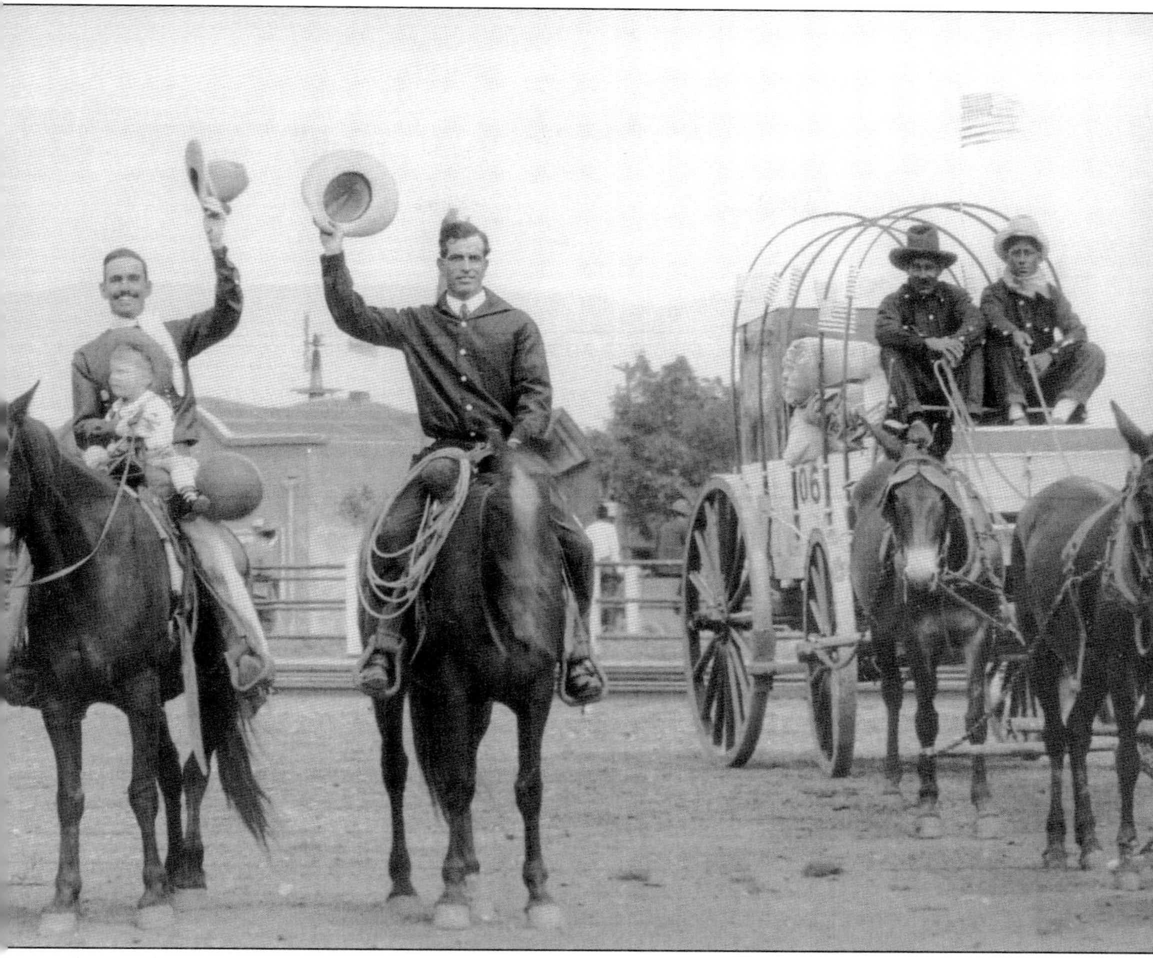

Herbert Kokernot Jr., holding his daughter, and Sid Mohler wave their hats as Don Gabino Ramiro and Pete Rodriguez (on O6 chuckwagon) look on before joining the Alpine rodeo parade in 1924. (Courtesy of the Museum of the Big Bend.)